Charisma, Converts, Competitors

D1385888

Charisma, Converts, Competitors

Societal and Sociological Factors
in the Success of Early Christianity

Jack T. Sanders

SCM PRESS

All rights reserved. No part of this publication may be
reproduced, stored in a retrieval system, or
transmitted, in any form or by any means, electronic,
mechanical, photocopying or otherwise, without the
prior permission of the publisher, SCM Press.

Copyright © Jack T. Sanders 2000

0 334 02795 0

This edition first published 2000 by
SCM Press,
9–17 St Albans Place London N1 0NX

SCM Press is a division of
SCM-Canterbury Press Ltd

Printed in Great Britain by
Biddles Ltd, Guildford and King's Lynn

to Ed and Becky

fondly and with admiration

Contents

Abbreviations

ASR	*American Sociological Review*
ABD	D. N. Freedman (ed.), *Anchor Bible Dictionary*, 1992
AJS	*American Journal of Sociology*
ANRW	W. Haase and H. Temporini (eds), *Aufstieg und Niedergang der römischen Welt*
BAR	*Biblical Archaeology Review*
BJS	*British Journal of Sociology*
BTB	*Biblical Theology Bulletin*
CBQ	*Catholic Biblical Quarterly*
FRLANT	Forschungen zur Religion und Literatur des Alten und Neuen Testaments
HTR	*Harvard Theological Review*
HTS	Harvard Theological Studies
ICC	International Critical Commentary
IDB	George Arthur Buttrick (ed.), *The Interpreter's Dictionary of the Bible*
JR	*Journal of Religion*
JRS	*Journal of Roman Studies*
JSNT	*Journal for the Study of the New Testament*
JSSR	*Journal for the Scientific Study of Religion*
JTS	*Journal of Theological Studies*

OBT	Overtures to Biblical Theology
SA	*Sociological Analysis*
SBLSP	Society of Biblical Literature Seminar Papers
SBLTT	SBL Texts and Translations
SBT	Studies in Biblical Theology
SecCent	*Second Century*
SJLA	Studies in Judaism in Late Antiquity
TDNT	G. Kittel and G. Friedrich (eds), *Theological Dictionary of the New Testament*
WUNT	Wissenschaftliche Untersuchungen zum Neuen Testament

Preface

This study is the fruit of my continuing interest in using insights from the social sciences and historico-sociological methods to try to enlighten aspects of early Christianity and second-temple Judaism. In my first attempt in this endeavour – *Schismatics, Sectarians, Dissidents, Deviants. The First One Hundred Years of Jewish-Christian Relations*, published in 1993 – I was able to determine that the multifarious kinds of relations and turns of events that existed or took place among non-Christian Jews, Christian Jews, and other Christians in the first decades of the Christian era could best be understood if one had some grasp of how and when societies identified and punished deviants, and of how social organisms evolve. Now, nearly a decade later, I continue to have a feeling of satisfaction about what I was able to discover in that study.

Since the appearance of that work, I have been able to complete several short studies, which have appeared here and there, on such subjects as the Corinthian congregation in Paul's day, Jesus as a charismatic leader of a new religious movement (on which more herein), the reception of the Torah in the wisdom movement in the late pre-Christian period, and the issue of whether early Christianity was primarily a Jewish phenomenon or not (also pursued further in this volume). Aside from what I have been able to discover in these studies, they have served to cement my conviction that we historians limit ourselves unnecessarily when we merely describe historical events and sequences, even when we seek to explain those events and sequences by historical observations. It is only when we learn from the social sciences – and this means primarily from sociology and anthropology – how and why societies and social movements behave and develop in certain ways that we can adequately understand the ancient societies and movements that we study. It thus seems especially appropriate, as we round on a new millennium, to examine Christian origins again in this new way, asking what role societal and sociological factors played in the success of the new religion.

This does not, of course, mean that we should slavishly take over certain 'laws' from the social sciences and use them as boxes into which we then force our historical evidence; rather, we must continue to analyse the evidence as closely as possible and then reach into the store of information available from the social sciences to see how that information may enlighten our evidence. Sometimes we may find rules or laws that seem to apply; but we are more likely to find models, which always have to be adjusted for each individual situation, or even more general patterns (as I think of them) that may help us to understand the evidence that we seek to clarify. It is this approach that I have tried to follow in the present study.

Part of the material in Chapter I, on randomness as an important ingredient of charisma, has appeared in a rather different format in *New Testament Studies*, Vol. 44; and a good part of Chapter III, the discussion with Rodney Stark over the Jewish component in early Christianity, appeared in somewhat more expanded form in *Social Compass*, Vol. 46. All translations of foreign words, phrases and longer passages are, unless otherwise noted, my own.

As always, there are many people who have assisted in this study in one way or another, and I cannot mention or even recall all of them here; but especially deserving of thanks are John Bowden, who encouraged me to put all this together in one place instead of resting content with a few scattered articles; Jean Duhaime and Paul-André Turcotte, who encouraged me to pursue my analysis of Rodney Stark's conclusions; Joanne Halgren of the University of Oregon Inter-Library Loan Department, who continues to provide an extremely valuable service for those of us here in the smaller academic depart-

ments; and my wife, Susan Plass, who is constant in her encour-
agement and support.

Eugene, Oregon
Summer 1999

Introduction

'It is evident that the cults that, through initiation and puri-
fication ceremonies, promised people a better life after death
were gaining ground [in Philippi in Paul's time]. The cults of
Dionysos and the hero-horseman had a special place near
those of the Kabiroi, the Egyptian gods, and the great goddess Cybele and her companion Attis'

(Chaido Koukouli-Chrysantaki)

Adolf Harnack's *Mission and Expansion of Christianity in the
First Three Centuries*, first published almost a hundred years
ago, was a watershed work. While it was hardly the first work
to address the historical question of the success of Christianity
in the Roman world, its scope and thoroughness made it a
standard for much of the twentieth century. Harnack described
the political and religious setting of Christianity's expansion,
the Christian message that won that world, the methods pursued by the missionaries (broadly understood), the progress of
the mission, and, in an appendix, the relationship between
Christianity's spread and that of other religions. While numerous later studies have contributed both refinements to and
corrections of Harnack's study, his approach – examining the
setting and analysing the message and methods of the Christian
mission – remains fairly constant.

One thing that seemed obvious to Harnack, and to many
succeeding historians of early Christianity as well, was that
Christianity triumphed due to its superior message. 'It was by
preaching to the poor, the burdened, and the outcast,' he wrote,
'by the preaching and practice of love, that Christianity turned

the stony, sterile world into a fruitful field for the church.'[1] He then proceeded to provide the evidence for that assumption.

A major flaw of Harnack's thinking, which still appears in most histories of early Christianity, was that he misunderstood the religious environment that Christianity entered when it moved out from its Jewish homeland. For Harnack, that religious environment was a *state polytheism*. Thus at the outset he understood Christianity as a religious movement unlike any other, and that meant unlike Judaism and unlike Roman state paganism. This approach, still followed by so many, overlooks the fact that Christianity was at first only *one of several new religious movements seeking adherents within the Roman Empire*. Consequently, while Harnack could note the presence of other new religious movements from the East,[2] he could write of them only that they aroused 'new religious cravings' among the populace that 'could not finally be satisfied apart from Christianity' with its superior message. In a few pages in his Appendix III Harnack dismissed the notion that Mithraism in particular was a rival to Christianity,[3] since it did not connect with Hellenism, was to be found mainly on the frontiers of the empire, and 'seldom managed to rise, even in the West . . ., to the higher levels of intellectual culture'. Furthermore, the witness of 'the Fathers of the church' is that they considered their main opponent to be state religion – that is to say, 'the state and its idea of religion'.

A much more recent historian of early Christianity, Robert Grant, also seeks (as did Harnack) to explain the progress of early Christianity within the empire in terms of stages of conflict with the state. While Grant is more aware of the pagan religious situation than was Harnack (as in his discussion in *Augustus to Constantine* of the situation in the empire when Christianity arose),[4] still he emphasizes only the way in which Christianity fought and cajoled its way past persecution to a rapprochement with the emperor. Thus Grant lets us see the *motivation* for Harnack's evidence that Christianity's main opponent was the state, i.e., that the apologists recognized that they had to overcome the antipathy (or worse) of the emperor and of the elites if Christianity was to be free to grow. This analysis of the apologists certainly marks an advance in our understanding of Christianity's success, but we should not allow the apologists' struggle to blind us to the other side of Christianity's effort, which was to win the hearts and minds of the populace in the face of competing efforts to do the same.

Christianity is still for Grant a movement apart, superior to pagan religions;[5] and he offers no explicit explanation of why Christianity surpassed its rivals in the minds of pagans in general and of the emperor in particular. In a number of places Grant points to parallels – noticed by various early Christians – between Christian and Mithraic worship practices;[6] but in the end he merely observes that as Christianity grew stronger, it 'could simply dismiss the resemblances'.[7] The religion of Isis he notes only once.[8] Grant's explanations of the reasons for Christianity's success have validity, and we shall want to return to them in Chapter III, but it behooves us to delve more deeply into other societal factors than the struggle with the state that may have contributed to that success, and to pose more directly the question of Christianity's rivals. If, after all, emperors prior to Constantine endorsed Mithraism,[9] would Christian appeals have caused Christianity to *surpass* Mithraism in imperial thinking?

It is not only historians of early Christianity, however, who tend to see Christianity as *novus ordo* within the early Roman Empire. Scholars of Roman religion sometimes do the same. The tendency is especially obvious in Walter Burkert's *Ancient Mystery Cults*, an otherwise thorough and carefully nuanced study of the main religious movements in the Hellenistic and early Roman Imperial periods that were mysteries in the proper sense, i.e., that had secret initiations – those of Eleusis, of Dionysus, of the Great Mother, of Isis and of Mithras.

At the outset Burkert scolds modern scholars for approaching the ancient mysteries with stereotypes in mind, one of which is that the mysteries are 'religions of salvation' and thus 'preparatory or parallel to the rise of Christianity'. Looking at the mysteries in this way leads, he explains, to misunderstanding

Christianity as 'just another – indeed, the most successful – of
the Oriental mystery religions'. Studying the mysteries with
that stereotype in mind obscures 'the often radical differences
between' the mysteries and Christianity.[10] It seems clear from
this formulation that Burkert is as interested in protecting
Christianity from association with the mysteries as he is in
clearing the way to a proper understanding of those religious
movements. Furthermore, since he has committed himself to
arguing that the mysteries were not religions of salvation,
Burkert has to resort to some rather strange explanations of
those texts and inscriptions that seem to indicate precisely that.

Burkert cannot, of course, overlook the fact that the oldest
and most renowned mystery of all, that of Eleusis, insisted that
'he who is uninitiate in the *sacra* (ἀτελὴς ἱερῶν) . . . has no share
(or: lot, αἶσα) . . . down under the murky gloom (ὑπὸ ζόφῳ
ἠερόεντι; *Homeric Hymn to Demeter* 481–82) – implying, of
course, the corollary, that the initiated *did* have a share in
Hades; nor can he overlook that 'the Hipponion gold leaf . . .
depicts the *mystai* and *bakchoi* [Dionysiac initiates] in the
netherworld proceeding on the sacred way toward eternal
bliss'.[11] Yet he feels obliged to distinguish these hopes clearly
from the Christian hope, arguing that the mysteries were essentially forms of 'votive religion', i.e., religious ways of meeting
'personal needs'.[12] And he reduces the hope for *post mortem*
well being to that: 'Mysteries were meeting practical needs even
in their promises for an afterlife.'[13] One has to wonder, however, just how this explanation distinguishes the mysteries from
Christianity, which also met personal needs – albeit in ways
superior to those of its competitors, as we shall have opportunity to observe in detail in Chapter III. Furthermore, Burkert
has to note that when Mithraism finally (late fourth century)
can say of its form of baptism (in bull's blood) that the baptized
is *in aeternum renatus*, it has taken over this notion from
Christianity, which Burkert describes as Mithraism's 'rival'.[14]
(That this 'baptism', incidentally, is late and has come into
Mithraism as a way of countering Christian practice and claims
has been well shown by Robert Duthoy.)[15] The mysteries,

Burkert concludes after presenting a wealth of evidence, did not provide 'a *redirection* of religion toward other-worldly concerns . . . At best they *continue what was already there*.'[16] This summary statement, however, seems to give up his original point that the mysteries were not religions of salvation and to argue instead that in their offer of a better or more fortunate or blessed existence after death, *the mysteries were not innovators*. Yet no one acquainted with the religion of more ancient Egypt, with its emphasis on survival in and beyond the tomb, would have proposed this in the first place.

In view of the evidence that Burkert presents so well, he finally, at the end of his chapter on 'Personal Needs', has to make his distinction between Christianity and the mysteries more precise. In the mysteries, he argues, 'there was no *dogmatic faith* in overcoming death . . ., as there was no devaluation of life'.[17] This is now a difference that may be too narrow to be visible. On the one hand, it is precarious to say that the mysteries had no dogma about overcoming death, in view of the dearth of texts and also in view of the fact that the *Homeric Hymn* seems to have provided a kind of dogma at least for the mysteries of Demeter.[18] On the other hand, 'devaluation of life' apparently refers to the aforementioned character of the mysteries as a form of votive religion (i.e., a type of religion that attends to personal needs), which character is supposed to distinguish them from Christianity – which was, by contrast, spiritual. Yet such a distinction severely distorts early Christianity because (as we just noted) Christianity also met personal needs.[19]

Beyond these proposed differences between Christianity and the mysteries, however, Burkert lays even heavier emphasis on the difference in organization. While there were communities of adherents to the mysteries, he argues, 'none of them approaches the Christian model of a church, *ekklesia*'.[20] Adherents to the mysteries did form associations that were called *thiasos* or *koinon* – in general, 'club' – but they did not form a church. He describes the difference:

The individuals remain independent, especially on the economic level, fully integrated into the complex structures of family and *polis*; but they contribute interest, time, influence, and part of their private property to the common cause. Such contributions are expected from the wealthy citizens, who receive remuneration in the form of honors bestowed on them . . . This type of association has a legal status and a place to meet; there is often common property; but there is no stable hierarchy or charismatic leadership.[21]

If one thinks, however, of the congregational situation revealed in I Corinthians, or of the complaint in James 2 that congregations treat rich and poor differently, then the type of association that Burkert describes could apply almost as well to Christianity. One difference is that it was difficult to be a Christian and be *fully* integrated into the structures of the *polis*; yet even here, as Paul's tortured discussion in I Corinthians 8 about eating sacrificial meat shows, the separation may often have been minimal. Certainly Christians also remained economically independent, and contributions were expected from the wealthier members of congregations. Christian congregations, to be sure, had no legal status and (in the period that we wish to examine here) little if any common property; but there was also no *stable* leadership, as Paul's various arguments both with locals and with the Jerusalem leaders of the church make painfully clear. (Mithraism was different, having 'a strict hierarchy of initiation grades'.)[22]

There are two other kinds of differences between Christianity and the mysteries that Burkert proposes that seem to reveal his orientation and the nature of his misunderstanding. On the one hand, he emphasizes that participation in a mystery ceremony, however significant ('moving through the city in a frenzied Bacchic *thiasos*'; meeting at Eleusis 'for blessed visions in the mystery night'), constitutes a 'unity of the group . . . in action and in experience, not in faith. There is no Credo.'[23] Again, he observes that when mystery congregations met together for a characteristic 'feasting or sharing an opulent meal', such activity 'arouses the suspicions of the *more puritan observer*' because 'there is no reduction to a purely symbolic level, as is characteristic of Christian communion'.[24] Burkert thus seems not to know that early Christians also met for common meals, and that these at least sometimes led to excesses (I Corinthians again); and we may indeed suspect that his view of early Christianity is derived not from knowledge of early Christianity itself, but rather from acquaintance with his (puritan) Protestant church in Zurich. There the credo and the symbolic eucharist are paramount. Of course early Christians were supposed to believe certain things, but then so were the adherents of the mysteries. It was, nevertheless, several centuries after its founding that Christianity actually composed a credo, and the arguing has never really stopped. And the impression that one gains of Christian congregations from I Corinthians and from James is really much more like what Burkert describes for mystery congregations (except for the highly structured Mithraic congregations) than it is like what he thinks Christianity was!

Burkert's sub-text on the distinction between Christianity and the mysteries is thus flawed because of his misapprehension of early Christianity, and his otherwise adequate analysis of the mysteries in fact shows us how *like* the mystery congregations Christian congregations often were.

Some years before Burkert's study, E. R. Dodds had presented a more adequate comparison of Christianity with its competitors, and he was also keenly aware of societal factors that abetted Christianity's success.[25] As to the religious alternatives to Christianity, Dodds reasoned that paganism as a whole had faded in the 'age of anxiety' (from the reign of Marcus Aurelius to that of Constantine), leaving Christianity as the most appealing alternative. That appeal resided first of all in Christian martyrdoms (Dodds writes primarily of the third century), so that 'Christianity . . . was judged to be worth living for because it was seen to be worth dying for'. Beyond this, it was also (first) exclusive, an approach that in an anxious age 'exerts a powerful attraction'; and, second, it 'was open to all', as were none of the other alternatives. Then there was the promise of heavenly reward. Unlike Burkert, Dodds recognizes that other religions also offered similar rewards, but he judges that Christianity 'wielded both a bigger stick and a juicier carrot' – that is, the Christian depictions of eternal punishment played more effectively on the anxieties of the age than did analogous portrayals on the part of Christianity's competitors. Finally, Christianity offered tangible benefits in this world that its competitors could not match, since 'a Christian congregation was from the first a community in a much fuller sense than any corresponding group of Isiac or Mithraist devotees'. Thus 'the Church provided the essentials of social security' as well as a 'sense of belonging'. This last Dodds considers 'perhaps the strongest single cause' of Christianity's triumph. Dodds has thus seen early Christianity as being a religious movement similar to others of the age but as more successful in attracting adherents; and his juicier carrot includes both the promise of salvation and practical benefits, offered by Christianity's competitors, but in less juicy versions.

Dodds' brief discussion has touched on several factors – e.g., especially Christian exclusivity and the tangible benefits that went with becoming a Christian – that some other investigators have later analysed in greater detail, as we shall have the opportunity to observe in Chapters II and III. Thus Dodds correctly sees the difference between Christianity and its competitors as one of degree, not one of kind. This is certainly to put us on the right road to understanding Christianity's triumph.

If we fail, as so many Christian historians have done, to see that Christianity was one of several new religious movements competing for adherents in the Graeco-Roman world, then we cannot understand how it came to best those competitors. Nowhere has this point been made more forcefully than in Jonathan Z. Smith's *Drudgery Divine*. Arguing largely with Arthur Darby Nock's work, *Conversion*,[26] Smith shows in some detail how Christian historians have often emphasized Christianity's Jewishness in order to distinguish it from paganism but then have invoked 'Pharisaism, rabbinism', or the like in order to distinguish it from Judaism[27] – thus maintaining Christianity's uniqueness. According to Smith, when one realizes that there were different forms of early Christianity – not just Paul's version of Christianity, which is endorsed by most Protestant historians of early Christianity – then one will come to see that 'most of the "mystery" cults and the non-Pauline forms of Christian tradition have more in common with each other' than historians have been wont to recognize.[28] Smith calls for a new approach: 'The entire enterprise of comparison between the "mystery" cults and early Christianities needs to be looked at again.'[29] This work is an attempt to meet that need.

The brief and cursory survey that this introduction has given of the work of several historians of early Christianity and of its competitor religions, whose work spans the last century, is intended to be indicative rather than comprehensive. We see the pronounced tendency to view early Christianity as unique, standing over against the aggregate of paganism; and we see that only one of our examples, Dodds, has pointed to societal factors that may have been important in Christianity's rise. Thus what we shall attempt in this study is the new approach for which Smith called (although perhaps not in the way that he would have intended). This means, first, that we shall attempt to place early Christianity within a more adequate heuristic context, that of a society in which a number of new religious movements, Christianity among them, were active. We shall also attempt to understand what societal factors may have abetted Christianity's success; and finally we shall attempt to place Christianity within a broader universal context defined by sociologists of religion as new religious movements *tout court*. When we have done this we should be able to give a much better explanation of Christianity's rise to dominance.

The *terminus ad quem* for this study is the end of the second Christian century (with some occasional glances into the third). To be sure, few at the end of the second century would have predicted Christianity's ultimate triumph; but we should be able to see, in those first two centuries, the emerging trends that led finally to that triumph.

The question of why Christianity was successful, however, takes us inevitably back to its origins in the ministry of Jesus. If we want to understand fully why the new religion succeeded, we need first of all to understand why people followed Jesus, and this is therefore the subject of Chapter I. We need next, then, to understand why Gentiles would be attracted to this new religion and why some found Christianity more appealing than its competitors. Chapter II explores this question from different perspectives. Finally, we need to understand what societal factors may have existed that assisted Christianity – or that it could exploit – in its march to triumph, and we shall examine these factors in Chapter III.

This work is by no means a history of early Christianity. It is rather an attempt to explain certain crucial elements in Christianity's success, and we may hope that the approach that we take here provides a new and better explanation of why Christianity triumphed in the Roman Empire. At the very least, our reliance on the social sciences will shed some new light on hitherto shadowed chapters in the history of that triumph.

I

Why Did People Follow Jesus?

'Jesus' miraculous deeds and powerful teaching attracted a large following of both Jews and Gentiles. In short, Jesus was a charismatic leader whose special powers of miracle-working and teaching were acknowledged and ratified by his followers.'

(John P. Meier)

1. Focussing the question

In attempting to understand early Christianity's success, we are inevitably drawn to the question of Jesus' appeal – that is, to the question of why people followed Jesus in the first place, i.e., the question of the origin of the movement. When we raise the question, 'Why did people follow Jesus?', we may be met with surprise. 'Is that not obvious?' some are likely to ask; 'He was the Son of God, and all right-thinking people responded positively to him.' But the answer is not obvious at all; for, without making any judgments about Jesus' nature, we really want to know about the people who followed, and the Gospels seem uninterested in explaining the followers' motives. It is thus the phenomenon of following Jesus that we want to examine. Yet we cannot inquire just about the followers, for we also have to understand what it was about the one whom they followed that made them want to follow him. Even if we take the un-critical, believing position with which we began, we still cannot escape asking what it was about Jesus that made (some) people agree that he was the Son of God (as in our formulation above) – that is, what it was about Jesus that compelled following. Our question, therefore, must receive answers from two directions:

from the side of Jesus, informing us about his appeal, and from the side of the followers, informing us about their response. Let us begin by noting how a few others have sought to answer the question.

2. Some answers to the question

First, when we ask about followers, we need to remember that we are not asking just about a close group of disciples. A number of authors point out the difference between close disciples and other followers,[1] and we may note the recent position of Hans Weder in the *Anchor Bible Dictionary*, according to whom the word 'disciple' first includes 'that quite large number of Jesus-followers whom one best calls adherents', a group to which 'in all probability even women belonged', and secondly the twelve.[2] E. P. Sanders thinks even of three groups: '(1) close disciples; (2) slightly more remote followers; and (3) still more remote sympathizers or supporters . . . Apparently [Jesus] intentionally called only a few to *follow* him in the strict sense.'[3] If Jesus did not actually call these more remote adherents, however, what was it about him that led them to give him their allegiance, if only in a limited sense?

A. Teachings and miracles

A number of authors (and here we can only sample from the myriads of works on Jesus) see Jesus' teachings and miracles as the factors motivating people to follow him. Thus Martin Dibelius writes that 'he arouses the people by the *preaching* of the Kingdom, but at the same time he lets them detect in the wrath of *judgment*, in the word of *counsel*, in the act of *healing*, the nearness of the Kingdom'.[4] Preaching, judgment and counsel belong to Jesus' message, to his teaching, while his healings are the miraculous side of his activity.

More recently, Paula Fredriksen thinks that the fact of Jesus' 'popular following' makes his miracle-working activity more historically likely. Healings, in her opinion, 'in an age of so many healers and miracle-workers, would confer no unique distinction upon Jesus; but coupled with his moral message and his call to prepare for the Kingdom, they may have enhanced his reputation as an authoritative prophet'.[5] It is the combination, in other words, of Jesus' healing miracles with his ethical and evangelical message that explain his having a following.

E. P. Sanders has added a more specific factor to Jesus' teachings, as an appeal to followers, than the general idea of the Kingdom of God. For him it was Jesus' acceptance of outcasts into the Kingdom that appealed, at least, to outcasts – like prostitutes and tax collectors. 'The promise of salvation to sinners,' he writes, 'is the undeniably distinctive characteristic of Jesus' message.'[6] That is to say that 'the wicked who heeded [Jesus] would be included in the kingdom even though they did not repent as it was universally understood – that is, even though they did not make restitution, sacrifice, and turn to obedience to the law'.[7] This appeal to outcasts, further, also explains the opposition that Jesus encountered.[8]

Seeing Jesus' successful appeal in terms of his miracles and his teachings, however, may be a trap of the synoptic tradition, which presents Jesus' career in terms of sayings (even if these sometimes become, as in Matthew, extended sermons) and deeds.[9] That is to say that we can explain everything about Jesus by referring to his words and deeds because the synoptic tradition presents his career in terms of words and deeds. We all realize, however, that this is a simplified presentation of Jesus' career brought about by the handing down of traditions about Jesus in the early decades of Christianity as either sayings or deeds.[10] On the one hand, of course, this is all we have, so there may be no other recourse. On the other hand, however, it is incumbent to try to work behind – or, as we shall attempt to do below – look around the tradition in an effort to reach more rounded explanations. As John Gager commented on a closely related subject, 'Nothing should escape examination, and it is precisely what seems self-evident that requires a second look.'[11]

B. Jesus' call

Most modern authors have emphasized Jesus' call when they have tried to explain why his disciples (as distinct from the more distant followers) followed him. Karl Rengstorf made this case quite strongly in his analysis of the Gospels' use of μανθάνω and related terms.[12] Rengstorf began his section on 'The Disciples of Jesus' with a discussion of the 'Call of the Disciples of Jesus',[13] and he opened with the statement that 'a fundamental mark of the μαθηταί of Jesus in the tradition is that they are called by Him to discipleship. This aspect dominates all the Gospel accounts of the way in which they began to follow Jesus.' Often Jesus says to a hearer, 'Follow me,' and he follows; but even in other cases where 'there is no formal call', still 'the tradition is quite unambiguous': 'Materially every such incident is exclusively marked by the initiative of Jesus.' Rengstorf further distinguished the commitment of Jesus' disciples to him from the commitment of a rabbi's pupils to the rabbi and from the pupils of a Greek philosopher to the philosopher.[14] 'The rabbi and the Greek philosopher are at one in representing a specific cause. Jesus offers Himself.'

Rengstorf is followed by, e.g., Eduard Schweizer, who explains that 'the call comes from Jesus. That is the beginning of it all.'[15] Schweizer adds, 'Grace becomes an event in such calling.'[16] So also Weder in the *ABD*: 'Someone became a disciple by Jesus' call reaching him . . . Apart from [Jesus'] call, there is no recognizable motive that could have turned the disciples to discipleship.'[17] Günther Bornkamm – who writes that the disciples 'do not become disciples by their own free choice, but by Jesus' "calling" . . . The Gospels state very clearly that the fact of someone becoming a disciple or being a disciple depends on Jesus' sovereign decision, and not on the free choice of individuals who are especially drawn to him'[18] – nevertheless also relates Jesus' call back to his teaching when he writes that 'the kingdom of God is the sole foundation of Jesus' call to follow him'.[19]

E. P. Sanders nuances this position somewhat more imaginatively. Emphasizing Jesus' call as the stimulus to discipleship, he proposes that 'we must suppose [the call narratives] to be abbreviated and idealized, and to leave out details in emphasizing the immediacy of the response' because it is clear that 'the future disciples already knew something about Jesus, so that when he called them they had some idea of who he was'.[20] Sanders explains the differences between Matthew and Mark, on the one hand, and Luke, on the other, in the narrative of the calling of the first disciples (Matt. 4.18–22; Mark 1.16–20; Luke 5.1–11) by proposing that Matthew and Mark have 'pruned away' any information about this prior knowledge and that Luke 'felt the lack of an explanation, so . . . he made up a story', which was that 'Jesus won the trust of the fishermen by telling them where to catch fish'.[21] Rengstorf had also proposed such prior knowledge of Jesus before the call.[22] We must admit, however, that there is no evidence for this prior knowledge, aside from Luke's embellished account, however reasonable the assumption of prior knowledge may seem.

It is worth emphasizing again that this discussion of discipleship as response to Jesus' call concerns those closest to Jesus. Thus Dibelius, in characterizing the distinction between Jesus' 'group of disciples' and 'a larger circle of adherents',[23] explained that 'the watchword to "follow" Jesus . . . holds good only for the inner group'. And we have already noted E. P. Sanders' three groups: disciples, followers and supporters.[24]

C. The people who followed

If we ask about the other side of the question, What was it about various people that led them to follow Jesus, whether as disciples or as more distant followers?, we find no answers. The Gospels are silent on this score, the writers being obviously uninterested in the question. They tell us from what walks of life some followers came (fishing, tax-collecting, prostitution), but they do not provide even that information for all the disciples. In quest of a sociological answer we might assume that Jesus' appeal struck root among a widespread and somewhat vague 'peasant class',[25] but even if we adopt that approach we are left with the problem that not all these 'peasants' followed Jesus, even at some remove. Bornkamm laments the fact that we have no psychological profiles of Jesus' followers,[26] and we surely join him in that lament. If there were a way to define the social location and the psychological state of persons who followed Jesus we could know a great deal more. We are left, however, only with guessing. Below, we may attempt some educated guessing, but we shall have to remember that it is only that. Even so, some educated guessing may help us, at the least, to think more creatively about the issue.

3. Rethinking the evidence

In 1968,[27] Martin Hengel proposed a new way of thinking about Jesus that adds to our understanding of what it was about him that caused people to follow him. Hengel proposed that we should understand Jesus as a *charismatic and eschatological prophet* who shared certain characteristics – especially the formation of a group of disciples – with other *charismatic leaders* in the ancient world. Hengel began with a problem saying, Matt. 8.22, 'Leave the dead to bury their own dead', and he emphasized what a radical 'break with law and custom' this saying implies.[28] Hengel found a context for such a radical statement in the definition of charismatic leaders given by Max Weber, who first identified the type. He quoted Weber: 'Those who are the bearers of the charisma – the master and his disciples and followers – must, if they are to do justice to their mission, stand outside the ties of this world, outside the everyday vocations and also outside the everyday family duties.'[29] With good sociological justification, then, for concluding that the author of the saying in Matt. 8.22 filled the role of charismatic leader, Hengel turned to a study of both Jewish and Hellenistic charismatic leaders, his Jewish examples being Elijah, Mattathias (the Hasmonean), Judas the Zealot, the anonymous Egyptian, and Theudas (cf. Acts 5.36–37; 21.38).[30]

His Hellenistic examples are 'teacher[s]' who were 'at the same time . . . *charismatic[s]* in the sense of the θεῖος ἀνήρ', like Pythagoras.³¹ Here, as he noted, is his best example, since especially 'Empedocles, related to Pythagoras', was both a teacher and a healer. But Hengel overlooked one other aspect of the similarity, that Pythagoras was both a teacher, as was Jesus, and the founder of something at least resembling a new religious movement (to use current sociological designators for what some readers might be inclined to call a sect). While Hengel, therefore, has come very close to discovering the best category or class in which to place Jesus and thus to understand him, he has a problem with his comparators. Aside from Elijah, who was a lone operator, Hengel's Jewish comparators are leaders of revolutions. While we may agree that leading a revolution is somewhat akin to starting a new religious movement (NRM), still we should prefer to find more analogous comparators if we can.

Geza Vermes takes 'charismatic' in a different direction and defines it in terms of the type of the (Galilean) Ḥasid. Vermes sees Jesus as being in line with Galilean charismatics known from rabbinic literature, especially Ḥoni the Circle-Drawer and Ḥanina ben Dosa.³² Ḥoni brought rain in a drought and Ḥanina stopped rain when he was getting drenched. Ḥanina was also once bitten by a poisonous snake that then died, leaving Ḥanina unharmed. Now, to be sure, Jesus performed nature miracles, but he did so in a context that is lacking for Vermes' comparative examples; for Jesus' miracles are related to his role as leader of the incipient Christian movement, whereas his Galilean counterparts act on their own and remain as something of oddities.³³

We may be helped here by a more modern sociological analysis. Theodore Long has clarified the distinction between two types of charisma – 'just any old charisma' (which approximates Vermes' model) and 'prophecy' (using Max Weber's term, which we shall examine in detail presently).³⁴ He writes, 'What distinguishes prophecy from ordinary life and other charisma is its backing; in God it claims the ultimate sponsor, the prototypical source of charismatic gifts.'[35] Prophecy entails a 'revolutionary force' that 'lies in the area of values, norms, and sacred customs'.[36] It 'stimulates the development of "new religions"'.[37] The prophet is therefore not 'just any old charismatic' but, as most sociologists of religion would say today, the charismatic leader of a new religious movement. Thus the rabbinic charismatics, who are idiosyncratic displayers of charismatic gifts and not leaders of discrete religious movements, also do not really form a class of comparators in which to place Jesus in order to understand him better. Pythagoras is a better comparator; but we should like to find more such.

Dale Allison has come closer to the goal of identifying the proper category in which to place Jesus when he defines him as a millenarian prophet (not quite, as we shall see, the same as Hengel's eschatological prophet).[38] Placing himself in the tradition of Albert Schweitzer and aligning himself with E. P. Sanders among current Jesus scholars, Allison argues convincingly for understanding Jesus as a millenarian prophet. Jesus, according to Allison – like (some) other Jews of his day – expected a final judgment, the resurrection of the dead, the restoration of Israel, and a great tribulation. He also held an imminent eschatology.[39] Allison then lists the following as characteristics shared by the 'pre-Easter Jesus movement'[40] and other – more recent – groups attached to millenarian prophets.[41] Such groups, first, 'commonly appeal . . . to the disaffected or unfortunate in a period of social change that threatens traditional ways and symbolic universes'. They also (2) 'typically interpret the present and near future as times of atypical of even unprecedented suffering and/or catastrophe'; they regularly (3) envisage 'a divinely-wrought comprehensive righting of wrongs, constituting "a holistic solution"'; and they hold (4) that 'reversal will come soon'. Further (5), they are 'revivalistic', (6) they 'characteristically promote[. . .] egalitarianism', and (7) they 'tend to divide humanity into two camps, the saved and the unsaved'. Millenarian movements also typically (8) break 'hallowed taboos associated with religious custom'; (9) they 'emphasize the value of an indigenous cultural heritage or selected portions of it'; and (10) they 'often replace traditional familial and social bonds with fictive kin'. The 'leaders regularly mediate the sacred through new channels' (11); and such movements involve (12) 'intense commitment and unconditional loyalty'. Thus (13), 'Millenarian movements more often than not coalesce around a charismatic leader' (and they sometimes expect the leader to return after death). 'The central beliefs of millenarians are formulated as fresh revelation, and they are authenticated by a prophet's miracles' (14), and (15) the movements 'sometimes take a passive political stance in expectation of a divinely-wrought deliverance'. 'Millenarian believers commonly expect a restored paradise which will return the ancestors' (16); such movements 'sometimes insist on the possibility of experiencing the coming utopia as a present reality' (17); they 'often grow out of precursor movements' (18); and they must in the end 'come to terms with disappointed expectations' (19).

Similarities between most of these points, on the one hand, and Jesus and his early followers, on the other, will immediately occur to many readers; but Allison argues that there is congruence on *all* points.[42] It would be unnecessarily tedious to repeat all Allison's evidence here, and to do so would prolong this work unreasonably, but we may note especially the following. The call to deny oneself and take up one's cross and follow Jesus (Mark 8.34 par.) implies that Jesus saw the present and the near future as times of suffering or catastrophe (point 2); and the several Sabbath-violation stories in the Gospels show that Jesus broke hallowed taboos (point 8). Further, Mark 3.31–35 par. clearly shows the point about fictive kin (point 10); and even though Luke departs somewhat here from Mark and Matthew, Luke 8.21 still makes the point that 'my mother and my brothers are those who hear the word of God and do it'. There is even an echo of the synoptic saying in John 15.14: 'You are my friends if you do what I command you.' We hardly need to cite the evidence for Jesus' demanding intense commitment and unconditional loyalty (point 12), but one may think at the least of Hengel's starting point (above), the saying about leaving the dead to bury the dead. Surely, finally, the Jesus movement focused on a charismatic leader (point 13), a subject that we are presently going to discuss in much more detail; and it grew out of a precursor movement (point 18), John the Baptist's.

Allison concludes, paraphrasing Albert Schweitzer and the Gospel of Matthew: 'He does not come to us as one unknown. We know him well enough. Jesus is the millenarian prophet. He is Wovoka. He is Mambu. He is Birsa. What we think of the least of these, his brethren, we think, to a large extent, also of him.'[43]

That Jesus was a millenarian prophet we need not deny. The one who spoke so regularly of the coming Kingdom of God, who designated twelve apostles, and who created a disturbance in the temple courtyard was surely such. And we have an advance here over Hengel's classification, for Allison's classification is made in a precise anthropological sense, and *it includes a wealth of comparators, although they are more modern and not Jesus' contemporaries*. As far as classifying Jesus goes, we might well rest here, and yet identifying Jesus as a millenarian prophet does not quite address the question as to why people followed him. Thus we need to return to the concept of charisma (which Allison notes but does not investigate further) and set our lens for a somewhat wider field of vision, to include other types of charismatic leaders of NRMs than millenarian prophets. It is when we understand how charisma works in the broader category that we shall be able better to say why people followed Jesus.

4. Charismatic leaders of new religious movements

Hengel, as we noted, quoted briefly from Max Weber in defining the type of the charismatic leader. Had he read some recent sociology and not rested content with quoting briefly from Weber, he would likely have seen that he could have improved his definition. We could say the same of, *mutatis mutandis*,

Vermes' and Allison's studies. We now turn to filling in this gap.

In the field of the sociology of religion today the literature on NRMs and the studies of their charismatic leaders are so enormous and multivalent that it is not, in fact, reasonable to try to survey them all here. Rather, we shall try to gain an adequate definition of the type, based on certain leading and comprehensive studies, and then to see if the definition does not help us to understand Jesus better, as well as to understand why people would have followed him, either as disciples or as more distant followers.

A. Defining the type

In what follows we want to remind ourselves of Weber's definition of the type, run quickly through the development of this concept since Weber, and then look closely at one charismatic leader of an NRM who has been well studied. When we thus have a defined pattern of what charismatic leaders of NRMs are like, we can decide whether Jesus fits the pattern better than he does that of Hengel's or Vermes' ancient charismatics.

(i) Theoretical discussion

Weber discussed charisma, charismatic authority, and Jesus as charismatic in a number of places, and when one gets all his statements on the subject together, one sees that he sometimes contradicted himself – something that is hardly surprising in view of the magnitude and the theoretical nature of his endeavour. (It is, incidentally, revelatory of the insulated nature of all academic disciplines today that an erudite biblical scholar like Hengel will quote a couple of sentences from Weber – especially on a topic like charismatic leadership, on which Weber had a variety of things to say scattered over several volumes – and will think that he has thereby cited the relevant sociological literature!) Weber did attempt, however, to provide a systematic presentation of his thought in *Wirtschaft und Gesellschaft*, and we may follow the pattern of most sociologists today and cite from it.

Weber began with the question of authority as an organizing principle of society, and he distinguished three types of authority – the rational, the traditional and the charismatic.[44] Of charismatic authority he wrote that 'the term "charisma" will be applied to a certain quality of an individual personality by virtue of which he is considered extraordinary and treated as endowed with supernatural, superhuman, or at least specifically exceptional powers or qualities'.[45] A person possessing such authority will have a devoted following 'based on an emotional form of communal relationship' and without any organizational layers. 'The prophet [Weber's term for what we are now calling the charismatic leader of an NRM] has his disciples; the warlord his bodyguard; the leader, generally, his agents. There is no such thing as appointment or dismissal, no career, no promotion. There is only a call.'[46] The 'want satisfaction' of such a charismatic movement is 'anti-economic . . . It repudiates any sort of involvement in the everyday routine world.'[47] Weber thus affirmed that 'charismatic authority repudiates the past, and is in this sense a specifically revolutionary force'.[48]

Later, Weber defined the prophet by distinguishing the type from other leadership types. Since 'prophet' means 'a purely individual bearer of charisma, who by virtue of his mission proclaims a religious doctrine or divine commandment', what primarily distinguishes the prophet from the *priest* is 'the personal call'.[49] But the prophet is also not a *magician*. Both, indeed, 'exert[their] power simply by virtue of [their] personal gifts. Unlike the magician, however, the prophet claims definite revelations, and the core of his mission is doctrine or commandment, not magic.' Nevertheless, 'outwardly, at least, the distinction is fluid', since the prophet may perform miraculous acts and the magician may practise divination,[50] and here Weber cited the ancient Israelite prophets. Recalling that Moses was considered a prophet, Weber then bounded off the *law-*

giver from the prophet, 'if one understands the [former] to mean a personage who in a concrete case has been assigned the responsibility of codifying a law systematically or of reconstituting it'; but the 'transition from the prophet to the law-giver is' again 'fluid'.[51] He cited Jesus to make the line between the two types clear: 'Jesus was not at all interested in social reform as such.'[52]

A more difficult line for Weber was that between the prophet and the *teacher of ethics*, a main example of which was the Indian guru, since 'the philosophical ethicist and the social reformer are not prophets in our sense of the word, no matter how closely they may seem to resemble prophets'. He added, 'What primarily differentiates such figures from the prophets is their lack of that vital emotional *preaching* which is distinctive of prophecy.'[53] Contrarily, the prophet was also for Weber not a mystagogue, even though mystagogues 'sometimes revealed new ways of salvation'. The difference here was that 'ethical doctrine was lacking in the mystagogue'.[54] For Weber, then, prophets – who exercised charismatic authority and who attracted devoted followings – fell finally into one of two categories, that of the ethical prophet, like Muhammad, who 'received a commission from God' and demanded 'obedience as an ethical duty', and that of the exemplary prophet, like the Buddha, 'who, by his personal example, demonstrate[d] to others the way to religious salvation'.[55]

Still later Weber turned to an analysis of religious groups, especially the world's 'great religions'. Of these, he took Christianity and Buddhism to be religions of world-rejection, as opposed to 'the world-conquest of Islam, or . . . the messianic expectations and economic pariah law of Judaism';[56] and it was in this context that he discussed Jesus at length.

Jesus was for Weber 'primarily a magician whose magical charisma was an ineluctable source of his unique feeling of individuality' and an interpreter of the Jewish law whose interpretation was in some ways stricter but in other ways less strict than the interpretation of the Pharisees, whom Weber considered to be 'erudite scholars . . . trained in casuistry'.[57] A portion of his description of Jesus is worth quoting at some length.

> Jesus' distinctive self-esteem did not come from anything like a 'proletarian instinct' but from the knowledge that the way to God necessarily led through him, because of his oneness with the Godly patriarch. His self-esteem was grounded in the knowledge that he, the non-scholar, possessed both the charisma requisite for the control of demons and a tremendous preaching ability, far surpassing that of any scholar or Pharisee . . . It should never be forgotten that these charismatic powers were the absolutely decisive components in Jesus' feelings concerning his messiahship.[58] . . . But Jesus held in general that what is most decisive for salvation is an absolute indifference to the world and its concerns.[59]

Finally, in a section on 'Charisma and Its Transformation', Weber discussed the structure and function of charisma as background to his discussion of the now famous concept of the 'routinization of charisma'. In order to bring charismatic authority into focus here, Weber contrasted it to both bureaucracy and patriarchalism and analysed how each of the three authority systems satisfies wants. Bureaucracy and patriarchalism, in his view, are 'oriented toward the satisfaction of calculable needs with ordinary, everyday means'; but 'all *extra*-ordinary needs, i.e., those which *transcend* the sphere of everyday economic routines, have always been satisfied in an entirely heterogeneous manner: on a *charismatic* basis'.[60] This means, of course, that charisma 'is *the* strongest anti-economic force',[61] but it also means that 'charismatic authority is naturally unstable' because the prophet must continually meet those extraordinary needs. The prophet 'gains and retains [his authority] solely by proving his powers in practice. He must work miracles, if he wants to be a prophet . . . Most of all, his divine mission must prove itself by *bringing well-being* to his faithful followers; if they do not fare well, he obviously is not the god-sent master.' Consequently, when Jesus was put to death, he naturally felt 'forsaken by his God'.[62] The obverse side of this situation, however, is the followers' acceptance of and submission to charismatic authority. 'The mere fact of recognizing the personal mission of a charismatic master establishes his power,' wrote Weber. 'Hence, in a revolutionary and sovereign manner, charismatic domination transforms all values and breaks all traditional and rational norms: "It has been written . . ., but *I* say unto you . . . "'[63]

From these statements we see that Weber (who, incidentally, certainly had Jesus in mind when he was describing charismatic leaders in general) thought of the charismatic leader as someone who knew himself to be divinely inspired and called, who attested his special status by performing miracles or other wonders and by attracting a following of persons who owed allegiance only to him, and who offered a true break from the status quo and introduced some radically new teaching or regimen. 'Charisma became . . . for Weber that ecstatic encounter which alone was capable of generating a vibrant force fully sufficient to break through established ecclesiastical structures with the bold, new promise of yet a better way toward achieving knowledge of God and salvation from the world.'[64] Hengel, as we noted already, applied this definition to Jesus and his followers. (Perhaps it will be well to point out that Weber did not mean revolutionary in the socio-political sense, as some apply the term to Jesus today, and as others have so applied it in former times.)[65] One implication of this radical newness is that it is unpredictable, for were the charismatic leader's new approach predictable, then of course it would not have the quality of radical newness about it that Weber notes, and it would lose its aura – that is, its charismatic aspect. Therefore we may say that Weber glimpsed the unpredictable nature of charismatic leadership, even though he did not employ just that term.

Before continuing we must note a *caveat*. A number of sociologists have pointed out that a charismatic leader cannot be charismatic all on his own, that charisma depends as much on the situation and on the (willing) followers as it does on the leader himself;[66] and this is surely correct. Weber, as a matter of fact, was hardly unaware of this side of the charismatic phenomenon; he wrote that Jesus' 'self-esteem involved the conviction that his power to exorcise demons was operative only among the people who believed in him'.[67] The high priest Caiaphas, for example, would hardly have described Jesus as a charismatic leader.

In its extreme form, the view that charisma is a projection of a collectivity goes back to Emile Durkheim, who wrote that 'if [society] happens to fall in love with a man and if it thinks it has found in him the principal aspirations that move it, as well as a means of satisfying them, this man will be raised above the others and, as it were, deified'.[68] Bryan Wilson, with his 'charismatic demand', is the most prominent contemporary exponent of this view.[69] On the other hand, however, Len Oakes is of the opinion that 'what all prophets have in common is their opposition to convention and their ability to inspire others with their visions'; and he adds, 'It simply beggars the imagination to suggest that men such as . . . Bhagwan Shree Rajneesh and Sun Myung Moon are not really, objectively, unusual people possessing exceptional abilities to inspire the kinds of mass followings they have achieved.'[70] Thus, for those who did experience Jesus' charisma, that charisma was extreme; and his followers made the most extravagant claims about him, as we know (miracles, messianic and divine titles). Given this understanding, some sociologists, while recognizing the truth of the two- or three-sidedness of charisma, have continued to analyse the nature of charisma in charismatic leaders of NRMs.

Robert Tucker emphasizes the interdependence of the leader and the followers when he declares, 'To speak of charismatic leaders . . . is to speak of charismatic movements; the two phenomena are inseparable.'[71] And Roy Wallis takes the same position: 'Charisma is essentially a relationship born out of interaction between a leader and his followers.'[72] Wallis at first seemed to agree with Bryan Wilson's view of that relationship, writing that charisma 'emerges out of a particular structure of social relationships';[73] yet he later came to propose that 'charisma has a greater role as an explanation of a *leader's* actions and their consequences than . . . as an attempted explanation of the behaviour of his *followers*'.[74] On this view charisma provided 'problems, opportunities, and resources . . . within which a leader must formulate his strategy and conduct his activities'. As we shall come to see below, when we look at a modern charismatic leader, a leader's charisma can by no means be defined solely as something projected on to him by a collectivity. The leader needs the followers, of course, and he would be nothing without them; but followers do not randomly simply put someone up as the embodiment of their hopes. Tucker says as much: 'The charismatic leader is not simply any leader who is idolized and freely followed for his extraordinary leadership qualities, but one who *demonstrates such qualities in the process of summoning people to join in a movement* for change and in leading such a movement.'[75]

A second aspect of charismatic leadership that some contemporary sociologists emphasize is the role of crisis in creating such leadership, and especially Bryan Wilson draws attention to this aspect. For him, 'the growth of anxieties and the disruption of normal life' provoke the charismatic demand that he sees at the root of charismatic leadership.[76] Tucker, further, writes that the charismatic leader 'is a leader who convincingly offers himself to a group of people in distress as one peculiarly qualified to lead them out of their predicament'.[77] It is thus a 'state of acute distress', of whatever kind, that 'predisposes people to perceive' a certain person as a saviour from distress,[78] and it is this situation of distress that gives the leader a 'peculiar sense of mission'. Indeed, in Tucker's opinion, it is charismatic leaders' 'self-confident' assurance that they can provide salvation (in whatever form) from the situation of distress that probably 'underlies their charisma and explains the extreme devotion and loyalty that they inspire in their followers'.[79] As we shall see below, to speak of social distress as a factor contributing to the rise of charismatic leaders of NRMs is more accurate than to speak of crisis.

A third aspect of charismatic leadership that has emerged in the recent discussion is that of randomness, for in fact randomness increases charisma.[80] Eileen Barker saw this clearly in her studies of the Rev. Sun Myung Moon. 'To a non-follower,' she wrote,

> the authority wielded by a charismatic leader may seem capricious, irrational, and totally incomprehensible . . . Charismatic leaders are unfettered by rules; no one can anticipate where they are going . . . reinterpretations or complete changes of doctrine can be revealed and contrary orders issued. *No one else can grasp and interpret the way, the truth, and the light with certainty*; the word of the charismatic leader is both unpredictable and unquestionable.[81]

Barker thus makes it clear that this randomness is a necessary ingredient of charismatic leadership. Without it the leader would have no aura of 'the other' about him; his charisma would be minimal.

Roy Wallis, also, has taken particular note of such randomness.[82] Writing of 'massive changes in the . . . character' of one NRM that he studied,[83] Wallis found that the leader's erratic and radical changes in the nature and direction of the movement were a means of maintaining charismatic control in the face of a threat of routinization.[84] This leader 'recognized that in order to maximize the mobilizability of his following in their mission, he would have to overcome the tendency of his lieutenants to seek to stabilize the membership for pragmatic reasons'.[85] That is to say that the leader fought off the 'routinization of charisma', to use Weber's term, by keeping even his lieutenants off guard. This would be analogous to Jesus' continually surprising the twelve. The leader's new moves were patently arbitrary, so that Wallis writes, 'The arbitrariness of his statements entailed that one should not even be committed to any particular thing he said but to [the leader] *regardless* of what he said!'[86] Thus Weber's principle of innovation has become, in this particular case, arbitrariness in the interest of maintaining charisma. In another case Wallis finds that a certain political leader, whom the news media and others often call charismatic, cannot be, because he is too 'constrained by tradition'. 'The greater the constraint,' he concludes axiomatically, 'the further the departure from charismatic authority.'[87]

Biblical scholars will immediately see the types of the priest and the prophet here, the one completely 'constrained by tradition', the other given to 'arbitrariness'. Interestingly, however, just in the context of that discussion Wallis provides a brief analysis of the charismatic aspect of the Hebrew prophets and finds that they, also, were probably too 'constrained by tradition' to merit the term 'charismatic' (thus differing with Weber). The biblical prophets are in any case 'more constrained than Jesus, Hitler or Moses David' (who was the modern leader under discussion in the preceding paragraph).[88] Michael Toth, whose primary interest is the leader of the second, 'routinizing' stage of a movement, emphasizes the same innovative quality in the original charismatic leader. While the leader of the second phase, in Toth's analysis, is 'more conventional, mundane, practical' than the original leader, 'the first leader is strange, fascinating, unusual, unearthly'.[89] The language will doubtless remind readers of this volume of Rudolph Otto's description of the Holy. Surely, however, that is just the way Jesus affected his followers. The routine and expected do not call forth such a response as Jesus received; the random and innovative, however, do. We biblical scholars, geared to rigorous historical method and intent on finding coherence in Jesus' 'message', have often tended to overlook just this numinous quality of Jesus which led his followers to experience in his presence the *mysterium tremendum ac fascinans*.

Finally, one further aspect of charismatic leadership that a few social scientists since Weber have emphasized is that the leader provokes not just a following, but hatred. Tucker considers the leader's 'capacity to inspire hatred as well as loyalty and love' to be 'probably a universal feature of the charismatic leader'.[90]

A few social scientists have attempted a psychological approach to understanding charismatic leaders of NRMs, and Len Oakes' profile is at least worth noting.[91] After very thorough studies of a number of contemporary leaders of NRMs, Oakes concluded that their careers all passed through five stages: early narcissism, incubation, awakening, mission, and decline or fall (which could include 'being jailed or assassinated').[92] While this profile, however, may be worth pondering, it would be fruitless to pursue it further here, in view of the impossibility of subjecting Jesus to any kind of psychological examination.

Now, before turning to Jesus, we need to examine the career of one modern charismatic leader of an NRM to see how well he fits the pattern and to give some more specificity to the type. As the comparison between this modern person (with some glances at a few others) and Jesus unfolds, we shall see the wisdom of the procedure; but here at the outset some theoretical remarks on the issue of commensurability may be appropriate. How can we consider it suitable to compare Jesus with any moderns? This is not a path that most historians are accustomed to following, and we have noted especially Hengel's and Vermes' reliance on comparators who were more or less contemporary with Jesus. Yet we also recall that Weber's main examples of the type of the prophet were Jesus, Muhammad, the Buddha, and Zarathushtra – the latest, Muhammad, being at least roughly 1200 years removed from the earliest, Zarathushtra. Surely we all see the appropriateness of comparing the founders of certain great world religions, even though they be separated from one another by centuries and by hundreds of miles. Comparison does not mean that one equates them all or makes them all fit into one Procrustean mould; but we compare them to see what we can learn about figures of that type. Certainly Weber's analyses were fruitful, and the more recent studies that we have surveyed have continued to improve on his definition(s); thus, if we want to understand Jesus, we are in fact remiss if we do not make use of modern comparisons. As Len Oakes observes, 'One might think that the comparative study of revolutionary religious leaders would be a priority for scholars wishing to shed light on the person of Jesus . . . But such studies are seldom undertaken.'[93]

Some New Testament scholars may fear that comparing Jesus with modern religious leaders risks giving up Jesus' uniqueness. (Indeed, the real point of Hengel's study was to show Jesus' uniqueness, not to show that he conformed to a type.)[94] But this issue should cause no concern, for of course Jesus was unique. That is a historical fact. So also were Weber's comparators and the more modern leaders to whom we are about to turn. Were it helpful in our immediate task of trying to answer why people followed Jesus, we could explore the ways in which Jesus was unique – from a historical, not from a theological point of view. Others have done that.[95] But our thesis here is that Jesus – all questions of uniqueness aside – conformed to a type, the charismatic leader of an NRM, and that such people have followers. Having surveyed relevant literature from the social sciences, we need now to demonstrate that thesis in detail.

(ii) Example and comparison

Our example is one who has been studied in great detail – by followers, by disaffected former followers, and by sociologists of religion and other outsiders – Bhagwan Shree Rajneesh. Certainly it is true that many persons, doubtless many readers of this volume, have thought of Rajneesh (Bhagwan is a later, self-adopted title)[96] as a pervert, a tax cheat and a charlatan; but did not many in Jesus' day think the same of him? The indictment against Jesus in Luke's Gospel is: 'Perverting our people and forbidding giving tribute to Caesar and saying that he was Christ, a king (or: that he was an anointed king)' (Luke 23.2). If we keep in mind that our comparison is only formal, having to do with the type of the charismatic leader of an NRM, and not one of similarity of character or of sincerity, then the comparison will prove enlightening.

In the discussion up to this point, we have defined four aspects of a charismatic leader of an NRM: his charismatic qualities, the situation of crisis or distress that calls forth his charisma and to which that charisma responds, the importance of randomness to charisma, and the hatred that a charismatic leader of an NRM provokes. Because of the nature of the evidence it seems advisable to divide the discussion of the first aspect into four: call, wonders, teachings, and calling disciples.

(a) The call

If by the term 'call' we think of the charismatic leader's hearing a voice (even in thought) or experiencing one single moment or event, at which time he knew with certainty that he should lead a new movement, then the term is misleading. It would probably be better to speak of a *sense of mission*. Rajneesh, an educated son of a middle-class Jain family, did experience, beginning at the age of nineteen, something analogous to a Christian conversion, but this experience did not start him on his career. Always a non-conformist, even as a child, Rajneesh began to display such bizarre behaviour (e.g., sitting in trees to meditate) that 'his concerned parents believed he was going crazy' and sought medical help. One physician, however, was 'a traditional Ayurvedic physician' who thought that 'the apparent breakdown was actually a kind of breakthrough'. His diagnosis seems to have been correct, since Rajneesh later said 'that on March 21, 1953, at the age of twenty-one, he did "reach home". He became enlightened.'[97]

His mission, however, developed over a period of time. He earned bachelor's and master's degrees in philosophy and then taught philosophy at first one and then another college. His non-conformist tendencies, however, soon led him to give up teaching philosophy in college to become an itinerant iconoclast, attacking even Gandhi.[98] This iconoclasm began to come to the notice of young Western adults, especially Germans, and 'by 1981 [Rajneesh] had established a commune in Poona, India'.[99] The commune grew, and Rajneesh's fame spread throughout Europe and the United States. Later Rajneesh and his followers left India to establish a commune in eastern Oregon. Aside from the constant motif of non-conformity and iconoclasm, however, what Rajneesh taught underwent periodic revision (we shall discuss some details of his teachings below), so that exactly what Rajneesh considered his mission to be is less than clear. A disaffected follower, Hugh Milne, writes that Rajneesh 'undoubtedly possessed remarkable gifts, but at the same time he was in the grip of a need for power and wealth that was nothing short of megalomaniacal'. These two sides to his personality meant that he was 'quite ruthless to an extent hardly known in the West. But he could also communicate a feeling of unconditional love that was, to everyone who experienced it, unquestionably the real thing.'[100] Yet his 'mission' appears to have been something that grew and developed, perhaps in response to the direction of charismatic demand (to use Bryan Wilson's term).

With Jesus we have a somewhat analogous situation, in that we have no definitive information about his call. The heavenly voice at his baptism, while reported by both the Synoptics and John, is surely a legendary or perhaps mythical element.[101] John Meier considers it part of the 'weighty freight of Christian theology overshadowing the . . . baptism proper'.[102] The baptism itself, of course, merely means that Jesus was first a follower of John the Baptist before setting out on an independent career, even if we can see in the baptism, with Meier, a 'basic break with [Jesus'] past life'.[103] We cannot view it as Jesus' 'call'. The baptism of Jesus is comparable to Christian conversion, or to Rajneesh's enlightenment. Perhaps the temptation, then? But here we face insurmountable historical questions. Bultmann considered the temptation narrative, again, a legend;[104] and Meier's reasoning seems conclusive: 'Granted the paucity of sources and their conflicting presentations of the temptation of Jesus,' he wrote, 'any judgment about a historical event is extremely difficult.' To this he added that, while there may be some kernel of truth to the temptation narratives – e.g., perhaps Jesus did retire to the wilderness for a period of reflection or meditation – still 'one must also recognize that the entire tradition of Jesus' temptation by Satan in the wilderness may be a symbolic representation of the apocalyptic struggle between

God and the devil which was prophesied for the last days and which – according to Christian faith – became a reality in the ministry . . . of Jesus'.[105]

Of course, as in the case of Rajneesh, one may gather at least some idea of Jesus' sense of mission from what he said – and from what he did. If we leave aside the many purposive sayings in the Fourth Gospel as reflecting Johannine theology rather than Jesus' own views, then of course we have the ambiguity of the synoptic material, which has received a variety of interpretations from (let us choose a watershed point) Albert Schweitzer until now. It would serve little purpose to review the history of the scholarly discussion of Jesus' *mission* here, but it may be helpful to survey the positions of a few recent scholars who have written on Jesus. If we note the positions of Norman Perrin, of Joachim Jeremias, of Geza Vermes, of E. P. Sanders and of Dominic Crossan, we shall have surveyed treatments of Jesus that are comprehensive, that have been widely noted by other scholars, and that present an interesting spectrum of conclusions about the nature of Jesus' mission.

For Perrin, 'the central feature of the message of Jesus is . . . the challenge of the forgiveness of sins and the offer of the possibility of a new kind of relationship with God and with one's fellow man'.[106] This new relationship was an anticipatory living in the Kingdom of God, so that 'discipleship begins and continues in the context of the experience of the activity of God as king'.[107] According to Perrin, Jesus made the possibility of this new relationship available in his parables. 'The ministry of Jesus makes the present of that ministry, and of the people confronted by it, God's present in a new and radical manner.'[108] Jeremias, Perrin's teacher, had laid great emphasis on Jesus' addressing God as Daddy (Aramaic *Abba*), thereby implying a special relationship with God.[109] For Jeremias, Jesus was calling the people of God together during a period of grace in advance of the coming catastrophe. At the time of this 'great turning point'[110] Gentiles would also enter the Kingdom.[111] Thus 'in the sayings of Jesus, the conception of the *basileia* is *stripped* not only of all nationalistic features but also of all *materialistic features'.*[112] This turning point would also be, in Jesus' expectation, the time of his coming as Son of man.[113]

Vermes' Jesus is primarily a Galilean Ḥasid, prophet, charismatic.[114] Jesus' christological titles (prophet, lord, Messiah, Son of man, and Son of God) are christological only in the later interpretation of Christianity; originally, and properly understood, they referred to Jesus' charismatic status.[115] Thus:

A powerful healer of the physically and mentally sick, a friend of sinners, he was a magnetic preacher of what lies at the heart of the Law, unconditionally given over to the rescue, not of communities, but of persons in need. He was always aware of the approach of the end of time and, at the moment known only to God, of the imminent intervention of our Father who is in heaven, who is to be revealed soon, the awesome and just Judge, Lord of all the worlds.[116]

E. P. Sanders, Vermes' Oxford colleague at the time, also sought to understand Jesus not as distinct from Judaism, but within Judaism. For him Jesus promoted a 'restoration eschatology'[117] that is most clearly seen in his overturning the tables of the money changers in the temple area and in his sayings about the destruction of the temple.[118] With that understanding in hand, Sanders then further interprets Jesus' ministry as offering God's grace to the 'truly wicked':

It seems to be the case . . . that Jesus offered the truly wicked – those beyond the pale and outside the common religion by virtue of their implicit or explicit rejection of the commandments of the God of Israel – admission to *his* group (and, he claimed the kingdom) *if* they accepted him. Putting the matter this way explains the connection between tax collectors and sinners in the Gospels (complete outsiders), attributes to Jesus a distinctive view of his own mission and the nature of the kingdom, and offers an explanation of what in Jesus' message was offensive to normal piety.[119]

Sanders raises the issue of coherence in the teaching of Jesus and votes to abstain:

> The nature of the sayings material will not allow us to be certain about the precise nuance which Jesus wished to give such a large concept as 'the kingdom of God'. We can see that 'kingdom' has a range of meanings in the Synoptics, but we cannot see just how much emphasis should be placed on each meaning. We never have absolute certainty of authenticity, and we probably have the original context of any given saying seldom, if ever.[120]

Crossan, finally, sees Jesus as a social revolutionary promoting an egalitarian programme. Jesus' ministry 'did not invite a political revolution but envisaged a social one at the imagination's most dangerous depths. No importance was given to distinctions of Gentile and Jew, female and male, slave and free, poor and rich.' Jesus, in Crossan's understanding, performed healing miracles and then asked to be fed. He said, in effect, that the Kingdom of God 'is, was, and always will be available to any who want it. Dress as I do, like a beggar, but do not beg. Bring a miracle and request a table. Those you heal must accept you into their homes.'[121]

If we look for common denominators here we find none beside the Kingdom of God. Beyond that, our sample of Jesus scholars does not agree entirely on anything; not on eschatology, not on who Jesus' target audience was, not on what he thought of himself. This situation is the result of the indefiniteness, the ambiguity present in the synoptic material, to which we alluded above. E. P. Sanders, in his statement quoted above on the meaning of the Kingdom of God, also sees the problem of recovering Jesus' exact definition of the term. Fortunately, however, for our purposes here we do not need to make one more attempt to define Jesus' mission, since the realization that he considered himself to have a mission is the important point. As a millenarian prophet and charismatic leader of an NRM, he was propelled by a burning sense of mission, one that – as far as we can tell, at any rate, from the Gospel materials – he would not abandon even when it meant his death. Nevertheless, Jesus' own concept of his mission may have changed during the course of his public ministry.

The great majority of New Testament scholars have been convinced that Jesus had, from his baptism until his death, one consistent, coherent complex of ideas that he was promoting. Normally we do not entertain the notion that he may have changed direction during his brief career. We must note, however, that if Jesus had such a clear notion, he failed to convey it to his followers in such a way that it could find its way into the synoptic tradition in a form that moderns could recognize. Otherwise we would not have such a diversity of opinions among scholarly works on Jesus. The fact that modern Jesus scholars, even when we discount those who still recreate Jesus in their own images (and after Schweitzer's exposé how can they yet do this?), can agree only on the *term* Kingdom of God should perhaps open us up to the fact that Jesus' own concept of his mission may not have been, from first to last, uniform, consistent and coherent. Perhaps he, like Rajneesh, was compelled by charismatic demand. At the very least we can be almost certain of this: Jesus', like Rajneesh's, attracting of a large following will surely have confirmed his own sense of his self-importance and of his mission.

When all this has been said, however, we should yet give attention to the interesting possibility raised by Ben Meyer that Jesus was propelled into his mission by John the Baptist's arrest. Meyer notes especially the Matthaean wording of Jesus' response to John's arrest. Mark had written simply, 'After John had been handed over, Jesus went to Galilee' (Mark 1.14), whereas Matthew has it that Jesus, 'hearing that John had been handed over, departed to Galilee' (Matt. 4.12; Luke 4.14 notes merely that Jesus 'returned' to Galilee but makes no mention of John). Meyer observes that the Synoptics leave 'unexplained why Jesus had remained in Judaea until John's arrest . . . and why the arrest should have had particular and decisive significance for him'.[122] (To be precise, since only Matthew implies particular and decisive significance, Meyer should have written that Matthew, not the Synoptics as a group, leaves this significance unexplained.) 'The lacuna,' he finds, 'is filled by data given in the Fourth Gospel,' where Jesus, with his own disciples, had been active as an ally of John. Meyer refers to John 3.26, where John's disciples query him about the one [i.e., Jesus] 'who was with you beyond the Jordan; . . . behold he is baptizing and all are coming to him'. Meyer reasons that, 'in view of [the] discontinuity [of Jesus' situation revealed in the query of John's disciples] with the tendency of the tradition to accent the independence of Jesus, this Johannine tradition may well reflect the historic beginnings of Jesus' career'.[123] In support of this conjecture Meyer further submits Jesus' sayings about the Baptist, especially Matt. 11.11, 'There has not arisen among those born of women a greater than John the Baptist; but the least in the Kingdom of Heaven is greater than he.' Thus, in Meyer's view, Jesus came to see John's career as an 'inauguration' and his own as 'transform[ing] the world'.[124] One recalls Günther Bornkamm's formulation that 'John [was] sent by God in the time of preparation for the end, and Jesus [was] the bringer of the time of rejoicing'.[125]

Many scholars who have sought to understand Jesus, of course, have seen Jesus beginning as John's disciple and then moving out on his own. We may take John Meier as representative of this view. For Meier the 'criterion of embarrassment' supports the authenticity of the tradition that Jesus baptized – that is, 'The entire Synoptic tradition was so embarrassed by the fact [of Jesus' baptizing activity] that it simply suppressed this aspect of Jesus' public life' (essentially Ben Meyer's point). Thus 'the main reason why the picture of Jesus baptizing is included in the Gospel [of John] may be that it was too deeply rooted in the Johannine tradition and too widely known to friend and foe alike simply to be omitted'.[126] The final redactor of the Gospel, however, 'considered the datum too dangerous to stand unchallenged', and so he added 4.2 at the conclusion of the narrative: 'And yet Jesus himself did not baptize, but his disciples.' Here the embarrassment re-emerges.

Nevertheless, Meier does not bring the tradition of Jesus' having been a disciple of John or of Jesus' baptizing together with Matt. 4.12, as does Ben Meyer. For Meier, Jesus' own ministry developed out of his participating in John's ministry, so that 'while Jesus . . . basically affirms and seconds the eschatological message of the Baptist [as in Matt. 11.11, which we just noted], he likewise indicates the important difference between John and himself. For Jesus, the end time John awaited as just-around-the-corner has arrived.'[127] Again we are reminded of Bornkamm's formulation, that the difference between the Baptist and Jesus is 'like that between the eleventh and the twelfth hours'.[128]

Yet the evidence that Jesus moved out from under John's leadership in his own independent direction is lacking any reference to a precise time when Jesus realized that he should do that, and putting the weight on Matt. 4.12 that Ben Meyer puts on it seems to be rather too much; although, proving Meyer wrong would be difficult, if not impossible. If, then, the most prudent course is to say that the evidence is abundant that Jesus had a pronounced sense of mission, even if we cannot be certain just what that sense was or whether it was consistent throughout his career, and that his sense of mission developed in some way out of his time as a follower of the Baptist, even if we cannot finger a precise time when Jesus came to realize and accept that mission, we nevertheless see that Jesus, in this particular, conforms to the type of charismatic leader of an NRM just in the same way in which Rajneesh conforms to the type.

(b) Wonders

There is no need to discuss Jesus' wonders, since they are such a prominent feature of the Gospel tradition, however much explanations of his wonders have varied and will continue to vary. Probably most New Testament scholars today would agree in general with the judgment of John Meier, who, introducing his discussion of the historicity of Jesus' miracles, points to Josephus' agreement with the Gospels when Josephus writes, in the *Testimonium Flavianum* (*Ant.* 18.3.3),[129] that Jesus was 'a doer of incredible (παράδοξοι) works'. For Meier this statement, taken together with the accounts in both the Synoptics and the Fourth Gospel, presents a 'rare' case of multiple attestation.[130]

What is noteworthy for us at this point is that Jesus, as a charismatic leader of an NRM, was in this way fitting the pattern, for other such leaders also possess extraordinary powers, perform healings, and the like. Hugh Milne, the disaffected follower of Rajneesh who was a principal bodyguard known as Shiva during his sanyassin (disciple) days, describes his first meeting with Rajneesh:

Here was my spiritual father, a man who understood everything, someone who would be able to convey sense and meaning into my life. It was a truly magical feeling. I was overawed, transported, and felt instantly that Bhagwan was inside my mind as nobody else had ever been able to be. From the moment his delicate brown hands with their perfectly manicured nails touched mine, I knew I was in another world . . . During that meeting, called a 'darshan', time stopped. I was flying, and every care had disappeared.[131]

Later, Milne writes, Rajneesh's followers experienced powers heightened even further:

Bhagwan gradually began to acquire for us the characteristics of a supernatural being. If you only just managed to catch a train because a taxi was inexplicably standing in the right place at the right time, it was all 'through his grace'. It was mostly Laxmi [Rajneesh's chief secretary in Poona] who spread the idea that Bhagwan was a Godlike person who could influence events – the weather, financial matters, relationships, trouble with the police or with passports. She would say, 'He will take care. Don't worry.' Bhagwan certainly did possess psychic gifts; of this I remain convinced.

However much he enhanced a belief in himself through showmanship and Laxmi's adoration, there was still something beyond the usual range of abilities. *He did have paranormal powers.*[132]

And Milne answered the question that he said 'many people' had asked, namely how he could become 'mesmerized by someone like Bhagwan', in this way.

Once you had been affected by his energy and experienced the sensation of being touched by it, you knew that there was nothing like it, no bliss to compare with it . . . It is similar to a drug-induced high, except that here there is no artificial chemical at work. Bhagwan's touch could be just as addictive as the strongest drug.[133]

We must be clear that Milne writes not just for himself – he was not the only one so affected by Rajneesh – but for hundreds, even thousands of Europeans and Americans who followed Rajneesh first to Poona and then to a former ranch near Antelope, Oregon. When these people encountered Rajneesh they encountered, as far as they were concerned, the divine.

Similarly with the Rev. Sun Myung Moon, leader of the Unification Church (Moonies). According to church tradition, on one occasion when Moon was jailed in Korea in his early years he was badly beaten and thrown out as dead. His followers were preparing to bury him when, miraculously, he began to breathe again.[134] Furthermore, before the mass marriages that he arranged for his followers, he led a 'Holy Wine Ceremony', during which original sin was removed from the couples, so that 'children born to the blessed couples will be born without fallen nature'.[135]

Rajneesh even discovered how to institutionalize this charismatic power. James Gordon, an American psychoanalyst who was a participant observer at different intervals both in Poona and in Oregon, explains how Rajneesh organized different

types of meditation groups for his devotees in Poona, one type
of which was the therapy group. These groups were supposed
to help the devotees rid themselves of emotional and psychological problems, and they employed a – from the Western
point of view – strangely direct method of accomplishing
that.[136] Participants had to face their emotional problems in
'cathartic confrontations' in which 'the ordinary limitations of
therapy groups everywhere else were breached and extended'.
This meant that people who had 'complementary problems'
were paired within the groups so that, for example, 'the girl
who had been raped had her counterpart in the man who feared
and hated and humiliated women', and these two would
express their problems to each other, even to the point of
violence. Thus 'a woman might be mocked, seduced, and on
occasion actually raped by a man who was just like the one who
had seduced her as a child. A terrified man might be told to
sleep with the domineering woman who reminded him of his
mother,' and so on.[137] Abhorrent as such practices doubtless
seem to most readers of this volume, the people who experienced them felt that the practices worked and that the therapy
sessions cleansed them of emotional problems. Even more to
the point, however, the healed experienced *Rajneesh*'s power in
such healings, which were directed by Rajneesh's lieutenants.
(We recall that Jesus' disciples could manifest his charismatic
power, and not only after the resurrection; for when he sent
them out it was with the gift [ἐδίδου αὐτοῖς] of 'authority over
unclean spirits' [Mark 6.7; cf. Matt. 10.1; Luke 9.1].) Gordon
writes that 'sometimes . . . after a particularly cathartic con-
frontation . . . group members were told [by the group leaders]
to "look at the picture of Bhagwan, into his eyes". "Surrender
more deeply to the group and the group leader", they were
reminded when they seemed resistant. The leaders were "mani-
festations of Bhagwan", "vehicles for his energy".'[138]

However we may evaluate Jesus' and Rajneesh's healing
and wonder-working powers, we see that *in the eyes of their
followers in each case*, they manifested such powers. In doing
so, they fulfilled the role of the charismatic leader of an NRM.

(c) Teachings

Jesus' teachings we also do not need to ponder, since that he was a teacher belongs to the bedrock of the Jesus tradition, and since his teachings make up such a large part of the Gospel tradition, however difficult it is for modern scholars to be certain about just what the point of his teaching was. (We recall the discussion above of the different ways in which a few modern Jesus scholars have construed Jesus' teaching.) Furthermore, it is perfectly clear from the Gospels that later Christians considered Jesus' teachings of paramount importance and that they understood the teachings to apply to their own circumstances (thus the differences among the Gospels in how Jesus' teachings are construed, even when individual sayings may be the same, or nearly so, from one Gospel to another).

With Rajneesh, we do not face the difficulty that we face with Jesus in recovering his original teachings, since his organization published his writings, and since many of his addresses were recorded and are available in print and on tapes. We might, in fact, dispense with any further discussion of this point, since it is so patently clear that both Jesus and Rajneesh were teachers; but it may be that if we turn our attention, at least briefly, to *what* Rajneesh taught, we may learn something more about charismatic leaders of NRMs and the way they teach; and that knowledge may lead us to some further insight about Jesus.[139]

At the heart of Rajneesh's teaching was the Eastern notion, so different from the Western concept of religion, of achieving enlightenment. Rajneesh claimed 'to have achieved enlightenment', and he promoted a Buddhist version of enlightenment, to understand one's own self – that is, to realize one's own 'Buddha nature'. 'Tacitly or explicitly – it varied from discourse to discourse – he promised his sannyasins [disciples]' an enlightened liberation similar to his, 'from the repetitive round of neurotic thought and behaviour, from life-denying apprehensions, and from fear of both death and life'.[140]

Yet, as the situation of his organization changed – from India to America and from flourishing to chaos – Rajneesh's teaching also shifted. James Gordon summarizes.[141] At the time of his enlightenment, Rajneesh followed a 'Tantric approach – pursuing a way to its limits'. He pursued a path of 'rebellious individualism'. Then, as a young philosophy teacher, his iconoclastic lectures made him appear 'like some itinerant anarchist organizer' but also made him attractive to Western young adults who were just maturing 'as the antiwar movement and the student rebellions in the West were exhausting themselves'. For these people 'Rajneesh was fresh', and he offered them the possibility of discovering themselves through enlightenment. What he taught was not really original, being 'in many ways similar to that of other mystics, . . . but he presented his message in a way that was more accessible and modern, more immediately relevant to the way that searching Westerners actually lived and felt and thought'.

The move to Oregon, however, meant the bringing to fruition of 'cross-fertilization between the energy of democratic America, and the contemplativeness of the East'. 'On Rancho Rajneesh, with the guidance of the visionary prophet Bhagwan, [Rajneesh's followers] would build heaven on earth.' Thus when Rajneesh first arrived in the United States he declared, 'I am the Messiah America is waiting for.'

Furthermore, early during his silent period (March 1981– October 1984), Rajneesh had his new chief secretary, Sheela, promote a new religion, the religion of 'Rajneeshism'.[142] This new religion would have three orders of ministers, with separate duties assigned to each; and it prescribed a standard (traditional Buddhist) mantra for daily recitation. He later explained that this new religion 'would be a kind of religiousness, not a dogma, a cult or creed but only a quality of love, silence, meditation and prayerfulness'. In Gordon's words, 'It was a "religionless religion".' This latter explanation that Rajneesh gave was apparently meant to ease the shock of the new religion for the sannyasins, now to be called Rajneeshees, inasmuch as Rajneesh had always taught previously that all religions were inadequate and only dimly grasped the understanding that he was promoting in its pure form. He now altered this last point, claiming that he had (in Gordon's words) 'an advantage over the other great spiritual teachers – Jesus, Buddha, Lao-tzu, Krishna' because 'they were unaware of each other. He had come afterward and had learned from their mistakes.' And the new religion of Rajneeshism 'would for the first time unite the meditativeness of the Eastern traditions with the activism of the West'. 'All other religions, he announced, "will disappear into Rajneeshism as all the rivers disappear into the ocean".'

During Rajneesh's silent period he ceased to give the daily evening lectures or homilies that had been his custom for so many years, and he merely sat on his dais while his followers worshipped before him. This, of course, increased the impression that he was some kind of divine being, and it is now time to note the meaning of the title 'Bhagwan' that he had earlier taken for himself. It literally means 'blessed one' 'but is used in India to describe an incarnation of God'.[143] Rajneesh explained at the time, 'When I call myself God I mean to provoke you, to challenge you . . . so that you start recognizing that you are also divine';[144] but the evening worship sessions during his silent period will have given a heightened impression of his 'Bhagwan-ness'. Nevertheless, when Rajneesh began to lecture again, now promoting his new religion, he insisted that 'he was an "ordinary man" and "ordinariness is blessed"'[145] – thus he seemed now to be defining Bhagwan to mean ordinary man. He added, however, that he was still different from others, but that the difference was 'not of quality, it is only of knowing. I know myself, you don't know yourself'; and he made an analogous distinction between his new religion of Rajneeshism and all other religions: 'All the religions,' he stated, 'are based on fear. They are antilife. No religion has accepted a sense of humor as a quality of religiousness . . . My religion is the first religion which accepts man whole as he is.'[146] Thus in spite of his claim to ordinariness, Rajneesh at the same time continued to place himself and his new religion within a different order of existence. The sociologist and participant-observer Susan Palmer was present at Rajneesh's lecture in October 1984 that broke his silence and records that he said at that time 'that he had travelled so deeply into the Absolute through his silence that he was now virtually indistinguishable from It'.[147]

All writers who have sought to analyse the Rajneesh movement over time have emphasized these shifts. As a further example of such analysis, we may note Palmer's division of his career into seven periods: initiating persons into discipleship, changing his title from Acharya (teacher) to Bhagwan, institution-building during the Poona period, the silent period, the time of prophecy and resistance (when he promoted the new religion, meeting resistance and even hostility from many of his followers), Sheela's betrayal (when her schemes caused the movement to begin to fall apart), and abdication.[148]

Let us now reflect a bit on these shifts in Rajneesh's teaching. If we ask, What was he thinking?, of course we cannot know what was in his mind; but we can make reasonable assumptions about the intent of the shifts. Let us begin with Bryan Wilson's charismatic demand, discussed above.[149] What Wilson meant was that charismatic leaders arise in a situation in which a society wants charismatic leadership. But charismatic demand works in another way, as well; for a charismatic leader must maintain his charisma over a period of time if he is to maintain his leadership, and Rajneesh was facing just this problem.

Above we noted Palmer's characterization of the Poona period as one of institutionalizing; but such institutionalizing, as we of course know, is identical with the routinization of charisma and is its nemesis. What had happened was that the Poona ashram had grown so large – Palmer reports 'an international crowd of one to two thousand participants a week'[150] – 'that the leader could no longer be personally available to his sannyasins, except for a small core group. Thus the problem of institutionalization arose.' Rajneesh thus faced a choice. Either he could become the CEO of an enlightenment *cum* therapy organization or he could make some kind of radical change to enhance his charisma. He chose the latter alternative.[151] He led the movement to a new site and articulated enhanced expectations for the future of the movement, and he tried a variety of methods to heighten his charisma: the Messiah for whom

America was waiting, silence, the daily 'drive-bys' in his ever-growing fleet of Rolls-Royces, and the new religion of Rajneeshism (although proclaiming his movement a religion may also have had a fiscal motive, since religious organizations in the United States are tax exempt).[152] What the Oregon site and movement might have become had Rajneesh not let Sheela run amok with her attacks on locals and sannyasins alike we will never know; but what destroyed the movement was Sheela's manic leadership, not a diminishing of Rajneesh's charisma.

With this principle in mind – that a charismatic leader must heighten his charisma from time to time or lose it – we should consider what we know of Jesus' teachings again. The principle raises the question about Jesus especially with regard to two aspects of his teaching: 1. whether he called himself Messiah and 2. how he explained his move to Jerusalem and the attack on the temple.

The results of form criticism are that Jesus did not call himself Messiah, either by that term (Greek, 'Christ') or by the term Son of man. Thus John Reumann can note, in his summary review of scholarship, 'a near consensus on *Messiah*, that Jesus did not employ or welcome the title or that he reinterpreted it . . . – a consensus save of those scholars who identify him as a political revolutionist'.[153] Scholarly opinion about the term Son of man, admittedly, goes in so many directions that they 'are almost too complex to analyse',[154] but even so most New Testament scholars today would reject attributing messianic content to any Son of man sayings in the Gospels considered authentic.[155] It is difficult to fault Douglas Hare's careful analysis leading to the judicious conclusion that Jesus used the term as a 'modest self-reference'[156] and that the christological use of the term came later. Bultmann thought that it was 'possible that belief in the messiahship of Jesus arose with and out of belief in his resurrection'. Peter's confession preceding the transfiguration was 'no counter-evidence – on the contrary! For it is an Easter story projected backward into Jesus' life-time, just like the story of the Transfiguration'.[157] E. P. Sanders considers it 'unlikely' that Jesus 'thought of himself as bearer of the title "Messiah"'.[158] Yet he has this to say about the title Son of man: 'It is not possible to come to a firm conclusion about Jesus' use of the phrase "Son of Man". He used it; sometimes he used it of himself; he expected the Son of Man to come from heaven; but it is not certain that he identified himself as that future Son of Man.'[159] Such uncertainty is about as close as modern scholarship comes to crediting Jesus with a christological use of the title.

Similarly with regard to the 'triumphal' entry into Jerusalem (Mark 11.1–10 par.). This event is also, of course, disputed; cf. Bultmann's judgment that the historical core might be no more than 'Jesus' entry into Jerusalem with a crowd of pilgrims full of joy and expectation (at the Kingdom of God that was now coming)'.[160]

It is inherently likely, however, that when Jesus went to Jerusalem at Passover he was making some move to increase his charisma. After Jesus had been healing people and teaching about the Kingdom of God round about the Galilee for some weeks or months (we still have no reliable information about the length of his activity in Galilee) he would surely have seen that his teaching and healing were under threat of being perceived as routine and that he had to do something to increase his charisma. He will surely also not have thought in those terms, and it is possible that he thought only in theological terms, as Schweitzer proposed (Jesus' deciding to go to Jerusalem and suffer was 'due to the non-fulfilment of the promises made in the discourse at the sending forth of the Twelve').[161] Whether we accept Schweitzer's reasoning in this matter – and most probably will not – still some disappointment on Jesus' part (the most probable way for him to have recognized a need for heightened charisma) is a reasonable motivation for the journey to Jerusalem. Just as *at least a part* of Rajneesh's decision to move from Poona to Oregon was a felt need to heighten his charisma, so *at least a part* of Jesus' motivation in moving from Galilee to Jerusalem was probably a felt need to heighten *his* charisma.

If our reasoning is correct on this point, then it would not be unreasonable to conclude either that Jesus saw to it that his followers came to the conclusion that he was Messiah or that he staged a triumphal entry into Jerusalem. However that may be, and we continue to note that the best analyses are against either, we must see Jesus' move to Jerusalem as, among other things, an attempt to heighten charisma. Even if he gave no explanation at all to the disciples (or, as a matter of fact, precisely if he gave no explanation) at the least their expectations will have been raised,[162] and Jesus will have been the author of those expectations, whatever exactly he said, did, hinted at, or implied, even if the implication lay only in what he did, not in anything that he said. The one action, of course, that cannot be historically doubted is the overturning of the money-changers' tables at the temple. This is the action on which E. P. Sanders lays such emphasis as the key to understanding Jesus,[163] from which he concludes that Jesus was leading a movement to restore Israel. Even, however, if this is the only certifiably dramatic deed or saying that we can find in the Gospel materials about the Jerusalem period, it is enough to show that Jesus acted to enhance his charisma at this stage of his career. Charisma enhancement will have been the most immediate result of the temple incident. The next result, however, may have been Jesus' execution.[164] Had he kept his charisma down, had he not done and said the things that he said and did to enhance his charisma, he might not have died at that time; but his fledgling NRM also would have gone nowhere. Could he have made a conscious decision to take the ultimate charisma-enhancing step and get himself executed? Are we back to Schweitzer? This remains a teasing, albeit undemonstrable possibility.

(d) Calling followers

Yet again we must qualify the model, for the calling turns out often to be only implied at best. Rajneesh gave lectures and people responded to them. 'As word of his rhetorical skill spread, he drew increasingly large crowds';[165] and in response to this reception, 'in 1964 . . . [he] began the ten-day meditation camps that would ensure his notoriety',[166] and these continued after the establishment of the fixed Ashram at Poona. Rajneesh did, however, clearly understand the response as a response to his message about enlightenment. '"I am here," he announced in his first evening lecture [at the inauguration of the meditation camps], "to wake you up."'[167] He could also maintain that he had called his followers, but such calling was not explicit; Rajneesh did not overtly invite people to follow him. We can see the two sides of this 'calling' in two reports. On the one hand, when the participant-observer James Gordon first arrived in Poona, 'no effort was made to seduce or recruit me. "You have come," the people at Reception seemed to say, "because you wanted to. We are here. Bhagwan . . . is here. Enjoy your stay. Make of it what you will."'[168] On the other hand, however, Milne reports this about the first meditation-camp lecture that he attended:

> He speaks, and all restlessness is at an end. 'I have called you here, and you have heard my call,' he starts. 'And you have come.' My Western scientific upbringing immediately objects to this. How could you possibly have called me from Oxford or Hampstead Heath? But if Bhagwan didn't call me, how do I come to be sitting here on this baking tennis court on a hill station in Rajasthan, surrounded by the motleyest crew of people ever assembled?[169]

Rajneesh considered that those who followed him had responded to his 'call', yet he never actually said to anyone, 'Follow me', or something similar.

While Jesus did say, 'Follow me', or something similar to some persons (the disciples as well as some who did not become disciples, e.g., Matt. 8.18–22 // Luke 9.57–62; Mark 10.17–22 par.), it seems that the objects of this calling were a select group and that Jesus himself distinguished between the small group whom he called to follow him and the much larger number who were attracted to his healing and teaching. We recall the discussion of this point earlier in the chapter.[170] Thus also for Jesus most people who 'followed' him in the sense of attending his sermons, believing in his mission (however they understood that), and perhaps benefiting from his healing power were not called – except in the same sense in which Rajneesh could say to people who attended his meditation sessions, 'I have called you here, you have heard my call, you have come.' Such people, like many of Rajneesh's followers, might have come to believe that they had responded to Jesus' call, even though they had never heard him utter the words, 'Follow me'.

(e) The situation of distress

On a cursory analysis, Rajneesh's charismatic leadership may seem unrelated to this criterion since most of his followers were affluent Westerners. Yet large numbers of them had certainly experienced social dislocation, as we have already noted; for the majority of his followers were Western young adults who were just maturing 'as the antiwar movement and the student rebellions in the West were exhausting themselves'.[171] These people, as those of us who were teaching or were students at the time can attest, were in need of finding purpose for their lives. They yearned for a movement to which they could devote themselves; and the pursuit of economic well-being, on which so many of them had been embarked, seemed shallow. Rajneesh's message of self-discovery satisfied that yearning for his followers. Thus we can certainly speak of a situation of distress – not necessarily of crisis – even if that distress was not brought on by economic or political oppression.

With Jesus the case is clearer. This case has been made most strongly by Richard Horsley, first in *Bandits, Prophets, and Messiahs* (with John Hanson) and later with more extensive application to Jesus in *Jesus and the Spiral of Violence*. Horsley estimates that the tax burden on Jewish peasant society was 'well over 40 percent',[172] and he points to other aspects of oppression as well. First, towns that fell behind in their tax payments to the Romans might be destroyed or the citizens enslaved.[173] There were also occasions of famine and drought,[174] and there was the cultural distress that the ruling priesthood (responsible for most administrative oversight under Roman hegemony, except during the time of Herod) was 'illegitimate',[175] i.e., not Zadokite. In such times of crisis it was, therefore, natural that bandits, prophets and messiahs would arise, since there were no normal channels for public participation in government. 'Such political decay in a "colonized" society,' Horsley writes, 'was simply the most visible aspect of the *extreme crisis* in which prolonged imperial domination placed a subject people.'[176] Horsley also emphasizes that following Herod's death in 4 BCE – thus at about the time, presumably, of Jesus' birth – there was 'widespread revolt'.[177] He relies, of course, almost altogether on Josephus for his analysis.

E. P. Sanders, however, has argued against Horsley's interpretation. In his analysis, Josephus' depiction of 'Roman misgovernment and Jewish restiveness as escalating steadily in the decades before revolt broke out in 66' (Horsley's spiral) does not accurately reflect historical reality; for when 'one counts the uprisings and tumults that Josephus himself names, one does not see a steady increase. Rather, uprisings occurred when there were changes in leadership or governmental procedures.'[178] Furthermore, according to Sanders taxes were not abnormally high; rather, rulers normally judged 'what the populace would bear' and levied taxes up to that level and no higher.[179] Beyond this, there was no consistent and widespread opposition to the ruling priests, although there were some priests whom the people hated.[180]

The most striking point of difference between Horsley and E. P. Sanders is in their respective evaluations of Herod. For Horsley 'Herod intensified the atmosphere of [Roman] repression', establishing fortresses around the country and 'maintain[ing] an army of foreign mercenaries' to help him hold on to his realm;[181] and he added extra taxes to pay for his elaborate building projects.[182] For Sanders, however, 'Herod was, on balance, a good king', judged 'by the standards of the day'. 'He raised Jewish Palestine to a new prominence . . ., he . . . obtain[ed] benefits for Jews outside of Palestine, he did not allow civil war', and, 'he kept Jewish citizens and Roman troops apart'.[183] But if Herod was, on balance, a good king, his son Antipas, Tetrarch of Galilee during Jesus' lifetime, may have been an even better ruler, for he also kept the peace. In fact, 'Josephus records no instance in which Antipas had to resort to force in order to suppress an uprising'; and that means that Antipas 1. 'did not publicly flout the Jewish law' and 2. 'was not excessively oppressive and did not levy exorbitant taxes'.[184]

How must we, then, evaluate the distress component of Jesus' charismatic leadership, in view of two such divergent views? First, E. P. Sanders is surely correct in his judgment of Horsley's – and Josephus' – spiral, since he has counted the revolts and has noted when they occurred (times of change). Spiral or no spiral, however, the fact that revolts did occur whenever the government changed, around the time of Jesus' life, and on other occasions when the government sought to effect cultural change shows the people's *general* extreme dissatisfaction with their rulers. On this point Horsley and Sanders do not really disagree. Thus whether we consider Herod, with Sanders, a relatively good ruler or, with Horsley, a harsh despot – and such judgments will always reflect the viewpoints of the interpreters – we have to conclude that people generally were not content with his rule or with that of his successors. In fact, they were so discontent with those rulers that they revolted at almost every likely opportunity. That they did so, incidentally, would appear to contradict Shaye Cohen's evaluation of Palestinian Jewry during the second-temple period, which was that people were generally content to live under foreign domination and 'seldom rebelled, even when provoked'.[185]

Thus we can confirm the principle that charismatic leaders of NRMs arise at times of social distress; and Jesus continues to fit that pattern, although there was no particular crisis at the inauguration of his public career.

(f) Randomness

Doing the unexpected is a key device of the charismatic leader of an NRM. Randomness, in fact, increases charisma.[186] Rajneesh regularly employed randomness as a way of impressing his followers with his charisma, and most of those who have written about him and his movement have noted this aspect of his leadership.

The introduction of 'dynamic meditation', for which Rajneesh's followers became so infamous, was a surprise. A devotee, Vasant Joshi, writes that the itinerant Rajneesh, leading a meditation group in Bombay on a routine visit to the city in 1970, 'surprised everyone who had come prepared for his regular "relax" meditation. He introduced for the first time his own technique of meditation, Dynamic Meditation.' Further, 'The day he introduced Dynamic Meditation, everyone was taken aback and fascinated at the same time. The Indian press expressed its shock at watching the participants scream, shout, take off their clothes.'[187] Rajneesh's standing with his followers, however, and his ability to control them only increased. Kate Strelley, who writes after she became disenchanted and left the movement, explains that when she first professed her devotion to Rajneesh and her desire to follow him anywhere, others thought that Rajneesh would respond, 'Oh *no*! No attachment.' 'Instead,' she explains, Rajneesh *characteristically did the unexpected* . . . He would go back and forth, reminding his followers that we were fooling ourselves if we believed we could anticipate him.'[188]

Hugh Milne recalls that on one occasion Rajneesh announced to one of his lieutenants that he would never speak in English again, only in Hindi; but then a year later he scheduled an hour's talk in Hindi to be followed by one of equal length in English. Milne comments, 'With Bhagwan what he said one minute could be completely contradicted the next.'[189] Again he writes, 'It was very hard, being with Bhagwan. We sannyasis (*sic*) were constantly changing our plans as a result of his contradictory orders . . . No one knew from one minute to the next what Bhagwan would do, what he would decide, where he would send you.'[190]

A few sentences from James Gordon's *Golden Guru* beautifully illustrate the principle and associate Rajneesh with it.

> Contradiction, confusion, and continual change – Masters have always used these techniques with their disciples. They create receptivity, an openness to seeing things as they are, as they break habitual patterns . . . If there were underlying principles and an operative technique at work in Rajneesh's counsel they were, in fact, *contradiction, confusion, and continual change.* 'Confusion,' he noted, in a lecture . . ., 'is my method. The moment I see you accumulating something, creating a philosophy or theology, I immediately jump on it and destroy it.'[191]

We have here clear and obvious examples of the principle that randomness increases charisma, and we saw above that this principle is generally recognized by sociologists who study NRMs and their leaders. Given Jesus' effect on his disciples – who did leave all to follow him, as he demanded – we must assume that Jesus also understood and employed the principle. To assume otherwise is to think that he was not a charismatic leader, that he did not fascinate and astound his audiences, that he was quite predictable, and that he was nevertheless a successful leader of an NRM. Viewed in such a way, 'Jesus . . . snaps nicely into sharp focus. This clarity, however, is purchased at the price of reality.'[192] Such an equation would not compute.

We can demonstrate the trait of randomness in Jesus' leadership from a group of problem sayings. If we examine six such sayings in the Jesus tradition, along with one problem saying of others about him and one problematic non-saying, we shall see the principle at work. With apologies to the myriad of Jesus scholars living and dead, we limit our discussion of scholarly positions on these sayings to the five scholars whom we discussed earlier,[193] along with the positions of the form critics Bultmann and Dibelius, as well as the vote of the Jesus Seminar.

Matt 11.7–19 // Luke 7.24–35, Jesus' sayings about John the Baptist, especially Matt 11.11 // Luke 7.28: 'No one is greater, among those born of women, than John; but the least in the Kingdom of God is greater than he.' Bultmann saw this collection of sayings as determined either by anti-Jewish or by anti-Baptist polemic and considered the latter part of the quoted verse a (later) Christian addition;[194] and Dibelius saw the collection as arising from a real interest in the relation of Christianity to the Baptist movement.[195] The Jesus Seminar voted grey (likely not said by Jesus).[196] Bultmann's proposal here certainly removes the apparent contradiction between the two statements of v. 11, since it assumes that some later Christian(s) added the second statement of the verse in order to blunt Jesus' appearing to say that John was greater than he. Our collection of authors on Jesus, however, has hardly taken up Bultmann's proposal. Perrin does not discuss the verse, but E. P. Sanders considers the saying authentic and agrees with J. C. O'Neill that Jesus is here contrasting the state of existence now with that in the coming Kingdom.[197] Jeremias compares the saying with other sayings in which Jesus says that, with him, 'more' is present – more than Jonah (Matt 12.41), more than Moses (Matt 5.21–48); and he connects these sayings especially with Matt 5.17, 'I have not come to destroy but to fulfill.'[198] This interpretation agrees with O'Neill/Sanders; but elsewhere Jeremias classifies the saying among the riddles.[199] Vermes, noting that the verse 'has baffled many an interpreter', first writes off the old-aeon/new-aeon theory as 'too theological for serious consideration by a historian' and thinks that the saying might refer to Jesus as Servant of God; and he concludes that it meant, 'John was very great, but I am greater.'[200] Similarly, Crossan takes Matthew v. 11 to mean that Jesus has moved beyond John (whom he earlier endorsed: Matthew vv. 7–9).[201] Yet Vermes later seems to endorse the O'Neill/Sanders position.[202]

Among the Jesus authors whom we are surveying here there is considerable support for the view that the saying means that John is the greatest man alive but that this greatness pales by comparison with the greatness of being in the Kingdom. Nevertheless, problems remain, for the saying does not actually say that but rather contrasts women's offspring (i.e., all humans) with those in the Kingdom. It is perhaps the saying's assumption that John does not belong in the Kingdom that led Vermes to declare it 'too theological'; thus Bultmann's proposal would seem to remain a live option. Or, one might conclude that if the saying is authentic, we are unable to fathom its meaning.

Mark 3.21: 'When those with him heard, they went out to detain him, for they said, "He is beside himself [or: He is crazy]."' Bultmann considered this saying a historical reminiscence,[203] but Dibelius thought it Mark's pragmatic preparation for Jesus' rejection of his physical family in 3.30–35.[204] Since the statement is not a saying of Jesus, the Jesus Seminar did not discuss it. Vermes apparently follows Dibelius, noting Jesus' tension with his family,[205] and Crossan also takes the statement to be a Markan addition.[206] Of course, as we have already noted, Vermes lays great emphasis on Jesus' charismatic character, an aspect which might include perceived craziness. Neither Jeremias, Perrin, nor E. P. Sanders discusses the statement.

While we have here some difference of opinion on this saying *about* Jesus, there is also widespread ignoring of it, largely due to the natural tendency to understand Jesus in terms of his sayings, not in terms of what others said about him or, as we shall shortly have occasion to note, what he did not say. It is especially noteworthy, however, that Vermes, who understands Jesus as a charismatic, accepts the saying as authentic, whereas the other interpreters of Jesus either ignore it or consider it inauthentic.

Mark 4.10–11 // Matt 13.10–11; Luke 8.9–10: 'When they were alone, those around him, with the twelve, put to him the question of the parables. And he said to them, "To you is given the mystery of the Kingdom of God; but for those outside everything happens in parables."' Nearly everyone considers this an inauthentic saying. Bultmann ruled it 'quite secondary',[207] and

Dibelius was of similar opinion.[208] The Jesus Seminar voted it black (definitely not an authentic saying).[209] E. P. Sanders and Crossan ignore the saying, and Vermes considers it 'a contorted and tendentious explanation'[210] and thus not authentic. Perrin rules the saying a *Satz heiligen Rechtes*,[211] which would certainly point to inauthenticity if that were correct. The saying, however, hardly follows the pattern of a *Satz heiligen Rechtes* (as you do now so it will be done to you later), and Perrin makes no attempt to justify his inclusion of the saying in that category. We see here, therefore, a good example of using unlikely exegesis in order to get rid of a problem saying. Jeremias seems to have the most difficulty with the saying. First he classes it among the riddles, then he says that it shows Jesus' special relationship with God, then he proposes that v. 11 was authentic but not originally connected with v. 10, and finally he suggests that it was normal in the Judaism of Jesus' day for religious teaching to be given in both an exoteric and an esoteric form.[212] Jeremias has therefore tried to straddle the fence between ruling the saying inauthentic, which he seems unwilling to do, and its obvious offence to most modern scholars: Jesus' apparently saying that he intended to give only riddles to outsiders but the 'true gospel' to his inner circle, when of course *we* know that he intended to speak clearly to all. The criterion of coherence with which most Jesus scholars work – i.e., that Jesus had a coherent 'message' – forces this saying out. But what if Jesus did not live up to our expectations of coherence? In conclusion, the weight of opinion is clearly on the side of inauthenticity for Mark 4.11, but those holding that opinion give different reasons for thinking the saying inauthentic.

Luke 16.1–9: Parable of the Unjust Steward. Cf. especially v. 8a: 'The lord praised the unjust steward because he had behaved wisely.' Neither Bultmann nor Dibelius could deal with this parable. Dibelius did not discuss it, and Bultmann considered its original meaning lost.[213] Among our Jesus authors there is a strong tendency to treat vv. 8–9 as if they were an appended conclusion, as is so often the case with the parables of Jesus, that does not embody the original meaning of the parable. This is the view of Jeremias, who takes vv. 1–7 to mean that one must act 'resolutely, where everything is at risk';[214] and Perrin follows this interpretation exactly.[215] Vermes also sees risk as the key.[216] The Jesus Seminar, however, voted vv. 1–8a red (certainly authentic) and vv. 8b–9 black.[217] E. P. Sanders and Crossan do not discuss the parable.

The unvoiced opinion of the majority would appear to be that Jesus could not have approved of injustice (ἀδικία). To have done so would have failed the test of coherence with his endorsement of justice and other virtues elsewhere. Yet the problem remains that even if Jesus in vv. 1–7 of the parable intended to emphasize that one must act resolutely where everything is at risk, the example that he used to illustrate that point is an example of immoral action. Verses 8–9 therefore *do* cohere with the rest of the parable; and these verses do not, in any case, look like the normal appended secondary conclusions to parables, where one often finds an allegorizing tendency, as in the interpretation appended to the parable of the Sower (Mark 4.13–20 par.).

Luke 18.1–8: Parable of the Unjust Judge. Cf. especially vv. 6–7: 'Hear what the unjust judge says. And will not God avenge his elect, who cry to him day and night, and be patient with them?' Dibelius does not discuss this parable, and Bultmann judges as in the preceding case.[218] The Jesus Seminar vote was pink (could be an authentic saying) for vv. 2–5 and black for vv. 6–8.[219] E. P. Sanders and Crossan also do not discuss the parable. Vermes also rejects vv. 6–8 as a Lukan addition and takes the point of the authentic parable to be that 'childlike determination persuades even God'.[220] Jeremias and Perrin, however – contrary to their opinion about the Unjust Steward – accept the conclusion as authentic, even though it forms an exact parallel to the conclusion of the Unjust Steward, including the adjectival 'unjust' in each case (ὁ οἰκονόμος τῆς ἀδικίας, ὁ κρίτης τῆς ἀδικίας). Perrin argues specifically for the authenticity of the conclusion and claims that it entails a 'how much more' ('*qal va-homer*') argument.[221] He is again following his teacher, Jeremias, who discusses the parable in four different places and proposes that it means that God 'hears . . . those in distress, *unlike* the judge who allows himself to be mollified by a complainant';[222] that 'even if God puts the patience of his elect to the test . . ., he will see that they get their rights ἐν τάχει (v. 8)';[223] that God can shorten the time of distress;[224] and that the Christian has a 'certainty of gaining a hearing'.[225]

The parallel phrasing that we just observed in the conclusions to the two parables appears to make it certain that the conclusions stem from the collector of the Lukan special parable collection, whether that collector be Luke or a predecessor. We probably ought also to reckon, however, with the possibility that the former conclusion is authentic, because it remains true to the intent of the parable, and that the collector has tailored the conclusion of the latter parable to fit the conclusion of the former. With the conclusion removed from consideration with the original parable, of course, Perrin's *qal va-homer* proposal falls out. Of Jeremias' explanations, there seems to be no basis for the first, and the second and third are based on the conclusion. This leaves his fourth explanation of the parable, 'certainty of gaining a hearing', which is essentially the same as Vermes' 'childlike determination' explanation. Perhaps this is what the parable means, but none of the proposed explanations takes account of the judge's stated motive, which is that he doesn't want a black eye (v. 5).[226] When we emphasize this aspect we see a certain continuity with the conclusion, although the term 'unjust' is rather too strong.

Mark 12.13–17: On tribute to Caesar, especially v. 17: 'Turn over Caesar's things to Caesar and God's things to God.' Bultmann considered the later church to be the author of this 'excellently constructed' apothegm because it concerns the disciples' behaviour.[227] Dibelius did not discuss it. The Jesus Seminar voted the concluding saying itself red but the entire preceding apothegm black, a decision that would leave us with a totally contextless and therefore essentially meaningless saying.[228] Perrin also does not deal with the saying, and Jeremias refers to Jesus' 'political temptation'.[229] Quite similarly Vermes thinks of Jesus being placed on the horns of a dilemma between a revolutionary/patriot position and a pro-Roman position. Jesus thus found a clever way out of being identified with an anti-revolutionary position.[230] E. P. Sanders, not surprisingly, agrees with Bultmann on the saying's inauthenticity;[231] and while his grounds for doing so are Bultmann's grounds, nevertheless he does remove from the corpus of sayings one that does not cohere with his interpretation of Jesus as a non-political figure. Crossan does not discuss the saying.

Mark 14.25: 'Not again will I drink of the produce of the vine until that day when I drink it new in the Kingdom of God.' Dibelius did not discuss this saying, and for Bultmann it was part of the narrative development of the original brief passion narrative.[232] The Jesus Seminar voted grey.[233] For E. P. Sanders the saying is obviously a *vaticinium ex eventu*, since 'all the sayings which attribute to Jesus the will to die correspond so closely with what happened . . . One might as well attribute to Jesus the doctrine of the Trinity or of the Incarnation.'[234] He refers to the criterion of dissimilarity. Vermes also rules the saying inauthentic.[235] Jeremias, however, refers to the glory of being in the Kingdom or of its nearness;[236] and Perrin follows, relating the saying specifically to the eschatological banquet.[237] Crossan (following Werner Kelber) sees a Markan addition and thinks that 'Mark is opposing an institutionalized eucharistic ritual that does not allow for Jews and Gentiles at the same table'.[238]

While the announcements of the passion may be *vaticinia ex eventu*, this saying is hardly one, since there is no account of Jesus' having drunk wine after his death. The judgments of all our authors regarding the authenticity or inauthenticity of this saying seem to rest on their determination, on other grounds, of what Jesus thought was going to happen to him (or, in Crossan's case, to the church).

Mark 15.2–5, esp. vv. 4–5: 'Pilate asked him again, "Do you answer nothing? Look how many things they are charging against you"; but Jesus still answered nothing.' None of our authors discusses this non-saying; and yet not to speak in one's own defence may be as important for understanding one's life and career as anything one may say. The non-saying remains one of the most enigmatic pieces of the Jesus tradition that we are examining here.

To sum up this survey, we see that the Jesus authors in our sample make little use of the form-critical works of Bultmann and Dibelius (and indeed! Dibelius is of little use for our test sayings). Only E. P. Sanders occasionally agrees with Bultmann's judgment, but the others rely on the form-critical handbooks not at all. Crossan advances several criteria for determining a saying's authenticity. First he deals only with those sayings that he places in what he calls the 'First Stratum' of the Jesus tradition. This means primarily Q and Thomas, although he includes a string of other sources including Paul, several non-canonical documents, and miracles appearing in Mark and John. To this he adds the criterion of multiple but independent attestation.[239] Jeremias' multiple explanations of several of our test sayings, while in a sense a noble attempt not to avoid difficult sayings, show his inability consistently to fathom the meaning of a saying; and Perrin either pushes the sayings into his eschatological pattern or ignores them. Vermes, similarly but in a different way, is intent on showing the Jewishness of Jesus and his sayings, and thus he either ignores our test sayings or relates them to near eschatology, in the manner of Perrin and Jeremias. Only in one case, that of the insider/outsider saying of Mark 4.10–11, does Vermes come down firmly on the side of inauthenticity; the saying just does not cohere with what he otherwise thinks Jesus' sayings are about. Of all our sample authors, E. P. Sanders has done the best job of trying to allow for a multivalent typology. Thus he takes the saying about John the Baptist and the Kingdom as an eschatological saying affirming the value of existence in the Kingdom, but he considers the saying about Jesus' being out of his mind to be further evidence that Jesus was a magician; yet he also avoids several of the sayings and considers the saying about drinking wine in the Kingdom to be a *vaticinium ex eventu*, which it is not.

Our survey of these authors' treatments of several sayings (including one about Jesus and not by him) and a non-saying has shown that modern scholars who attempt to carry out a historical analysis of Jesus invariably seek coherence, even when they occasionally realize that such coherence may be a misdirected goal.[240] And it appears that it is this quest for coherence that leads them to ignore prominent elements in the Jesus tradition, to explain them away, or to misinterpret them. When we come to realize, however, that Jesus was a charismatic leader of an NRM, then we can see Jesus, and some of the problem components of the Jesus tradition, in quite a different light.

Understanding that Jesus was a charismatic leader of an NRM and seeing that, as such, he apparently employed randomness to increase his charisma, we must cease trying to make of the 'teaching of Jesus' a coherent 'message' and recognize that Jesus said contradictory things. He may very well have said that John the Baptist was the greatest man on earth and then have qualified that by saying that anyone in the Kingdom of God was greater. He may have been at times so *in*coherent that his friends and relatives considered him out of his mind. It would fit the pattern of a charismatic leader of an NRM exactly for Jesus to have said to his close associates that he taught in parables to keep the crowds from understanding, and then to have gone on teaching the crowds. His answer about paying taxes probably has no profound meaning that the modern scholar can tease out; it is, however, a way of puzzling the questioner, thus increasing Jesus' charisma. Similarly, it is probably a mistake to continue to try to explain the parables of the Unjust Steward and of the Unjust Judge in such a way as not to offend common morality; for what better way to keep one's followers off guard than to use examples of immorality in reference to God? And for Jesus to say that he would drink his first post-Passover wine in the Kingdom is just as likely as anything else that he may have said. Possibly, his silence during his trial before Pilate falls into this category, as well. None of these sayings has to cohere with the others or with any selected corpus of Jesus' sayings. *If Jesus had sought such coherence he would not have been the leader that he was.*

The incoherence of the body of Jesus' sayings ought to have been clear to us at least since 1954, when Hans Conzelmann ushered in the discipline of *Redaktionsgeschichte*; for at that time New Testament scholarship began to deal explicitly with the fact that each evangelist had so formed the Jesus tradition as to create a distinctive picture of Jesus, different from the pictures painted by the other three evangelists. The implication of that process is that the pre-Gospel tradition lacked coherence and was subject to many diverse, even contradictory meanings. (This point remains even if we add Q and any *Ur*-Gospels that may have existed prior to the four canonical ones to the list of Gospels that formed the tradition in distinctive ways.) And *the tradition presented this incoherent and contradictory face because Jesus had given it no coherence.* Had he done so he would not have affected his followers as he did, and there would have been no church to try to puzzle out the coherence of his words and deeds, a task in which it has been engaged for quite a few years now. *The attempt to make Jesus coherent in the individual Gospels was a part of the routinization of charisma.* Jesus could have worked out a coherent eschatological theology, and had he done so he might have been remembered alongside Philo and Maimonides. But he was not a coherent philosopher; he was a charismatic leader of an NRM.

When we adequately understand Jesus as the charismatic leader of a new religious movement,

> He will not be a Jesus Christ to whom the religion of the present can ascribe, according to its long-cherished custom, its own thoughts and ideas, as it did with the Jesus of its own making. Nor will He be a figure which can be made by a popular historical treatment so sympathetic and universally intelligible to the multitude. The historical Jesus will be to our time a stranger and an enigma.[241]

(g) Hatred

For the sociologist Robert Tucker, we recall, hatred is 'prob-ably a universal feature of the charismatic leader'.[242] This otherwise-overlooked element in charismatic leadership of NRMs is so obvious a part of Jesus' leadership that again, as in the case of his teachings, it hardly needs comment. The Gospels refer to opposition to Jesus from the beginning of his career and from various groups, especially from Pharisees during his Galilean period and from the chief priests during his Jerusalem period. Even if much of the Pharisaic opposition, especially what we find in Matthew, is a retrojection back into the life of Jesus of the later Christian situation,[243] and even if the conflict form of most of the conflict sayings in the synoptic tradition can be shown to be the contribution of the early Jewish-Christian congregation,[244] it still seems quite a stretch of the imagination to conclude that the whole notion of conflict and opponents was merely invented by the early church and had no basis in the life of Jesus. E. P. Sanders argues that 'Jesus' presumption to speak for God would have been resented', and that, 'further, Jesus had attracted enough of a following as a healer to be accused of healing by means of an evil spirit'. He adds, 'These matters may well have made the Jewish leaders wary and suspi-cious of him.'[245]

The kind of opposition that Jesus experienced during his Galilean ministry, however, will not explain his being executed. Different persons and groups may have opposed him in Galilee, but the crucifixion represents the ultimate act of hostility toward Jesus. According to E. P. Sanders, again, what con-vinced the authorities to get rid of Jesus was his overturning the tables of the money changers at the temple. This act 'would have been seen as presenting a challenge to the rest of Judaism in a way that cannot be called just "religious" or "political"'. Jesus' claim to speak for God and to accept sinners into the Kingdom of God had 'challenged the leadership in all respects'. Thus when he overturned the tables he struck 'a blow against the temple, even if a physically minor one, [which] was a blow against the basic religio-political entity: Israel'.[246] This act was, in Sanders' opinion, the straw that broke the camel's back. Because of other hostility to Jesus (for the reasons mentioned in the preceding paragraph), 'the gun may already have been cocked, but it was the temple demonstration which pulled the trigger'.[247] Otherwise, Sanders explains that the temple demonstration would perhaps not have got Jesus killed had he been just a solitary individual; but the fact that he had a following (not necessarily a large one) made his act appear more ominous.[248] Ben Meyer, in the *Anchor Bible Dictionary*, offers a nearly identical explanation of Jesus' death.[249]

Rajneesh, like Jesus, attracted a group of devoted followers who were scorned by the general populace; and, like Jesus and his group, Rajneesh and his group found themselves in trouble with the law. (The trials continue.) Whereas the Roman government put Jesus to death, the more civilized government of the United States deported Rajneesh, who soon died.

As soon as Rajneesh and his followers took over the former Big Muddy ranch in Wasco County, eastern Oregon, alarm went up among the ranch's rural neighbours, and among other Oregonians, as well. The strange practices of the Rajneeshees, especially the sexual aspect of dynamic meditation, created a considerable amount of apprehension and at least some hostility. Early in 1985, however, the Rajneeshees, numbering in the hundreds, took over the nearby town of Antelope, former population thirty-nine, and renamed it Rajneeshpuram. Within months only fifteen of the original inhabitants of the town remained.[250] When the Rajneeshees also immediately took over the school system,[251] the state superintendent of schools withdrew state funds from the school system, on the grounds that the schools had become religious schools (which governments in the United States may not support).[252] At that time, local opponents of the Rajneeshee presence could be 'quietly confident about the future. State and federal law enforcement authorities [were] gearing up to move on the ranch. There [were] rumours that a grand jury [was] about to be convened on the immigration charges against Rajneesh and the

Sannyasins. [The Oregon attorney general was] continuing to pursue the church-state case.'[253] Of course, Rajneesh's followers struck back in ways unavailable to Jesus' followers, and in ways that Jesus' followers would not have used, in any case. They filed law suits, they poisoned a number of people, they planned assassinations.[254] The end result, however, was that on 8 November 1985 Rajneesh admitted that the evidence that he had committed immigration fraud 'was sufficient to convict him' – a subtlety of United States law that allowed him 'to maintain his innocence'; and 'he received a ten-year suspended prison sentence and paid a fine of $400,000 . . . He agreed to leave the country within five days and not to return for five years without written permission from the U. S. Attorney General.'[255] After being rejected in a number of other countries, Rajneesh returned to India, where he enjoyed some months of leadership of a much smaller group than he had had in Oregon before his death.

It is unnecessary at this point to reflect on the differences in morality and judgment between Rajneesh and Jesus. They will be obvious to all readers of this volume (and more so to those who follow the details in Milne's or in Gordon's book). It is sufficient to note that both Jesus and Rajneesh followed the rule that charismatic leaders of NRMs provoke hatred – and let us not forget that the hostility against Rajneesh was there from the moment he set foot on Oregon soil; it was not merely a response to the later plots. We might, however, return briefly to the causes of the hatred that Jesus provoked. That hatred was not irrational or Satan-inspired; rather, those who hated Jesus had cause to hate him, even if Christians later judge them wrong and Jesus right. Jesus' violent and symbolic act against the temple, his saying about destroying and rebuilding the temple (Mark 14.57–58; 15.29; Acts 6.14),[256] and his acceptance of religious outcasts (prostitutes and tax collectors) were direct challenges to all reasonable interpretations of Jewish righteousness. Naturally the people who had an investment in the system and in the continuation of traditional religion opposed him.

Thus in every way Jesus fits the type of the charismatic leader of an NRM. But what about the followers?

5. The followers of such leaders

In the next chapter we want to examine the process of conversion in some detail, and there is no need to anticipate that discussion here. Nevertheless, we may note that there is widespread agreement among sociologists that people who follow leaders of NRMs are, in general, seekers,[257] although such seeking may be either more or less intense. That is to say that people who follow leaders like Rajneesh are not (entirely) satisfied with the previous meaning systems – the 'symbolic universes', to use Peter Berger's and Thomas Luckmann's term[258] – guiding their lives and are open to more meaningful concepts. Furthermore, the people who follow such leaders feel free to do so and either have or are in the process of forming some kind of relationship with those already in the movement; thus 'the probability of being recruited into a particular movement is largely a function of two conditions: (1) links to one or more movement members through a pre-existing or emergent interpersonal tie; and (2) the absence of countervailing networks'.[259]

We have already noted, in our discussion of the 'situation of distress', what sorts of people followed Rajneesh. They were predominantly affluent young Western adults who were seeking meaning for their lives as the civil-rights and anti-war movements were coming to an end. Just who these people were we can see more clearly in an article by Ted Mann, who relies on his own interviews as well as on previous studies of the Rajneeshees.[260] In general, Mann finds that the followers of Rajneesh were, while not 'misfits', nevertheless 'loners; outside the commune setting they often would not "fit in"'. Mann found, further, that most Rajneeshees were 'socially marginal . . . They were not strongly affiliated with established organizations, either professional or occupational, or with unions, traditional religions, political parties, nor with accepted volun-

tary associations or conventional family groupings.'²⁶¹ Mann
cites especially a survey that was part of a German doctoral dis-
sertation. The surveyor took responses from a total of 1900
persons, divided unequally into four groups.²⁶² He found that
nearly 70% of people working at the ashram at Poona were
'between 26 and 35 years of age, while 8.3% were younger',
and that people in the other groups were rather younger than
those working at the ashram.²⁶³ The majority over all were
female and from urban backgrounds.²⁶⁴ Mann's own interviews confirmed that followers of Rajneesh were seekers. He
classifies them 'as mostly freshman seekers. This means they are
under 40, are seeking with great eagerness and are often willing
to make a strong commitment.' (By contrast, 'veteran seekers'
are 'over 40, predominantly women', and move frequently
from one group to another.)²⁶⁵ Many followers of Rajneesh had
also had prior involvement with some version of the 'human
potential' movement that attracted many young adults in the
1960s and 1970s.²⁶⁶

What we do not see in Mann's article or in any other studies
of the Rajneesh movement is the element of existing or emergent ties that new followers had to people already in the movement. Sometimes there was a word-of-mouth publicity effect,
but people did not journey to Poona because their brothers
were already there (as, in the case of Jesus, with Peter and
Andrew) or because they were led into incipient romantic relations with members of the movement, as was sometimes the
case with the Moonies.

What does this have to do with those who followed Jesus?
Perhaps nothing. Were Jesus' followers seekers, dissatisfied
with existing religious alternatives? This description may fit the
disciples but not the more distant followers, but we could not
prove it. Were they affluent? In general, decidedly not. Were
they rootless independents, moving frequently from place to
place and from job to job? For Roman-period Galilee such a
life-style would have been impossible. Had they had prior
involvement with a human-potential movement? Absurd. Were
they young? Aha! probably so – the disciples, in any case. Of

the whole group, including Jesus, only Peter is mentioned in the Gospels as having been married (Mark 1.30 par.). Paul states in 1 Cor. 9.5 that 'the rest of the apostles and the brothers of the Lord and Cephas' were married, but these marriages may have come after Jesus' death. Because most adults in Galilee in Jesus' day and age were married, and because marriage generally came at a relatively early age,[267] we may be fairly sure that the persons in Jesus' innermost circle of followers, at least, were young; and we may be reasonably certain that they were, in some sense, seekers. Reared in villages and small towns, they could not have been loners and misfits in the sense in which Rajneesh's followers were, although it is possible that the disciples' ties to family and local groups were not strong. Beyond this, our modern comparators do not help us to understand what motivated people to follow Jesus, and we are left with a dearth of evidence regarding the followers themselves. We therefore return to Jesus himself.

6. Summing up: the attraction of Jesus

On all points – displaying charismatic qualities (being called, performing wonders, providing teachings, calling disciples), responding to a situation of distress, using randomness to maintain charisma, and provoking hatred – there is abundant evidence that both Jesus and Rajneesh met the criteria of a charismatic leader of an NRM fully. None of this, of course, is to say that Jesus and Rajneesh shared the same moral plane, that their missions or teachings were equally valid or relevant, or that they are equally deserving of our esteem. The purpose of this examination and comparison has been simply to show why people followed Jesus, and that should, in general, now be clear. He was a charismatic leader of a new religious movement who appealed, by his charismatic activities, to persons in a situation of distress; and he maintained his charismatic leadership precisely in the way in which such leaders always maintain their leadership – by his wonders, by his teachings (which need not always have been free of mutually incompatible elements), and by his randomness, by keeping his followers off guard.

In his filling of this role Jesus had no models – not the Hebrew prophets of centuries earlier, not the messianic revolutionaries with whom he was more or less contemporary, not the rabbis of a later day, and certainly not the cynic sages of his own. And he had not read Max Weber or Roy Wallis. Rather, he had to find his own way, surely led along by charismatic demand. In this he was supremely successful, far more successful than he doubtless ever dreamed that he would be, the most successful such figure ever to live, and the evidence of whose success continues to grow, to baffle, and to astound.

When the MS for this work was completed and just ready to go to the printer, an important new article by Rodney Stark appeared relevant to the subject.[268] Stark considers the prophetic (in the sociological sense) leaders Joseph Smith, Muhammad, Jesus and Moses and asks about the sociological factors important for their receipt of revelations. He finds, among other things, that there must be a 'supportive cultural tradition' for the receipt of revelations, that revelations often occur during 'periods of social crisis', and that reinforcement by a support group is necessary for the career of the recipient to progress. This article throws additional light on Jesus as charismatic leader of an NRM.

II

Why Did Gentiles Become Christians?

'Most studies of conversion to date have been too narrow in orientation, employing theories too restrictive in disciplinary perspective and assumptions too deeply rooted in religious traditions.'

(Lewis R. Rambo)

1. Preliminary remarks

The question that we want to address here is that concerning the motives and causes for Gentile conversion to Christianity in the early decades of the new religion as it left its Jewish matrix and became a universal religion. What was it about the early Christianity that was attractive to Gentiles? And what was it about the situation of those Gentiles that disposed – or pre-disposed – them to conversion? Before turning to an examination of the early Christian evidence of conversion, however, we need to review modern scholarship briefly on the subject, and we need also to acquaint ourselves with a few of the modern studies, that exist in considerable abundance, of conversion to new religious movements (NRMs). This review is necessary in order for us to have the most adequate conceptual framework possible for evaluating the evidence. When we then turn to the evidence itself, our interest will be on conversion to Christianity in the Greco-Roman context, not on Jewish conversion. Not only did we examine Jewish conversion to some degree in our discussion of why people followed Jesus, but there is little actual evidence for such conversion (although we know that it certainly existed) in the early church after the time of Jesus.

Of course, the early chapters of the book of Acts record mass conversions of thousands of people in Jerusalem; but these narratives are clearly fanciful and idealized, as can be seen most readily by contrasting the cumulative effect of the conversion narratives through Acts 6.7 with the persecution narrative in Acts 8. The conversion narratives would lead us to believe that a large proportion – if not nearly all – of the population of Jerusalem became Christians within the space of a few days, whereas when the persecution breaks out it empties Jerusalem of all Christians save the apostles, yet the population of Jerusalem seems hardly diminished. This contrast remains when in the concluding narratives we learn both that there were tens of thousands of Jewish Christians (Acts 21.20) and that 'all the multitude of the Jews' (Acts 25.24) opposed Paul before the Roman governor – statements that appear to contradict each other. Consequently, almost no modern scholars think that there were mass conversions to Christianity in Jerusalem in the days of the apostles.[1]

We proceed, therefore, to a review of scholarship on conversion and then to an analysis of conversion to Christianity in the Greco-Roman world.

2. A brief history of the recent discussion of the issue

Arthur Darby Nock's landmark work, *Conversion*, has focussed the modern discussion. Nock distinguished between *conversion* to Judaism and to Christianity and *adhesion* (adherence) to other religious movements, like the religions of Isis and of Mithras. The difference was that conversion meant 'the re-orientation of the soul of an individual, his deliberate turning from indifference or from an earlier form of piety to another, a turning which implies a consciousness that a great change is involved, that the old was wrong and the new is right';[2] where-as, in the case of the other religions, 'a man used Mithraism [for example], but he did not belong to it body and soul; if he did, that was a matter of special attachment and not an inevitable concomitant prescribed by authority'.[3] It was this latter qualification that allowed Nock to maintain his distinction between conversion and adhesion in the face of the devotion of Apuleius' Lucius to Isis.[4] As Nock's discussion developed, however, he had some difficulty holding firmly to the distinction, as when he wrote that Christianity, like Mithraism, might gain adherents in similar ways,[5] and when he observed of such texts as the Chaldaic Oracles and the Hermetic literature, including the Asclepius, that 'we have . . . a feeling of otherness from the world and a concept of conversion'.[6]

Nock also sought to analyse the *mechanics* of conversion in considerable detail. For him the other religions, like those of Isis and Mithras – 'cults' in his terminology – won converts or adherents by a variety of means. One individual might bring another to a meeting or service;[7] in the case of Judaism the exclusive and absolute teaching may have been influential;[8] there was the 'direct appeal to the eye' of public processions and ceremonies;[9] there were 'supposed miracles . . . and the literary propaganda which made them known and enhanced their value';[10] and beyond this were the public expressions of 'hymns and votive offerings and works of art'.[11] But Nock also sought to explain the receptiveness of the general Greco-Roman population to these stimuli, which receptiveness he attributed to '(1) the picture of the universe which arose, above all from astrology, (2) the interest in immortality, (3) an inquisitiveness about the supernatural resulting in a general increase in the tendency to believe'.[12] Then, anticipating modern sociological theory, he observed that 'demand creates supply, and this demand was met by the rise of private mysteries'.[13] This point – that the soil, so to speak, was ready for the Christian seeds – is one to which we shall want to return.

Yet early Christianity, according to Nock's analysis, lacked most of the appeals to which that receptiveness responded. There were no outdoor sermons or other displays, and only the authorities, like those responsible for arresting Ignatius, could finger Christians.[14] What was visible to the public was the martyrs, and martyrdom was effective. Thus Nock laid down an axiom (taken from Tertullian), 'The blood of martyrs is the seed of the Church.'[15]

More recently, Ramsay MacMullen has sought to improve on Nock's analysis.[16] He opens his study by showing that conversion to Christianity is not always, and perhaps not generally, a 'body and soul' distinction, and he offers the example of 'Saxony and the neighbouring parts of Germany around 1600',[17] where people who were Christians nevertheless followed practices that were clearly 'pagan' in origin. MacMullen thus emphasizes that instead of a black-white distinction between Christian and non-Christian (as in Nock's model), Christianity could blend 'into the secular and even the non-Christian without clear demarcation'. Indeed, MacMullen seems to have seen the reality of Christian existence here, in contrast to Nock's more idealized view of conversion, and he offers this definition of conversion: 'that change of belief by which a person accepted the reality and supreme power of God and determined to obey Him'.[18] We note that this definition leaves practice entirely out of the picture.

As motivation for conversion to Christianity, MacMullen proposes miracles and (like Nock) martyrdoms.[19] Also like Nock, he lays emphasis on the fact that after the Pauline mission 'the church had no mission, it made no organized or official approach to unbelievers; rather, it left everything to the individual',[20] and he proposes that people like Justin and Tatian became individual converts as the result of their quests.[21] Modern sociologists would call such people 'seekers'. There are thus for MacMullen two classes of early Christian conversions, the lower-class type that responded to miracles and the like and the upper-class type that found Christianity at the end of an intellectual quest.[22] Finally, he notes that many persons, albeit a minority within the Christian whole, will have progressed in their understanding of and commitment to Christianity sufficiently to have reached Nock's conversion point.[23]

Throughout his discussion MacMullen notes the importance of individual, often chance encounters – in the market place,[24] 'in quite obscure settings of everyday',[25] perhaps in homes.[26] Without using the term, he has thus seen that conversions take place most often in the context of pre-existing *networks*. Yet he also thinks that mass conversions must have been necessary in order to account for the growth of Christianity.[27]

(Eugene V. Gallagher has offered an important corrective to MacMullen's analysis, in that he notes that it is not the real historical core of the miracle stories, as MacMullen proposes,[28] that prompts early Christian conversion, but the stories themselves. 'Though the frequency,' he writes, 'with which miracles produce conversions in the [*Apocryphal Acts of the Apostles*] could support MacMullen's claim that the performance of miracles was the primary spur to conversion in early Christianity, such use of the conversion stories in the AAA should be tempered by a recognition of their present status as reconstructions of past events designed to communicate their authors' present point of view.'[29])

Finally, MacMullen proposes a rather different 'soil' from Nock's in which Christianity could take root. The interest in immortality, according to him, was more apparent than real,[30] and Greco-Roman beliefs appear in general to have been 'a very spongy, shapeless, easily penetrated structure' that 'positively [invited] a sharply focused and intransigent creed'.[31] Thus where Nock found positive aspects of Greco-Roman belief to which Christianity appealed, MacMullen finds only negativity that was bested by Christianity.

Two years after the appearance of MacMullen's book, Beverly Roberts Gaventa also sought to improve upon Nock's analysis, by offering a tripartite model. Gaventa distinguishes three types of conversion: 'In addition to those experiences that grow out of the past (alternations), and those that result in an affirmed present at the expense of a rejected past (conversions), there are experiences that we may call transformations.'[32] Alternation she understands as 'parallel' to adhesion,[33] and neither alternation nor transformation requires the rejection of the past involved in conversion (where she stays with Nock's definition). The third element, transformation, is 'a radical change of perspective in which some newly gained cognition brings about a changed way of understanding' – that is to say, 'a re-cognition of the past'.[34]

At this point we may affirm that Nock, MacMullen and Gaventa have given us a helpful framework in which to view cases of conversion. Nock's work focussed the issue sharply, and both MacMullen and Gaventa have improved on Nock's definition of conversion, the former by emphasizing the spectrum of belief and practice among new converts, and the latter by a helpful expansion of Nock's two-type model. Of Gaventa's tripartite model we may note that while one might initially think that alternation, at least, and probably transformation would apply only to Jewish conversions, this is by no means necessarily the case, and Gaventa herself apparently considers the conversions of the Ethiopian eunuch and of Cornelius in Acts to be examples of alternation.[35] (She clearly sees, however, that all the conversion stories in Acts are not 'ideal or typical account[s] of conversion', but that the accounts are rather subservient to Luke's narrative purpose.)[36]

Nock's explanation for the success of Christianity, that while the cults and philosophical schools answered various longings of people in the early centuries of our era, Christianity answered the entire complex of their needs,[37] and MacMullen's emphasis on the effect of miracles, on intellectual quests, and on the efficaciousness of individual contacts, are points that we shall have to examine further below.

We should briefly note a few still more recent works that address conversion in early Christianity. Martin Goodman, *Mission and Conversion*, investigates the causes of mission, not of conversion, and proposes the idiosyncratic notion that, while Christianity developed the concept of a universal mission, few if any Christians expected converts to join a particular congregation (pp. 94–104). That early Christians did not think as Goodman proposes is seen in the fact that all early Christians known to us, except for the itinerant apostles and similar itinerant leaders of the church, belonged to local congregations. In a different kind of approach Thomas Finn, *From Death to*

Rebirth, attempts to set Christian conversion within the context of Greco-Roman culture. This work is, however, unfortunately flawed for two reasons. On the one hand Finn considers paganism to be a single entity alongside Judaism and Christianity. Thus conversion to, e.g., the religion of Isis becomes conversion *within* a religion parallel to a Jew's becoming an Essene. This way of construing things obscures the fact that Christianity was a new religious movement alongside the Isis religion and similar religious movements, something that Nock already understood. On the other hand, Finn is overly interested in ritual and takes baptism to be, for Christianity, 'the hinge on which conversion turns' (p. 141; cf. also p. 145). This focus on a ritual event causes Finn to miss the nature of conversion, even though he endorses (pp. 15, 33) an early version of Lewis Rambo's model (see below).

Robin Lane Fox, in his massive historical treatment of the success of Christianity,[38] had earlier made the same mistake of lumping all pagan religions together. (Lane Fox's work was originally published in the same year in which Gaventa's book appeared.) While on the one hand he recognized the vitality of pagan religion (pp. 27–261; cf. esp. the summary on p. 261), he argued (pp. 265–335) that Christianity offered a winning alternative that addressed the 'faults in pagan society' (p. 335). Lane Fox seems hardly aware of Christianity's competitors among the NRMs of the day; Isis is mentioned only twice in the entire book.

Finally, however, a recent comprehensive handbook on Roman religions by Mary Beard, John North and Simon Price brings important new perspectives to the discussion. The authors see quite clearly that conversion to early Christianity must be viewed alongside conversion to the other NRMs (which they call 'new cults'), and they have given a considerable discussion to the phenomenon of conversion to these NRMs in the early empire.[39] The authors first discuss the appeal of the NRMs and propose that the appeal can best be explained 'under the term "transformation": for all these new cults claimed to make much more of an impact than traditional religions on the everyday world and on the after-life of their adherents'.[40] This transformation the authors see first of all in 'a new sense of community' that the NRMs offered that was 'stronger' than that offered by traditional religious groups. Such membership was 'marked by special initiatory rituals'. Thus, membership in the NRMs 'affected, in different ways, the everyday life of their members'.[41] That is to say that 'what was distinctive about the new cults was their drive toward a strong religious identity through strictly controlled rules of behaviour'. Furthermore, the NRMs 'created new statuses and new ways of life that may have started within the walls of the sanctuary, but extended outside those walls too'.[42]

In the second place, transformation in *some* (albeit not all) of the NRMs had to do with 'the fate of the initiate after death'. Those NRMs that possessed this trait emphasized it by 'construct[ing] death much more sharply as a "problem" – and, at the same time, offer[ing] a "solution"'.[43] These authors thus implicitly reject Nock's distinction between conversion and adhesion and implicitly posit Gaventa's transformation as the explanatory principle for adhesion or conversion, which they do not distinguish.

Beard, North and Price then turn to a discussion of the members of the subject NRMs. First pointing out that 'male members of the senatorial order appear conspicuously absent from' the NRMs in Rome,[44] they further observe that, 'outside Rome, members of local élites (. . . holding the rank of "town councillor") were involved in these cults much more widely and fully'. Thus, 'at Pompeii . . . town councillors became priests of the' Isis religion.[45] Mithraism was equally respectable, although in another way, since its adherents were mostly 'soldiers, up to the rank of centurion, [and] imperial slaves and ex-slaves'.[46] Furthermore, 'by A.D. 200 Christians were found in Rome at every level of society', and they cite the scolding of *Herm. Man.* 10.1.3 that 'many second-century Roman Christians were "absorbed in business affairs, wealth, friendship with pagans, and many other occupations of this world"'.[47] The authors here take note of the Christian ideal of

poverty and cite Celsus (below, p. 103) on the lower-class
membership of the church; but they also astutely note that
poverty was, in Christianity, 'clearly vested with symbolic,
religious significance', thus making it 'difficult . . . to trace
accurately the presence of the poor (in strictly economic terms)
in early Christian communities'.[48] In the opinion of Beard,
North and Price, then, the main NRMs in the early empire
attracted a broad spectrum of class and status groups, although
Christianity was apparently slower in doing so than were some
of its competitors. Again, they refuse to assume that there were
conversions of different orders among the various NRMs,
although they are aware of individual differences in some cases.
(See the next paragraph.) The individual differences, however,
do not lead them to propose that conversion or adherence to
one or another of the NRMs was qualitatively different from
conversion or adherence to the others.

The authors next take up the role of women in the NRMs,
and they observe that the possibilities for women's participation varied. Mithraism, of course, admitted no women; but
most of the other NRMs did make a place for women that they
would normally not have had in the traditional religions of the
day. This is true for the worship of the Great Mother, of Isis,
and in both Judaism and Christianity. Nevertheless, men
retained the primary positions of leadership in all the NRMs.[49]
The authors conclude their discussion of membership by
attacking the notion (without referring directly to Nock or to
MacMullen) that 'significant sections of the population of
Rome had long been searching for some kind of spiritual satisfaction which was eventually offered by the new cults'. Rather,
they propose, the NRMs on the one hand created 'the very
needs which they satisfied' and on the other hand offered a
transformation that 'was rooted and legitimated in the social
and political lives of [the] adherents'. In other words, the
'everyday experience [of the converts] . . . found an echo in
the promise of the cults to transform lives'. Unfortunately for
this last proposal, however, Beard, North and Price offer only
the example of Mithraism, which allowed soldiers and freed-

men the opportunity for advancement, something that the broader culture considered 'both desirable and possible'.[50] Nevertheless, something that we shall want to consider further below is the degree to which Christianity and our comparator NRMs stood in tension to the culture. Did people become Christians in part because Christianity offered a transformation rooted and legitimated in the social and political lives of its converts?

Turning next to the issue of 'homogeneity and exclusivity', Beard, North and Price observe the relative continuity of each of the NRMs across the geographical spectrum, although they are aware that, e.g., 'Isis in Gaul *must* have been a significantly different phenomenon from Isis in Egypt'. They speculate that the use of more or less standard books in the Isis religion, in Judaism and in Christianity may have abetted this uniformity, but they think that 'the crucial point must be that these cults defined themselves as international',[51] a point to which we shall return at the end of the next chapter.

The authors finally, again without specifically rehearsing Nock's adhesion-conversion antithesis at this point, confront the theory head on by proposing that all the successful NRMs under study were *to some degree* exclusive, and in this they are surely correct. They ask first, 'Would it be possible at any level to accept the tenets of both the cult of Isis and of Mithras?' and they answer in the affirmative; but the 'at any level' must be emphasized.[52] Their examples of exclusiveness are the castrated priests, the *galli*, in the service of the Great Mother and certain devotees of Isis, e.g., Apuleius' Lucius, whose 'newly shaven head [at the end of the *Metamorphoses*] . . . emphasizes that Lucius had no time for any other deity but Isis'.[53]

It is clear that Beard, North and Price have moved the discussion of Gentile conversion to early Christianity to a new level by insisting that all conversions to NRMs in the period with which we are concerned must be analysed together as part of a general phenomenon. Scholars who want to understand early Christian conversion can no longer give prior preference to the notion that Christianity was somehow unique in winning converts in Greco-Roman society. The correctness of this new approach will be more obvious after we take into account sociological (and related) studies of conversion to NRMs in recent times.

3. Conversion to new religious movements in recent times

Since the 1960s the study of new religious movements (NRMs) has occupied many social scientists and has well-nigh consumed the energies of sociologists of religion. So many analyses of various aspects of conversion, including many by participant observers, have appeared in these four decades that it would be impossible to review even a significant fraction of them here, so our best approach is to look at major alternatives. We may conveniently begin with a textbook, Thomas Robbins' *Cults, Converts and Charisma*.

Summarizing a wide range of sociological studies, Robbins notes first the necessity to distinguish between recruitment and conversion.[54] Conversion he defines in Nock's way but then also cites a study of one NRM that made clear that 'recruitment tended to be rather sudden whereas conversion was a gradual evolutionary process'. It is possible, therefore, to construe conversion *per se* as a form of 'the more general process of *socialization*'.[55] This insight alerts us to the possibility that some persons may join a group with little or no understanding of the group's theology and with little or no commitment. (MacMullen, we recall, made very much the same point.) Commitment or 'true' conversion may follow; or, alternatively, increased understanding may lead the new recruit to drop out of the movement – an aspect of the dynamic of early Christianity that is probably too often neglected. Nevertheless, in the rest of our study we shall of necessity have to ignore the distinction between joining and being converted, since the evidence simply does not allow us, at this remove, to make judgments about who were the 'true' Christians and who merely signed on. It will be best to bear MacMullen's opening observation in mind, for which Paul especially also gives evidence, that joiners may make progress in the religion until they reach the point of true conversion. It is possible that the distinction between recruitment and conversion is misleading and is, even unwittingly, informed by a Christian theology that insists that in conversion 'certain things are to be rejected and certain things are to be embraced'.[56]

Robbins next refers to two studies by John Lofland and N. L. Skonovd in which they proposed six conversion motifs: intellectual, mystical, experimental, affectional, revivalist and coercive.[57] In intellectual conversion the convert is attracted by the literature of the NRM or by other indirect means. Mystical conversion is characterized by 'high subjective intensity and trauma',[58] and it may involve visions or less dramatic – though no less sudden – feelings leading to the impetus to join. Lofland and Skonovd did not attest any examples of such conversion that were devoid of prior knowledge of the NRM, but such prior knowledge itself is for them insufficient to explain the mystical experience. Experimental conversion is normally one of a long, slow process in which the convert gradually 'tries out' the NRM. Affectional conversion is invariably related to 'interpersonal bonds' and is a type of conversion in which the supportive aspect of the NRM is prominent. Revivalist conversion entails 'managed or manipulated ecstatic arousals in a group or collective context';[59] and by coercive conversion Lofland and Skonovd mean brainwashing.

Complicating the picture further, Lofland and Skonovd proposed five variables that need to be noted for each of the six types of conversion. We may most conveniently see how those variables interact with the six motifs by consulting the chart on the following page.[60]

In intellectual conversion (MacMullen's seeker type), as we see, there is little or no social pressure on the convert, the process of conversion is neither short nor long, the convert's emotional arousal is neither high nor low, the affective content is one of illumination or enlightenment, and belief precedes

	Intellectual	Mystical	Experimental	Affectional	Revivalist	Coercive
Degree of Social Pressure	low or none	none or little	low	medium	high	high
Temporal Duration of Conversion	medium	short	long	long	short	long
Level of Affective Arousal	medium	high	low	medium	high	high
Affective Content	illumination	awe, love, fear	curiosity	affection	love (and fear)	fear (and love)
Belief-Participation Sequence	belief-participation	belief-participation	participation-belief	participation-belief	participation-belief	participation-belief

participation. In revivalist conversion (MacMullen's mass-conversion type) there is strong social pressure, the process of conversion lasts only a short time, the convert's emotional arousal is high, the primary emotional response is love (and fear), and participation precedes belief. The type of conversion that most closely conforms to MacMullen's individual-contact type is the affectional, and we see here that the conversion process is usually long and that, again, participation precedes belief. We may omit coercive conversion from further discussion since, while there certainly was coercive conversion to early Christianity – most notably in the case of a *pater familias'* ordering all his household to convert – such coercive conversion did not follow the pattern of modern brainwashing.

Here is, then, a more refined way of thinking about conversion than MacMullen's, although we see that MacMullen was on the right track. Of Nock's adherence-conversion distinction, however, or of Gaventa's tripartite refinement of that distinction, there is nothing. Lofland and Skonovd appear to reckon with degrees of commitment,[61] not with degrees of rejection of the past. However, valuable as Lofland and Skonovd's analysis of conversion is in opening our eyes to the variety of ways in which ancient people may have become Christians, their approach will not provide much help in answering our Why? question.

More to the point at hand, then, is a proposal made by Lofland and Rodney Stark in 1965, a way of understanding conversion that has become 'the most influential sociological model of conversion-commitment processes in religious movements',[62] namely a 'value-added process model' that entails seven stages of conversion. According to this model conversion is accomplished when a person (1) experiences *acute and persistent tensions*, (2) within a *religious problem-solving perspective*, which leads the individual (3) to define himself as a *religious seeker*, after which (4) he encounters the movement at a crucial *turning point* in his life, and (5) forms an *affective bond* with one or more converts, after which (6) *extra-cult attachments become attenuated*, and (7) the convert is exposed to *intensive interaction* within the group and ultimately becomes the group's 'deployable agent'.[63] What makes this model so engaging for our interest here is that, as further sociological studies have shown, the model works only for groups that are 'highly stigmatized'. Other groups that 'do not drastically transform the social roles of converts' and do not involve the attenuation of extra-cult attachments do not follow this pattern.[64]

Where, then, can we place early Christianity among these types of conversion? Were we to stay with Nock's distinction we should be inclined to endorse the value-added process model, but MacMullen's analysis would incline us to the opposite view. For Gaventa, however, conversion to early Christianity was spread over both conversions involving rejection of the past and those that did not involve such rejection; and she specifically included non-Jewish conversions within the latter category (for her, two categories, to be precise). Was early Christianity at some times and places highly stigmatized and at other times and places not? Gaventa's model would imply that it was, and she is likely correct since, as MacMullen also realizes, the real situation is likely to have been more complex than we may have been wont to recognize.

We need to note two other aspects of Robbins' summary discussion of sociological studies of conversion, namely, social networks, and defection and deconversion. There is a great deal of evidence that conversion follows lines of social networks, and Robbins quotes a widely noted summary maxim: 'The probability of being recruited into a particular movement is largely a function of two conditions: (1) links to one or more movement members through a pre-existing or emergent interpersonal tie; and (2) the absence of countervailing networks.'[65] The latter condition means that the potential convert is 'structurally available'. Yet structural availability is subject to other conditions, especially the religious movement's 'goals and beliefs about the world';[66] or, more broadly, there must be a real appeal of the movement to the structurally available person. As Robbins puts it, 'A married man with a family might be "available" for a romantic liaison with Brooke Shields but not with Margaret Thatcher.'[67]

The matter of networks is worth pausing over. If our image of conversion is informed by the accounts of mass conversions in the early chapters of Acts and by the existence of large evangelistic rallies conducted by modern American preachers, we shall surely miss what is probably the most important ingredient in conversion, namely that the convert has or develops an affective tie to someone in the movement before joining. It is well known, of course, that modern evangelistic rallies win most of their converts not at the rallies themselves, but through prior evangelistic contact – and such contact readily follows affective lines. Protestant evangelism aside, however, it is also the case that many recent studies of NRMs have shown that most converts are won through networks. Twenty years ago Stark and William Sims Bainbridge published a study in the *American Journal of Sociology* that is now almost a classic on this subject.[68] Stark and Bainbridge showed that the 'Moonies', for example – the followers of the Rev. Sun Myung Moon – were initially stymied in their attempt at further growth when they first moved from Eugene, Oregon, to San Francisco. 'Only when the cult found ways to connect with other newcomers to San Francisco and develop serious relationships with them did recruitment resume.'[69] Stark's and Bainbridge's best example, however, was the Mormon Church (officially the Church of Jesus Christ of Latter Day Saints). Young Mormon men are encouraged by the church to go in pairs to places away from their homes seeking converts, and these young men, in their white shirts and ties, have visited or sought to visit many Americans and Europeans in their homes. Such random visits, however, turn out to be a waste of time for the church. After examining statistics 'for all [Mormon] missionaries in the state of Washington during the year 1976–77', Stark and Bainbridge found that only .1% (!) of all conversions during the year were the result of 'door-to-door canvas', whereas 34% of conversions came from meetings with potential converts arranged by other Mormons, and fully 50% of all conversions occurred when 'contact with missionaries took place in the home of [a] Mormon friend or relative' of the potential convert. (Other conversions followed from referrals.)[70] Stark and Bainbridge also sought to discover whether any kinds of conversions occurred in significant proportion *apart from* such networks, and they found that only adoption of such occult beliefs as astrology and the validity of tarot cards fell outside the pattern.[71]

To this evidence we can also add that of the movement now known as Nichiren Shoshu of America (NSA) and formerly as Soka Gakkai.[72] Some aspects of this NRM are strikingly reminiscent of some aspects of early Christianity. Just as early Christianity may be seen as originally a Jewish reform movement that severed its ties to Judaism and moved into the broader world, so NSA began as a reform movement within Nichiren Shoshu Buddhism, a branch of Japanese Buddhism, and then came to the Americas as a virtually distinct movement. (The breach with Nichiren Shoshu Buddhism has since been healed.) Soka Gakkai even held a conference very much like the early Christian Apostolic Conference, at which time the issue of accommodation was debated. The decision, likewise, was similar to that reached at the Apostolic Conference (albeit not identical): The movement could adopt foreign practices (flying the American flag, allowing statues of the Virgin Mary in homes) as long as the essence of the religion remained the same. NSA, while not as large as the Mormon Church, maintains a similar growth rate, and the experience of conversions via networks is the same as that for the Mormons and for the Moonies. Out of a total of 345 conversions counted by David Snow, Louis Zurcher, Jr, and Sheldon Ekland-Olson in their and in others' studies, 82% were the result of social networks, 17% of recruitment activity in public places, and 1% of information in the mass media.[73]

The evidence from NRMs in modern Western societies is clear: conversions come primarily through personal contact within social networks. Can we assume the same for antiquity?

Not, to be sure, in the absence of evidence or in the face of evidence to the contrary; but the studies of modern NRMs make it reasonable to think that many ancient conversions to Christianity, and to the other NRMs of that day as well, likely came about as a result of contacts and affective relationships within networks.

We need not linger on the matter of defection, only note it, although it is worth pointing out that the attrition rates of modern American NRMs are 'extremely high'.[74] We historians perhaps normally do not take into account that in the early days people might have left Christianity as readily as they entered. Should we perhaps revise our opening judgment about the stories of mass conversions in Acts and propose that there may have been such conversions but that most of the converts then left the movement before the events described in Acts 7 and 8? Such a course of events would not be impossible but still seems unlikely.

A modern sociologist who has sought to understand early Christianity explicitly is Anthony Blasi, and in a discussion of early Christian adherence Blasi distinguishes three types of adherents – 'the activist, the person who identifies with the movement, and the person who agrees with the movement but does not identify with it' by labelling himself a Christian.[75] Blasi adds that 'the latter two categories differ from one another only insofar as Christian "identifiers" would know themselves and acknowledge themselves to be Christians while the "agreers" would not'. Yet he has to admit that we know little of the identifiers and agreers in early Christianity and that we have knowledge of only some of the activists. Helpful, therefore, as this analysis is in filling in our image of early Christian congregations, it does not advance our understanding of conversion itself.

A few paragraphs ago we noted the possibility of greater complexity in the matter of conversion to early Christianity than scholars who have studied the issue may have seen. It is now time to complicate that theoretical complexity further by looking at two studies, Newton Malony's psychological model

of converts and Lewis Rambo's thoroughly inclusive sociological study of conversion.

Malony proposes that there are five possible psychological
motivations for conversion.[76] The first is the problem-solving
motivation, by which he means the Lofland-Stark value-
added process model that we examined above. Other motivations, however, are friendship-finding, meaning-seeking, role-
discovering and preparation-lacking. How the first three of
these may be motivations for conversion is obvious. People
who feel alone in the world may welcome the friendship that an
NRM provides, those who feel that traditional systems do not
provide adequate explanations of life and the world (seekers)
may welcome the meaning system of an NRM, and others may
be attracted to the status of assigned roles in the NRM. (More
on roles below.) By 'preparation-lacking' motivation Malony
means that potential converts have not been prepared to resist
the appeals of NRMs.

Malony, of course, was considering the modern American
and European situation, not the ancient; and the vast majority
of subjects for his model were 'older adolescents', the primary
convert group for modern NRMs, for whom especially
friendship-finding, role-discovering and preparation-lacking
motivations are particularly appropriate. (The other two
motivations do not seem to be age-related.) Nevertheless, these
motivations may be relevant for the situation in antiquity that
early Christianity confronted. We can likely, in any case, be
certain that persons who were *not* seeking solutions to life
problems, who had an adequate circle of friends and family,
who were satisfied with traditional meaning systems, and who
had established life roles to play would not have been the most
likely candidates for conversion to early Christianity or to any
other NRM.

Rambo, a sociologist, presents a 'holistic model of conversion'.[77] He first emphasizes three aspects of conversion: 1. It
is 'a process over time, not a single event'; 2. it 'is contextual
and thereby influences and is influenced by a matrix of relationships, expectations, and situations'; and 3. 'factors in the

conversion process are multiple, interactive, and cumulative. There is no one cause of conversion, no one process, and no one simple consequence of that process.'[78] Rambo finds five types of conversion: 1. apostasy or defection (from previous commitment); 2. intensification, i.e., 'the revitalized commitment to a faith with which the convert has had previous affiliation'; 3. affiliation, i.e., 'movement . . . from no or minimal religious commitment to full involvement'; 4. institutional transition, i.e., moving 'from one community to another within a major tradition'; and 5. tradition transition, i.e., the 'movement of an individual or a group from one major religious tradition to another'.[79] A comparison of these types with Gaventa's three types is instructive. While Rambo does not make Gaventa's distinction (following Nock) between alternation and conversion, his affiliation and tradition transition would be present in both, and vice versa. Similarly, both Rambo's intensification and institutional transition are different ways of thinking about what Gaventa called transformation; and Gaventa, of course, did not discuss apostasy. Rambo, like Nock and Gaventa, conceives of conversion as moving from a previous state to a new religious context, whereas Lofland and Skonovd sought rather to analyse the experience of conversion. When we return to our evidence below we shall do well to keep both perspectives in mind.

The rest of Rambo's book analyses seven interlocking aspects that may go into any conversion: context, crisis, quest, encounter, interaction, commitment and consequences.

A part of any *context* may be resistance and rejection – for example, after many decades of Christian missionizing in Asia, 'in Japan, Christians comprise less than 1 percent of the population. Chinese Christians are a tiny fraction of 1 percent.'[80] Yet a new religious option may appeal to identifiable enclaves within the population.[81] Conversions may also proceed along established paths – that is, following existing 'lines of social cleavages'; and conversions are also dependent on congruence – that is, on 'the degree to which elements of a new religion mesh with existing macro- and microcontextual factors'.[82]

Noting that Lofland and Stark were 'among the first . . . to note the importance of *crisis* in the conversion process', Rambo points out that crises differ. They may be mild or severe, brief or prolonged, etc., but he sees 'two basic types': 'crises that call into question one's fundamental orientation to life' and those 'that in and of themselves are rather mild but are the proverbial straw that breaks the camel's back'.[83] Here Rambo connects apostasy to conversion by observing that 'some conversions require explicit and enacted rejection of past affiliations, but all conversions implicitly require a leaving-behind or a reinterpretation of some past way of life and set of beliefs'. When we recall the social difficulties that early converts to Christianity experienced (exclusion from much of public life), then we see clearly the connection of apostasy to conversion, the leaving of one way to cleave to the Way. But Rambo, in placing this observation under the heading of crisis, meant to show that the leaving may prompt the joining, that 'leaving a religious tradition' is a 'catalyst for crisis and conversion',[84] an aspect of modern conversion that is probably irrelevant to our study.

Here we may note that one of the most discussed issues in the modern sociological study of conversion to NRMs is that of deprivation. Thus in his summary Robbins notes that 'many of the theories' that scholars have put forward to explain such conversion are 'crisis theories and/or modernization theories' that 'tend to pinpoint some acute and distinctively modern dislocation which is said to be producing some mode of alienation, anomie or deprivation to which Americans are responding by searching for new structures of meaning and community'.[85] And Stark reports that before he and Lofland observed conversion to the Unification Church (Moonies), sociologists normally 'examined the ideology of a group to see what kinds of deprivation it addressed and then concluded . . . that converts suffered from those deprivations'.[86] On more adequate analysis deprivation seems not to be a factor – or at least a significant factor – leading to conversion, and so some sociologists refer at times to *relative* deprivation.[87] In the light of this ambiguity in the current scholarly analysis of deprivation as a motive for conversion, Robbins appeals for 'a cautionary viewpoint' that 'would also highlight the constancy and continuity of movements of "religious outsiders" throughout American history'. The implication of that caution would have to be that we must not assume that people who join NRMs always do so because of some deprivation or crisis in their lives; although, we should certainly be alert to evidence for such motivation.[88]

We first saw the importance of the *quest* in our review of MacMullen's views; but whereas MacMullen thought of only a few intellectuals as pursuing such a quest, Rambo thinks that 'many, if not most, conversions' are 'active' rather than 'passive', i.e., come about as the result of seeking, at least in some form and at some level.[89] A seeker is thus available to the missionary enterprise of the religious movement, but this availability has to coincide with the nature of the movement if conversion is to work. Thus availability must be structural (we recall Robbins' adultery joke), emotional, intellectual and religious. Regarding intellectual availability Rambo explains that 'it is rare for someone to be converted to an option that embraces an intellectual framework radically different from the person's previous viewpoint'; and religious availability is similar, meaning that 'a person's religious beliefs, practices, and life-style are to some degree compatible with the new option'.[90] The seeker, finally, must be motivated by one or more psychological needs (enhancing self-esteem, or the like).[91]

Rambo next discusses *encounter*, where he first defines the role of the 'advocate', thus employing a term that fits a broader field of activity than does 'missionary'. After first noting that advocate strategy in different groups can run from the 'extensive' to the 'minimal' and that advocate style can be 'diffuse' (seeking to convert whole groups) or 'concentrated' (targeting individuals),[92] he observes that advocates' 'modes of contact' are extremely diverse.[93] Finally, he emphasizes that, to be successful, the advocate must represent desirable benefits, namely 'a system of meaning', 'emotional gratifications', 'techniques for living', 'convincing leadership', and possibly 'power', i.e., feeling 'filled with power', having 'access to power', or the like.[94]

Following this discussion Rambo deals with the nature of missionary encounter itself, pointing out that, at first, a new movement normally has only a few converts but that, 'as increasing numbers of people adopt the novelty, there is a bandwagon effect, characterized by more and more interest in and less and less resistance to the innovation'.[95] Then he points to missionary and convert adaptations that are part of the encounter process. An advocate may be tolerant of the potential convert's life and belief, may translate, i.e., 'communicate the new religious message in a manner that is understandable', may assimilate – that is, may 'utilize the traditions and rituals of an indigenous culture' – may Christianize – that is, cleanse rites and practices of 'un-Christian' elements – may acculturate ('go native'), or may incorporate by introducing indigenous concepts into the advocate's Christianity.[96]

Potential converts, on the other hand, may oscillate between old and new beliefs, may then eliminate 'more and more elements of their tradition that were considered incompatible with Christianity' ('scrutinization'), may combine, i.e., work out compromises with advocates over new and old beliefs and practices, may indigenize, by which Rambo means taking over equivalent practices to replace ones given up, and, finally, may retrovert.[97]

The next stage in Rambo's conversion model is *interaction*, and here he discusses the ways in which the NRM 'encapsulates' the convert. The modes of encapsulation are relationships, rituals, rhetoric and roles. Rambo is persuaded that while some conversions may not involve relationships, most do;[98] and he means, of course, that the potential convert must establish some kind of meaningful relationship within the NRM before conversion can succeed. Ritual is crucial because, by offering 'a form of knowledge that is distinctive from, but as important as, cognitive knowledge', it 'helps people to learn to act differently'.[99] And of course rituals like baptism that strongly mark the transition from the old ways and the old group(s) into the new are important.[100] The importance of rhetoric is that it helps the convert to conceptualize and to interpret the changes involved in conversion;[101] and roles, finally, of course integrate the convert into the movement.[102] (We recall that role-discovering was one of the psychological motivations for conversion proposed by Malony.)

The importance of *commitment* and *consequences* will be so obvious to most readers that Rambo's observations on these aspects of conversion require little discussion. One point worth noting is his emphasis on the importance of 'sustaining surrender'. Some groups, in his observation, are better at this (usually through ritual) than others; thus the less successful groups will also be less successful at holding converts in an active relationship with the movement. Furthermore, the convert's testimony is important to commitment; it helps to cement the conversion. But such testimony also involves 'biographical reconstruction', i.e., viewing one's past life through the lens of the new self-understanding.[103] Consequences are likely to be affective, intellectual, ethical, religious, or social/political;[104] the convert, indeed, *is* not the same person as before.

Rambo's analysis has not met with widespread acclaim among sociologists, primarily because it is so all-encompassing and multi-faceted. Thus Lofland writes in his review of Rambo's book that it is, on the one hand, 'likely the single most comprehensive compendium of the literature on conversion'. On the other hand, however, it is an 'everything-is-sometimes-true view' that fails to specify 'when forms and aspects of conversion occur and when they do not'.[105] This does not mean, however, that Rambo has failed in his attempt to place between two covers *all* facets of conversion, and he seems to have done so. He has provided the broad, theoretical model that allows us to evaluate *all aspects* of individual conversions; and, as we have noted at different points in the review, his analysis has subsumed the primary aspects of conversion to which Nock, MacMullen and Gaventa have called attention.

Before going forward, we need to take note of what is, just as this work is going to print, the latest attempt to provide a comprehensive treatment of conversion to NRMs, Lorne Dawson's *Comprehending Cults*. While most of Dawson's work is so specifically orientated towards developments in the United States in the last forty years that it has little relevance for our interest here, his discussions of why NRMs arise and of who joins them are worth noting. Dawson divides his discussion of the first issue into a consideration of NRMs as *responses* to cultural change and as ways of *continuing* cultural patterns. Regarding the first tendency he observes that many sociologists have pointed to 'the decline in the social prominence of conventional religions' as the background for the rise of NRMs in recent times[106] – a tendency that might tend to support the notion that there was a malaise, from the Hellenistic period on, brought on by increasing internationalism and individualism that prepared the ground for the rise of Christianity, and of other NRMs as well. Yet Dawson balances this observation with the alternate view that not only America, but the Western world generally, has 'a long lineage of alternative religious and philosophic groups'.[107] According to this view, then, there is nothing new in the *existence* of NRMs, only in the details of the individual movements. Dawson thus inclines toward the view that a major social or religious dislocation is not necessary for NRMs to arise.

On the issue of the converts themselves Dawson is somewhat more specific and offers five 'broad generalizations'.[108] 'First,' he notes, 'the members of most NRMs are disproportionately young', and the NRMs are not able to retain many of their converts as the converts age and take on family and social responsibilities (just as we have repeatedly noted the likelihood that there were numerous defectors from early Christianity). Then, new converts to NRMs are 'on average markedly better educated than the general public', perhaps because the novel and sometimes esoteric teachings of NRMs are a challenge to understand.[109] Converts come, further, 'disproportionately from middle- to upper-middle-class households'.[110] Dawson's final two generalizations are, rather, ambiguities. Some movements attract many more women than men, while others do not; and some appeal largely to persons from religious backgrounds, while others, again, do not.[111]

While these generalizations probably do not offer us much that will help us to understand ancient conversion to Christianity – we have already noted the likelihood that Jesus' followers were young; we shall return in the next chapter to Wayne Meeks' (and more recently Rodney Stark's) argument that early Christianity did not recruit primarily from the poorer classes; level of education will be impossible to assess – in the end Dawson offers a quite salutary concluding evaluation. He writes,

> From a social-scientific perspective, there is still a crucial and easily overlooked element of mystery about why people choose to be religious . . . So a full explanation of why people choose to convert still eludes our grasp. In these circumstances we must duly appreciate that people may well convert for precisely the reasons the religions themselves say they do: because they have achieved some form of enlightenment or insight into their salvation.[112]

With that awareness firmly in the backs of our minds, let us turn to the ancient evidence to see what, if anything, we can learn about societal or sociological aspects of early Gentile conversion to Christianity. We shall surely want to keep Rambo's paradigm in mind, which means that we shall need to be alert to the degree to which context, crisis, quest, encounter, interaction, commitment and consequences led to individual conversions. And we shall also want to watch for any evidence that seems explicable by one or another of the other sociological principles that we have reviewed in this section. It is to that inquiry that we now turn.

4. The early Christian evidence

A. Acts

Let us first get all the relevant evidence before us. When we turn to the book of Acts for evidence for the conversion of Gentiles to Christianity, we find that the author is primarily interested in – to use Rambo's terms – encounter, interaction and commitment, while demonstrating almost no interest in consequences and very little in context, crisis and quest. People respond to the apostles either following wonders (as in the case of Sergius Paulus in Acts 13.12 or that of the Philippian jailer in 16.30) or as a result of the preaching of the word, as in the keynote conversion of Cornelius in ch. 10 or in the conversion of many citizens of Antioch in ch. 13. While miracles leading to conversion may be performed in view of a crowd, as is the case with the early work of Philip in Samaria (8.6), or before only one observer (the Philippian jailer), normally Acts represents the proclamation of the gospel as a public event in the presence of sometimes large numbers of people. In a few cases, however, the preaching takes place in an individual or small-group setting (Philip with the Ethiopian eunuch in ch. 8, Peter with Cornelius, Paul and his companions with Lydia and a few others in Philippi; cf. esp. 16.13, 'We sat down and spoke with the women who had gathered [there]').

Most Gentile converts in Acts seem to come from among the group of the 'God-fearers', those Gentiles who have some attraction to Judaism and who may be found at synagogue prayer services, but some do not come to Christianity by this route. When we make this division, however, then we immediately note that the only Gentile converts who are attracted to Christianity by wonders are those who do not belong among the God-fearers. Thus Samaritans (if we should call them Gentiles) respond to Philip's ministry in Acts 8.6–7 because of 'hearing him and seeing the signs that he did; for many of those who had unclean spirits that cried with a loud voice came out (*sic*), and many paralytics and lame were healed'. Sergius

Paulus, further, a proconsul (13.7–12), 'saw what happened and believed', where what happened was Paul's blinding Elymas/bar Jesus, a 'Jewish magician and false prophet' (v. 6). To be sure, Acts calls what Paul did 'the teaching of the Lord' (v. 12), but it is not the kind of teaching that, e.g., Peter gave to Cornelius. The Philippian jailer, whom we have already mentioned, asked about salvation after the prison doors were miraculously opened and Paul and Silas did not leave. No other Gentile conversions in Acts come about as the result of wonders, not even that of Cornelius, whose vision prompted him to send for Peter but who believed only after hearing Peter's preaching. All other conversions of Gentiles to Christianity in Acts, most of which are conversions of God-fearers, happen in response to apostolic preaching, whether on a large or a small scale.

The most common strategy for reaching Gentiles in Acts is that of preaching in a synagogue (Paul), but other contacts are varied: the Ethiopian eunuch and the Philippian jailer are chance encounters; Philip in Samaria probably attracted attention first by his healing miracles.

The author of Acts also provides very little information about the backgrounds of the converts other than to locate them in their social worlds. Cornelius is a God-fearer and Roman centurion, Sergius Paulus is a proconsul, others are simply Samaritans or a jailer, many are God-fearers. Only the Ethiopian eunuch may be defined as a seeker, for he was attempting to understand Isaiah when Philip encountered him. Apparently he is also a God-fearer.

Acts also presents almost no information about the aftermath of conversion, although the author apparently wants to give the impression of ever-increasing success in the mission. Such a cumulative effect is explicit, however, only in the case of Jewish conversions in Judah, for the author notes the ever-larger groups who become Christians in the first four chapters and then reminds us in 21.20 that we should remember 'how many tens of thousands' of Torah-faithful Jews have become Christians. In any case, we learn almost nothing of the consequences of Gentile conversions beyond the further 'advice' that the missionaries give to the new Christians in Lystra, Iconium, and Antioch that they should 'abide in faith' in the face of 'many afflictions' (14.22). Probably quite significant here, however, is the note that Paul and Barnabas 'commissioned elders' (v. 23). Although the author mentions this commissioning only here, he elsewhere mentions elders in the church(es) with some frequency, so that we can see that he reckons with a continuing structure of leadership in local congregations after the time of first conversions.

Now, of course, we have to confront the question of whether the author of Acts has given us an accurate picture with regard to early Christian conversion. We know that the picture is inaccurate in at least one respect, the representation of Paul as normally seeking converts first in a synagogue. It has long been recognized that this characterization is so in conflict with Paul's own statements that it cannot be true and must be a schema that the author retrojects on to the earlier period about which he writes. (This remains true even when a number of recent scholars attempt to show – or merely assume – that the picture must be correct.) How Paul sought out potential converts will likely remain for ever an unanswered question, although we shall see below that Paul himself provides some clues for evaluating the way in which Acts characterizes early Christian conversion.

B. New Testament epistles

Not only does Paul not corroborate the Acts account in the matter of finding converts as the result of synagogue preaching, but he also does not corroborate the descriptions in Acts of preaching to large crowds. To be sure, Paul mentions preaching as a main part of his missionary endeavour; in Gal. 1.23 and 2.2 he refers to his preaching 'the faith' in the one case and 'among the Gentiles' in the other, and especially in I Corinthians 15 he rehearses the content of his preaching (vv. 1–11; Gal. 3.1 seems to refer briefly to this same content), but he gives no indication of how large an audience he may have had on any occasion, and what we now know about the spread of NRMs via networks might incline us to think of very small groups or of individuals. Likewise, his remarks in I Thessalonians 2 – where he says for example in v. 9 that he was 'working night and day not to burden some [of the Thessalonians] and preached the gospel of God to [them]' – provide no information at all about the size of any groups. The fact that he had a full-time job, as we should say, and preached at the same time certainly makes the possibility of his networking and talking to small groups more credible, but there is no proof.

What is clearer, however, is that some persons were attracted to Christianity by Paul's miracles. This he says fairly plainly in I Cor. 2.4, when he asserts that his 'argument (λόγος)' and his 'preaching' were 'by demonstration of Spirit and power', not in 'persuasive reasonings (λόγοι) of wisdom'. In I Thess. 1.5 he says the same: 'Our gospel did not come to you by word (λόγος) only but also by power and by the Holy Spirit and in much certainty.' Should we think that, in a culture in which healing miracles took place, Paul meant by this contrast only that he was bombastic? No; surely he meant that he provided visible proof of the power of his gospel. He may well allude to this same aspect of his missionary activity when he reports in Gal. 2.9 that the Jerusalem Christian leaders 'recognized the grace (or: gift, χάρις) given' to him.[113] With regard to such miracles also we may well think of small audiences, such as households, rather than of the civic demonstrations that Acts describes, but again the evidence is insufficient to allow us to draw a firm conclusion. Nevertheless, Paul seems to have relied on miracles, probably healings, as well as on preaching in order to win new Christians. Whether any of the miracles to which he alludes in I Cor. 2.4 are the same as those that appear in Acts would be impossible to say.[114]

There are two other things that we learn about Gentile conversion to Christianity from Paul, namely the insignificant status of converts and that conversion was a process, not an event. The latter is most ably demonstrated by I Cor. 3.1–2, 'I

was not able to speak to you as to spiritual persons (πνευ-
ματικοί) but as to fleshly persons (σαρκίνοι), as to babes in
Christ. Milk I gave you to drink, not solid food; for you were
not yet able.' Indeed, most of what Paul writes in all his letters
involves the assumption that Christians are in process – that
they have become Christians, but that they still need to learn
what it means to be Christian, both as regards belief (as in the
discussion of the resurrection in I Corinthians 15) and as
regards practice, as is the case here ('jealousy and strife', v. 3).
As Gaventa writes, 'Despite the fact that Paul understands this
transformation [of becoming a Christian] to be real and
significant, it is never a finished or completed event but is on-
going.'[115] Such an understanding of conversion as process
supports MacMullen's point that converts grow into the faith,
and it confirms the sociological distinction between recruitment
(joining a movement) and conversion (coming to share the
ideology and goals of the movement), and we should thus
now think of most conversions, not merely conversions to
Christianity, as happening in this way.[116] Only Lofland and
Skonovd's first two types of conversion, intellectual and mystical, put the process in reverse order, with belief preceding
participation.

The insignificant status is a bit of a problem. Paul says in I
Cor. 1.26–28 that among the Corinthian Christians

> not many are wise in human terms (κατὰ σάρκα), not many
> are powerful, not many are well-born; but God chose the
> foolish of the world in order to shame the wise, and God
> chose the weak of the world in order to shame the strong, and
> God chose the low-born of the world and the despised, the
> nothings, in order to render the somethings of no effect.

One of the problems with this statement is the gender of the
nouns. Paul begins with (gender-inclusive) masculine nouns
for 'wise', 'powerful', and 'well-born'; but then he brings in a
neuter for 'foolish', shifts back to masculine for 'wise', but then
uses neuters for the remaining groups. It seems impossible,

however, to see any deliberate theological motive for these shifts, especially in view of the contrast between 'foolish' (neuter) and 'wise' (masculine). And Paul does, after all, begin this statement by advising, 'Look at your calling, brothers.' All the 'things', then, that God has chosen appear to be the Corinthians whom God called. What Paul says here about the insignificance of Christians in society finds later corroboration in Celsus' criticism of Christians (as a number of authors note). 'Their injunctions are like this,' Celsus wrote about 180, '"Let no one educated, no one wise, no one sensible draw near."'[117] Meeks cites other disparaging remarks from Celsus.[118]

A problem here, however, is whether what Paul says comports with reality. Is Paul, in other words, skewing the facts here a bit for the sake of effect, in the context of his broader polemic against the wise in Corinth who have a wrong theology? It was, in large part, the work of Meeks' justly acclaimed study to show that we should not take Paul's statement here as simple sociological description, for in fact the early Christians in Paul's churches represented a socially mixed group. Meeks first reported on a number of earlier studies that had tended to show that the people in Paul's churches belonged to the urban middle class, and he then carried out an astute study both of prosopography in Paul's letters and of indirect evidence,[119] concluding that the social make-up of the churches was mixed. The names and apparent wealth of a few pointed to high status, but much of the evidence located other persons elsewhere in society. Meeks' conclusion, which was not totally firm and which he therefore 'ventured', was 'that the most active and prominent members of Paul's circle (including Paul himself) are people of *high status inconsistency* (low status crystallization) . . . Their *achieved* status is higher than their *attributed* status.'[120] These people were 'independent women with moderate wealth, Jews with wealth in a pagan society, freedmen with skill and money but stigmatized by origin, and so on', who 'brought with them not only anxiety but also loneliness, in a society in which social position was important and usually rigid'.[121] Modern sociologists of religion would say that such people suffered relative deprivation and were therefore prime candidates for conversion to an NRM.[122]

If Paul's labelling Christians the nothings of the world is, then, not an entirely accurate social description, what Meeks has shown is how the label might nevertheless resonate with them, which is of course what has to be explained. (Otherwise they would have exclaimed, 'Surely he doesn't mean us!') Especially *after they had become Christians* and had gained a status and security that they had not experienced before (so, in general, Meeks), they might very well have been able to agree that formerly they had been nothings. Beyond this, we should not lose sight of the likelihood that the term is, indeed, a part of Paul's polemic in his argument with the wise in the Corinthian church.

Col. 2.13 and Eph. 2.5, with slightly different wording, explain that Christians are persons whom, though formerly dead in their transgressions, God has made alive together with Christ – a homiletical attempt to sustain commitment through an intellectual and probably also an affective appeal. Somewhat similarly James 4.4 and I Peter 4.3–4, with a detailed list in the latter instance, remind the readers of the life-and-death difference between Christian and Gentile life, thus enforcing the understanding of Christian existence as distinct from normal existence in the surrounding society.

Ephesians 4.11 amends Paul's list of charismatic offices in I Cor. 12 by adding evangelists. Presumably these persons have taken – or are taking at the time of the writing of Ephesians – the role of the earlier apostles; but we still receive no clarity about exactly what that role was, i.e., whether the evangelists spoke to large crowds or contacted people through networks. In the absence of contrary evidence, we shall probably do best to assume networks, as also in the case if II Tim. 1.8, which advises the recipient not to be 'ashamed of the witness of our Lord', a witness apparently intended for potential converts.

I Timothy 3.6 lists 'neophyte' – presumably a new convert – as an improper candidate for bishop, 'so that [the bishop] not become blinded and fall into the devil's judgment' – a danger sufficiently vague to prevent our determining whether the author has lapsing in mind; nevertheless, we see here again the notion that converts must grow in their understanding of their new religion. The author of Hebrews also expresses the developmental aspect of conversion when, in his discussion of apostasy in 6.1, he refers to the 'discussion of the beginning in Christ' that Christians returning after leaving the faith would have to 'leave' again in order to proceed again to 'completion'.

I Peter brings a new element into view, namely that Christians by their *examples* may bring Gentiles to conversion. In I Peter 2.11–12 the author admonishes staying away from pagan life-style, but then advises that Christians should turn a good face toward non-Christians, even when the latter abuse Christians, so that 'by good works they may gain enlightenment and glorify God on the day of visitation'; then in 3.1 he proposes that women may be especially effective simply by 'being obedient to their own husbands, so that if some are not convinced by reason (τῷ λόγῳ), they will be won by the women's behaviour apart from reason'. The author of I Peter thus seems to assume the attempt to talk to non-Christians but to encourage a more encompassing attitude toward evangelization, winning converts by good example.

Finally, the view of the author of the Apocalypse is worth noting here not for what we learn about conversion to early Christianity in that work, but for its unusual position, namely that it is too late for any more conversions and that sinners and righteous should remain in their respective conditions (Rev. 22.11).

Aside from this last oddity, then, a fairly uniform picture of some aspects of conversion emerges. The early Christian advocates proclaimed the gospel of Christ's death and resurrection, probably to small groups reached through networks, to persons of low status but nevertheless often of some means. Paul also attracted attention to the gospel by miracles, but others who followed him seem not to have performed miracles. New Christians were expected to sever their ties with Greco-Roman culture and to grow in their understanding of Christian theology. Where Acts disagrees with this picture (preaching in synagogues and, both there and otherwise, to large crowds), the author has probably misconstrued early Christian history. If there were areas within Christianity during the first century where conversion appeared otherwise, we do not learn of them.

C. 'Sub-Apostolic' literature to the end of the second century

(i) Apostolic Fathers

As we round into the second century, we find first that the works contained in the Apostolic Fathers present us, to the degree that we can learn anything about conversion from them, with a picture similar to the one that we found in the epistles in the New Testament. I Clement 7.5–7 is particularly straight-forward, explaining that even in former days God provided preachers of repentance in response to whom people were saved. Thus, 'Noah preached repentance, and the obedient were saved. Jonah preached catastrophe to the Ninevites, and they repented . . . and received salvation' (7.6–7). Obviously the author considers this pattern paradigmatic. Much of his letter, further, offers advice on Christian living and thus resembles Paul's letters in revealing the assumption that Christians need advice – that is, that their belief and practice need to improve. We may note especially 30.1, where the author reminds the Corinthian Christians to 'flee slander, polluting and unholy couplings, drunkenness and rioting and abominable passions, and loathsome adultery and abominable arrogance'; and 62.2, where he gives the positives: 'faith, repentance, noble *agapē*, self-control, prudence, and patience'.

Beyond this, there is little in this collection about conversion, except that Ignatius, in Ephesians 10, mentions the influence of example, using language very similar to that in 1 Peter that we noted in the last section. 'Pray unceasingly,' he advises in 10.1, 'on behalf of other people, that they may encounter God. Leave it to them perhaps to be made disciples to you by works.' Since

Ignatius never mentions the 'by reason' of I Peter as the alternative or even normal approach to gaining converts, we might conclude that evangelism as such has ceased; and that impression is strengthened by the observation that neither Ignatius nor Polycarp, for all that they discuss the responsibilities of Christian leaders, ever mentions evangelizing as such a responsibility.

(ii) Apocryphal Acts of the Apostles

Let us turn now to an examination of the Apocryphal Acts of Andrew, of John, of Paul, and of Peter – works on which MacMullen relied in his analysis of early Christian conversion – to see what information they provide about conversion.[123] Beginning with Andrew, we note at the outset that the recovery of the original is so difficult as to be admittedly impossible. Two modern authors – Jean-Marc Prieur and Dennis Ronald MacDonald[124] – have struggled with the textual tradition and have come to similar although not identical results regarding the contents and order of the original work. As a matter of convenience we may follow J. K. Elliott's preference for Prieur's order, without implying a decision regarding whether the Acts of Andrew and Matthias should precede (so MacDonald) or follow (so Prieur) the work otherwise known simply as the Acts of Andrew.[125] In any case, the Acts of Andrew and Matthias contains only one conversion, a group conversion following Andrew's removing of a curse.

The bulk of Andrew is known from an epitome given at the end of the sixth century in Latin by Gregory of Tours. Especially the first part of this version is filled with highly stereotyped narratives that contain the sequence miracle-conversion or miracle (with preaching)-conversion, and perhaps we may content ourselves with noting only two of these. In ch. 3 of Gregory's epitome a young slave dies, and his master asks Andrew to restore him. Andrew does, and everyone believes and is baptized. Again in ch. 12 a lad asks Andrew for the *via veritatis* and becomes a Christian in response to Andrew's preaching. This angers the townspeople, who set fire to the house where Andrew and the boy are, but the boy douses the fire with only a small quantity of water. Then all except the boy's parents become Christians. Schneemelcher notes of these accounts, 'These conversions resulting from preaching and miracles are repeated in stereotyped fashion by Gregory.'[126] We can hardly disagree, nor can we think that we have here anything like historical accounts.

We find a rather more interesting narrative at the beginning of the Acts of Andrew according to Prieur's arrangement, which is followed by Elliott (= Sinai Greek MS. 526). This segment begins with the request of one Stratocles to leave imperial service in order to pursue philosophy (1) and then presents the conversion of Stratocles after Andrew exorcises Stratocles' servant. When the demon departs (5), promising to leave not only the servant but the 'whole city', the servant rises from the earth, and Andrew and he have a brief conversation, after which 'Maximilla [an earlier convert] encouraged the apostle to speak, on account of Stratocles, so that he might believe in the Lord' (6). Stratocles then remained with Andrew 'night and day' (8), and finally he, Maximilla, and other characters 'were considered worthy of the seal in the Lord' (10).[127] Here, then, we clearly have a story of a seeker who was first attracted to Christianity by a remarkable miracle but who then sought further instruction and finally demonstrated sufficient faith for the congregation to allow him ('were considered worthy') to become a Christian, i.e., to be baptized.

In John, first the author mentions an important Ephesian official, Andronicus, who begins by being a sceptical critic of John (31) but who, after John's amazing healing of all the sick in the city (36), is then a follower of John (37). Doubtless an account of Andronicus' conversion has fallen out between John 36 and 37, and indeed Schäferdiek assumes some displacement of the text at this point.[128] Then, when John prays for God to reveal his 'mercy' (41) to the unbelieving Ephesians, the Artemis temple falls down, and the altar and several old statues (ξόανα) fall into pieces (42), after which the Ephesians declare

(43), 'We know only the god of John, and now we bow before him, having received mercy from him.' Apparently, that is, they become Christians. Finally, in John 48–54, we find an account of a young man who kills his father. Confronted by John, he is overcome by grief and agrees that, if John will raise his father from the dead, he will break off an adulterous affair in which he is engaged. John goes to the corpse and commands it to 'get up and give . . . glory to God', whereupon the corpse replies, '"I am getting up, lord", and he got up' (52). The young man then emasculates himself, gives his severed parts to his mistress and bids her depart, and becomes such a committed Christian that 'he did not depart from John' (54).

The main conversion attributed to Paul in the Acts of Paul is that of Thecla. As a matter of fact, this conversion is unique among the Apocryphal Acts in several ways. Most notably, it is not a miracle that brings Thecla to Christianity, but Paul's preaching (Acts of Paul and Thecla 7), which he does not even direct to her! (She eavesdrops.) Furthermore, she is not converted all at once, but rather she is 'led on in faith' (7), after which 'her faith grew' (18), so that she represents Lofland's and Skonovd's intellectual type of conversion, in which there is typically a medium duration of the conversion process.[129] Finally, when Thecla is burned at the stake, divinely produced water saves her (22); and when she escapes beasts in the arena by jumping into a pool, announcing first that she is 'baptizing [her]self', she is saved by divine fire.[130]

The Martyrdom of Paul recounts the conversion of 'the prefect Longus and Cestus the centurion' (3). Paul, under sentence of death, explains 'the word' to Longus and Cestus, and they are sufficiently convinced by his explanation and by his courage in the face of death (4) to ask for salvation (5). When the executioner finally beheads Paul, milk spurts from his body (5); and later, raised from the dead, Paul confronts Caesar, where 'the centurion' is also present (6). Longus and Cestus then visit Paul's grave on the following morning and find Titus and Luke (as Paul had prophesied [5]), who give them the 'seal in the Lord' (7), which completes their conversion. Here, then, we have conversions that are motivated by a combination of factors – a martyr's courage, the explanation of the gospel, and miracles attending the martyr's death.

In the Acts of Peter, 'because of what they witness the weak, including the believers and the neophytes, are strengthened, and many are converted to the Christian faith, which promises them life for eternity'.[131] In the first such account (Acts of Peter and Simon 5) a ship's captain, Theon, has a dream about his passenger Peter that calls to mind Cornelius' dream in Acts 10. He invites Peter and recounts the dream to him, whereupon Peter explains to him the '*magnalia dei*', and Theon requests and receives baptism. The entire story seems to have Acts 10 as its model. In the second story (9–11) a Roman Senator, Marcellus, is converted after a dog 'takes on human voice' (9) and announces Peter to Simon. Marcellus overhears (10) and makes confession to Peter, requesting forgiveness of sins. Peter then baptizes Marcellus (11), who 'believes from his whole heart (*praecordia*) in the name of Jesus Christ the son of God, by whom all things impossible are possible'. Next, Peter restores a smoked tuna (*sarda*) to life, leading many to 'believe in the Lord' (13). Acts of Peter 26 presents a possible but uncertain case when the crowd observing a resurrection from the dead 'immediately cried out together, "*Unus deus, unus deus Petri*"'; but we are not actually told that the crowd all become Christians. Yet immediately after this (27) another resurrection prompts the observers to 'accept [the miracle] to [their] sanctification' (*in sanctificationem acciperunt*). Finally, a long resurrection scene implies conversion when it concludes (29) on the note that the observers 'worshipped [Peter] like a god' (*adorabant eum tamquam deum*).[132]

Except for the conversion of Thecla and of Theon, the latter of which is fairly clearly modelled on the narrative in Acts 10, all the conversions reported in the Apocryphal Acts follow on fanciful miracles, even when other elements play into the conversion process, as in the case of Paul's conversion of Longus and Cestus. Surely, therefore, we must recognize the relevance of Gallagher's modification of MacMullen's analysis (which we noted above), that it is in the *reports* of conversions following upon miracles, not in the miracles themselves, that we see the motivation to conversion.[133] The problem that remains after this realization, however, is attestation, for we do not possess accounts of conversions stemming from the reading of the Apocryphal Acts. However many Christians may have believed these tales, we simply have no information about their success as evangelical aids – if indeed that was their purpose; for their purpose may well have been primarily to fortify Christian faith, not to lead Gentiles to conversion. The Apocryphal Acts of the Apostles have then, in the last analysis, provided us no information about early Christian conversion. This leaves MacMullen's theory, that the conversions of non-intellectual persons were based on miracles, without most of its support. Surely miracles, when they did occur, influenced some people's conversions, as we learn from Paul if from nowhere else; but we have no basis for making a class distinction.

(iii) Apologists

Of the several second-century writers classified as Christian apologists, only four present us with material relevant for our discussion of conversion. (One of the others, for example, is Aristides, who proposes a hierarchy of world religions, with Christianity at the top.) They are Aristo, Justin, Tatian, and the anonymous author of *Diognetus* – to use Quasten's order.[134] Of these, only Aristo, Justin and Tatian are apologists properly speaking, since they write in order to defend Christianity against its detractors and persecutors, whereas *Diognetus* is an evangelical tract. The other three, nevertheless, do provide certain perspectives on conversion.

The *Epistle to Diognetus* is a direct evangelistic appeal – whether to a real person Diognetus or to other unknown person or persons is impossible to say – that hopes to lead the reader(s) to conversion. The author begins (1) by addressing Diognetus as a seeker. 'Since I see you, most excellent Diognetus, applying yourself zealously to learn about the religion (θεοσεβεία) of the

Christians', he begs to be allowed to lay out the case for Christianity, which he then proceeds to do. He first shows why pagan religion is folly (it is idolatry; 2), and then he argues that Judaism is equally foolish, since it requires sacrifice (3; yet surely not in the author's lifetime!) and furthermore imposes certain purity regulations (4). Next he presents a positive explanation of Christianity (the 'apologetic' section of the tract): Christians obey the laws (5.10), they love everyone (5.11), etc., and, 'to say it simply, what the soul is in the body, that Christians are in the world' (6.1). Furthermore, Christians accept martyrdom unflinchingly (7.7). Then the author gives a brief exposition of Christ's revelation of God (8) and of Christian soteriology (9), at the conclusion of which he offers the appeal that God 'demonstrated in the former time the powerlessness of our nature to attain life, but now he has shown his salvation powerful to save even the powerless' (9.6). Finally, he appeals to his reader(s) to accept Christianity (10.3). 'When you have come to know this,' he asks, 'will you not think [your] joy to be fulfilled? Or how will you not love the one who first so loved you?' And he concludes, 'Let your heart be knowledge and your life the true Logos finding room in you' (12.7). Conversion of 'Diognetus' is the logical outcome.

If this little gem is not quite, as Quasten judged it, deserving of 'rank among the most brilliant and beautiful works of Christian Greek literature',[135] nevertheless we shall have to agree that it is a well-thought-out and winsome appeal to a seeker (or seekers). This is the kind of presentation that would likely have been effective with seekers and with others already interested in Christianity or for some reason favourably disposed to Christianity because of, e.g., network or family contacts with Christians. In a network or family context, such an approach as *Diognetus* could equally well have been oral.

Justin, however, shows us the effectiveness of chance encounter. According to the autobiographical opening of his *Dialogue with Trypho the Jew*, Justin had followed a Stoic, then a Pythagorean, then a Platonist, under the tutelage of the last of whom he 'stupidly hoped to perceive God forthwith'

(*Dialogue* 2). Then off by himself with his thoughts (3), he was accosted by a stranger who engaged him in philosophical dialogue. After some Socratic-type discussion, the stranger concluded that 'those philosophers . . . cannot even say what the soul is', with which conclusion Justin agreed (5). After further showing that traditional philosophers were lacking in true knowledge, the stranger declared that 'there were some a long time ago who were much more ancient than all those considered philosophers, blessed and just and devoted to God (θεοφιλεῖς) . . . They call them prophets . . . And they glorified God the maker of all and father, and they announced the Christ from him, his son' (7). After the stranger said 'many other things' (8), Justin felt 'a fire lit in [his] soul, and desire (ἔρως) seized [him] for the prophets and for those men who are Christ's friends'. Justin the seeker had become a Christian as a result of a form of Christian preaching during a chance encounter. (In his *Second Apology* 12, Justin also explains that he had come to admire the Christians, while still in his Platonic phase, because they were 'fearless' in the face of death and of other ill treatment.)

While the author of *Diognetus* and the evangelist/philosopher who converted Justin chose the approach of friendly persuasion with a potential Gentile convert, Aristo and Justin preferred to argue when it was a matter of discussion with Jews. The bulk of Justin's *Dialogue*, as also Aristo's (from what little we know about it),[136] deals with the presentation of Christianity to Jews, a matter that does not concern us here.

With Tatian, finally, we have yet another insight into early Christian approaches to conversion, for he, rather than writing to convince others to become Christians, composes an apology showing Christianity's superiority to Greek religion and in the process describes his own path to Christianity as a seeker. Originally an Assyrian, Tatian became a disciple of Justin in Rome but later left the Catholic church to found the Encratite sect.[137] In his *Discourse to the Greeks* 29 he briefly describes his path to Christianity. He first says that he had 'taken part in mysteries' and further had 'tested the rites organized every-

where by effeminates and hermaphrodites' – doubtless referring
to rites similar to those described by Lucian in his *Syrian
Goddess*, esp. 51–53, and so beautifully satirized by Apuleius
in *Metam.* 8.25–28. After, then, further charging that various
gods seemed primarily interested in bloody violence, he says
that when he 'was by [him]self [he] sought (ζητέω) in what
manner [he] would be able to learn the truth'. In the process of
his research he 'happened upon certain barbarian writings,
older as regards the doctrines of the Greeks, but also more
divine as regards their error' (29.1). He then mentions the
creation of the world and foreknowledge (29.2), implying that
it was the Jewish scriptures that he had read. This narrative
leads Tatian to go on at length, with some digressions, to prove
that Moses preceded famous Greeks, and that Moses is 'older
than heroes, cities, spirit beings' (*daimones*, 40.1). Here Tatian
reaches the end of his *Discourse*. Obviously, therefore, we must
assume that he encountered these scriptures within a Christian
context, since the truth that he found there led him to become
not a Jew, but a Christian.

Tatian's spiritual odyssey to and through Christianity, as
well as his mentioning that he discovered the Jewish scriptures
'by [him]self (κατ' ἐμαυτόν)', show him to fit the type of the
seeker exactly. Since both he and Justin followed this path,
probably we should assume that it was not uncommon, at least
in the second century, for intellectuals to come into Christianity
in this way, as MacMullen proposed. We note that while
Justin's path of seeking that led him eventually to Christianity
lay through philosophy, Tatian's lay through the mystery religions, and that both, nevertheless, found the truth that they
were seeking in the (Christian interpretation of) the Jewish
scriptures. Only Justin mentions that those scriptures prophesied Christ, but we are forced to assume some such understanding also in the case of Tatian, although he does not express it
explicitly.

(iv) Summary of the Christian evidence

When we now run up the sum of our evidence we find that we know something about Gentile conversions to early Christianity, but that there is much more that we might wish to know. We know that miracles, most likely healings, and martyrdoms played some role in attracting interest in the new religion; but we also have learned that miracles and martyrdoms alone did not lead to conversions, that preaching of the gospel was normally also required.[138] In other cases the preaching alone seems to have sufficed, although we are woefully uninformed about the contexts of that preaching – assuming that we are correct in discounting as idealized historiography the Acts accounts of large crowds. From Paul we learn that the main content of the preaching concerned Jesus' crucifixion and resurrection, and the speeches in Acts confirm that impression. Somewhat later (Justin, Tatian), the pattern seems to have begun with an exposition of the Jewish scriptures, proving that God had foretold Christ and salvation in ancient times. We also learn that, around the turn of the first-second centuries, the evangelical impetus of Christianity seems to have declined and that Christian leaders stressed the importance of example. Justin's conversion, some decades later, was the result of a one-on-one chance encounter.

Reading the Jewish scriptures also convinced some persons to become Christians, something that could have occurred only within a Christian context. The successful line of reasoning seems to have been that 1. these great scriptures are older than anything that the Greeks have and that 2. they have given accurate prophecies, especially about Christ. An outside observer cannot come to those conclusions without Christian interpretation.

About those Gentiles who became Christians we know even less than we know about the process. Many were, as Meeks puts it, persons of high status inconsistency (lonely, anxious),[139] but there were also a few who had real status, as well as people of genuinely low status, like slaves. Some intellectuals were clearly seekers. Then there is the matter of the God-fearers. Aside from Acts, none of the early Christian literature that we have surveyed gives the slightest hint even of the existence of these people, let alone of their being a major component of Gentile conversions to Christianity. While we need not, therefore, doubt that many Gentiles were attracted to Judaism in various degrees,[140] we may strongly doubt that such people composed a major missionary field for Christians. This conclusion leaves begging, of course, the question as to why the author of Acts so construed the success of earliest Christianity among Gentiles. Perhaps he knew of some such conversions in his own day and assumed that there had formerly been many others.

Finally, an aspect of conversion that has surfaced in several places is the need for continuing instruction after baptism. Without that aspect of Gentile conversion, becoming a Christian would have meant a thousand things to a thousand people and would have been, in the last analysis, merely an ephemeral experience.

5. Christianity's competitors

Christianity, however, was not alone in winning converts, was not the only NRM in the Roman Empire; and we need to give some attention to those other NRMs, the movements with which Christianity competed.[141] In doing so we are anticipating to some degree the question at the head of the next chapter; but it seems appropriate here, in the context of the discussion of conversion to Christianity, to examine conversion to the competitor NRMs in order to learn what we can not only about why people became Christians, but why, ultimately, more joined the Christian movement than the other movements.

Since Alexander's time, in fact, it had been the age of NRMs, a new phenomenon in the ancient world. Before Alexander, when one visited a foreign country one sacrificed to the local gods, as for example Gentiles visiting Jerusalem did. By the time

Christianity emerged on the scene in the Greco-Roman world, however, a devotee of Isis could worship at an Isis temple almost anywhere around the Mediterranean and up into Gaul, just as Catholics or Methodists can today travel to most places in the world and find Christian congregations in which to worship that bear at least a considerable similarity to their home congregations. Those religious movements – especially the religion of Isis and the Mithraic mysteries (the latter coming into the empire only about the same time as Christianity), but some of the other mysteries as well – gained adherents, as did Christianity. If we prefer, with Nock, not to call beginning to participate in one of these NRMs conversion because they were not exclusive in the way in which Christianity and Judaism were – i.e., because one could 'adhere' to more than one such NRM – nevertheless we shall see that we can only with difficulty distinguish the phenomenon of such adherence from Christian conversion.[142] (While our concern here is to compare Christianity to other NRMs of the day, we should of course recall that established pagan religion did not always die and wither away to make room for the NRMs. The cult of Asclepius, for example, remained vigorous until well into Byzantine times.)[143]

We are, of course, woefully bereft of sources. For all the mysteries, including the Mithraic, there are no direct sources for conversion as such (unless we count Tatian's brief reference to his earlier initiations). What we do have is book 11 of Apuleius' *Metamorphoses*, which, simply because of its character, is widely thought to present at least a somewhat accurate account of conversion to the religion of Isis and of initiation into her (and Osiris') mysteries.[144] Lucian gives some information at least about priests in his *De Dea Syria*, and there is also some relevant iconographic evidence for Mithraic initiations. A few scattered remarks by Justin and Tertullian provide some information about initiation into Mithraism but nothing about what led men to affiliate with that movement. Livy, book 39, gives a long account of the suppression of Dionysus worship in Italy in the second century BCE, but one hardly learns anything there about conversion to the movement. The many inscriptions that survive also are silent on the matter of conversion.

Apuleius' Lucius, an aspiring magician who changed himself into a donkey and then was prevented by circumstances from turning himself back into a man, finally in desperation appealed to the (apparently indefinite) goddess. The goddess revealed herself to him as Isis – the beneficent creatrix and ruler of all, who is known inadequately by other names (Mother of the gods, Demeter, etc.; Apuleius *Metam.* 11.4) – and she advised him what to do to return to human form. In this transformation Isis also secured the collaboration of one of her priests. At the time of the revelation Isis demanded that Lucius, in exchange for his liberation from his asinine state, be 'tied and bound' to her until 'the end of [his] last breath' (*Metam.* 11.6), and the priest at the time of Lucius' transformation further clarified that Lucius should become a priest of Isis (11.15). After a period during which Lucius devoted himself daily to the worship of the goddess he was initiated into her mysteries (11.23–24), and he describes the initiation in some detail. Next Lucius moved to Rome, where he was Isis's 'constant worshipper' (11.26). Here he found that he should be initiated into the mysteries of Osiris, Isis's divine companion (11.27), and later into what we should call priestly orders – 'the supporters of the great divine rites' (*sacris initiare diis magnis auctoribus*, 11.29). Osiris then appointed Lucius to the priestly college of the Pastophores (11.30).

Lucian's account (*Dea Syr.* 51) concerns only those who become priests – Galli – of the goddess; and the account is very brief. They castrate themselves and take 'female garments and women's ornaments'.

The Mithraeum at Santa Maria Capua Vetere contains fresco scenes of an apparent initiation in which a naked man or boy is blindfolded and an officer of the mystery holds a torch to his face.[145] From several sources, further, we know of seven grades or ranks within Mithraism, although it is far from clear if everyone started at the bottom grade, Raven, and advanced to the top, Father.[146] Justin (*Apol.* 66.4) reports that initiates to Mithraism received bread and water, but this gives us only minimal additional information about the ritual of initiation.

From inscriptional evidence we do learn what kinds of people became Mithraists. They were by and large army men or imperial slaves or freedmen, or clients of such people.[147] Thus the social status of men who joined Mithraism was about the same as that of people who became Christians.[148] Furthermore, becoming a Mithraist was not a response to deprivation of any kind; rather Mithraism, with its ranks, reiterated 'ordinary social experience' and gave men the opportunity to 'display their status and achievements'.[149] In these ways Mithraism was distinct from the other NRMs, including Christianity; but beyond this our evidence is insufficient to allow us to make any claims about the situation of the converts to these NRMs just prior to their conversions.

6. Social-scientific evaluation of the evidence

Let us now bring together the two threads of this chapter, the social-scientific and the historical. First of all, on the psychological side, we see that there is almost no evidence. We may speculate – and may indeed in our minds be certain – that those Gentiles who became Christians were psychologically ready, in one or more of the senses that Malony proposed, for what Christianity had to offer. The problem is, of course, that we are woefully lacking evidence for such motivations, except that we see some evidence that some converts had been seekers (Justin, Tatian). Even if we accept that Thecla is not totally a fiction and may represent a type, still we do not learn anything of the psychological motivation that may have inclined her to listen to Paul's preaching in the first place. Perhaps the nearest that we get to evidence of psychological motivation is the demonstrable presence of Meeks' status-inconsistency, which might very well have produced at least some of Malony's motivational types. With sociological evaluation of the evidence, however, we are on much firmer ground.

If we recall Rambo's matrix, then we see how well, in general, it fits the evidence that we have of early Gentile conversions to Christianity – or perhaps we should say that we see how well our evidence fits into the matrix. While the Lofland-Skonovd model can help us to ponder the different types of conversions to Christianity that may have occurred, looking at the character of the conversion experience itself, as we noted above, does not help us answer our question. The Lofland-Stark value-added process model would be of more help if we had more complete information about a number of conversions, but that is what we do not have. We may suspect that many early Christian conversions followed converts' acute and persistent tensions, that these converts encountered Christianity at crucial turning points in their lives, and that they formed affective bonds with Christians, but we do not have the evidence to support those suspicions. To be sure, we may say that, in general, people who became Christians were structurally available for conversion to Christianity (Robbins), but that category, in and of itself, is rather broad. Thus Rambo's all-inclusive approach to the process of conversion suits both our interests and the evidence best.

The *context* for Gentile conversion to Christianity was, of course, opportune. We do not have to understand this opportunity theologically, emphasizing with Paul and with many older historians of Christianity that God had 'at the right time' (Rom. 5.6) inaugurated Christianity,[150] in order to agree with the point; for the opportunity is a historical given, as well. The Greco-Roman world was awash with NRMs from Egypt, from Anatolia and from Syria, as Nock pointed out. However numerous the adherents to these religions may or may not have been – and there is no way to know, although we do know that they had numerous sites – we see that the first decades of Christianity occurred during a time when it was not unusual for people to take up the worship of new, international gods. (Although to speak of the gods as 'new' is not quite correct, for, while they may have been new in the sense of being recently imported from elsewhere, they all laid claim to great antiquity.)

Nor do we need to decide one way or the other on the much-debated issue of whether there was a widespread 'failure of nerve' that opened the way for these new religions. Whatever reasons people had for turning to NRMs, the more important fact is that doing so was a recognized option when Christianity came on the scene.

To be sure, some type of *distress* must lie behind conversion, and we most likely see such in Meeks' status inconsistency (a variety of relative deprivation). Persons entirely comfortable with their stations in life are unlikely to turn to NRMs, and in the first decades of Christianity (and before) most persons of high status did not – although there are a few notable exceptions. We have also seen good evidence of the role of the *quest* in early Christian conversions. Here Rambo probably steers us toward the right understanding better than MacMullen when he points out that many, if not most, converts are seekers. Why should we think that only intellectuals came into Christianity in this way, merely because we have the autobiographical descriptions of Justin and Tatian and nothing similar from *hoi polloi*? Do we not see, in this matter, how modern sociological analysis can help us to 'fill in the blanks' in our often meagre historical information? If it were in fact true that most of the Gentile converts to early Christianity came from the ranks of the God-fearers, then we would indeed have evidence of a preponderance of seekers among the converts. The absence of adequate evidence for the theory of God-fearer conversions, however, should not deter us from drawing the likely conclusion that most of those Gentiles who first embraced Christianity were seekers. If we cannot demonstrate that for others than a few intellectuals, it is at least probable for the majority, especially in view of the fact that so many people were also joining the other NRMs.

Under the subject of the quest we need also to consider the *availability* of potential converts. We have no evidence on the basis of which to judge emotional availability, but the discussion of structural, intellectual and religious availability brings us back to the point of contention between Nock and

MacMullen that we noted in the first section of this chapter. For Nock there were religious aspects in the culture to which Christianity appealed, whereas Greco-Roman religion for MacMullen was a spongy mass for which Christianity provided some backbone. The argument, as we have seen, can be made both ways, even if we might be inclined to think that MacMullen's position is an example of special pleading. In the light of our evidence we may rather recall Rambo's criteria for intellectual and religious availability.

Regarding intellectual availability Rambo observed, as we noted above, that 'it is rare for someone to be converted to an option that embraces an intellectual framework radically different from the person's previous viewpoint'; and one is religiously available when one has 'religious beliefs, practices, and life-style [that] are to some degree compatible with the new option'. Regarding the former condition, we recall that the Christian who led Justin to conversion spoke to him in terms of philosophy, and Justin in turn sought to promote Christianity as the right philosophy. With regard to religious availability, Tatian's example is instructive, since he, having been initiated into several mysteries before he encountered Christianity, probably saw Christianity as the true mystery offering a blessed existence after this life. The examples of Justin and Tatian remind us again that there were other philosophical and mystery-religion alternatives competing with Christianity in Greco-Roman society. Paul, we remember, had couched a part of his argument in I Corinthians in mystery language in order, apparently, to convince his readers that Christianity was a mystery (I Cor. 2.6–7). Paul's language in I Corinthians 15 about the seed that dies in the ground in order to produce a stalk of grain, moreover, may well be an attempt to make a connection with the grain imagery of the Eleusinian mystery. To be sure, Paul writes here to people who are already Christians, but we nevertheless see an example of how Christianity could make religious contact with persons accustomed to think in terms of the mysteries. Thus for a Gentile to become a Christian in the early decades of the movement was not the radical religious and intellectual break with the past that modern Christians often think it was. Of course Christianity was different from other religious and intellectual alternatives, but it was not totally different.

Since Rambo realizes that *advocate* styles can be quite diverse, we can only readily confirm that we have seen good evidence of such diversity in early Christianity; but his list of *benefits* certainly rings true for all of early Christianity. Christian theology, including its scriptural underpinning, provided a thoroughgoing system of meaning, and evidence of emotional gratification turns up everywhere; we may think of the fire in Justin's breast or of the frequent occurrences of χαίρω and χαρά (rejoice, joy) in the New Testament. Christianity excelled at offering techniques for living; and first the apostles and later the bishops provided convincing leadership. Everywhere, finally, we see evidence of some manifestation of power, even when it is not a matter of miracles; although, on this point, early Christianity certainly faced stiff competition from the Isis religion because of Isis's much-touted omnipotent benevolence and beneficence.[151]

Rambo's pointing to missionary and convert *adaptations* opens our eyes to aspects of the growth of early Christianity that we often overlook when we take a strictly historical approach. One of the best examples of an advocate's attempting to engineer convert adaptation, while himself adapting, occurs in I Corinthians in Paul's discussion of 'idol food' and of sexual morality.[152] In I Cor. 5.11 Paul explained that Christians were 'to have no contact with someone called a brother who should be a fornicator or greedy or an idolater or a reviler or a drunk or a robber'; and in 6.9–10 he expanded the list by saying that 'neither fornicators nor idolaters nor adulterers nor effeminate males [i.e., the objects of pederasts] nor homosexuals nor thieves nor greedy persons nor drunks nor revilers nor robbers will inherit the Kingdom of God'. In chs. 8 and 10, further, he expanded on the prohibition against idolatry. In ch. 8 he first proposed that Christians should be permitted to eat meat of animals sacrificed to the local gods, since Christians know that in fact these local gods are really no gods at all (v. 4); but then he advised against eating such meat because doing so might set a bad example for other Christians, for 'knowledge is not in everyone' (v. 7). In ch. 10, however, Paul labelled the local gods not 'no gods', but rather 'demons' (v. 21), and he encouraged the Christians to 'flee from idolatry' (v. 14). In either case the advice was the same: Don't eat it. Paul also expanded on his sexual prohibitions in ch. 7.

In his paraenesis on each subject, Paul was endorsing normal Jewish morality. Thus he was clearly calling for the Corinthian Christians to adapt their life-styles, in these respects, to Jewish life-style. That Christian life-style should be the same as Jewish life-style in these matters may be so obvious to us today that we overlook the fact that *not all early Christians agreed* – most immediately the Corinthian Christians, who had not been living according to the rules that Paul now proposed; but there were others, even Christian leaders, like 'the woman Jezebel' in Rev. 2.20, who was leading the Christians in Thyatira 'to err in committing sexual immorality and in eating food offered to idols'. Whether these are supposed to be two sets of practices or one (sexual immorality serving as a metaphor for idolatry) is immaterial here; the Christian prophetess was nevertheless encouraging behaviour that Paul condemned in I Corinthians and that the author of Revelation also condemned. Other Christians, like the Jerusalem leaders whom Paul opposed in Galatians 2, wanted Christianity to remain much more Jewish and insisted on circumcision for all converts to Christianity. Thus some Christian leaders required more adaptation to Jewish lifestyle on the part of Gentile converts and some required less.

Paul, however, was also adapting in that he broke with Jewish tradition on certain matters, namely circumcision, Sabbath and dietary laws. Thus in this way, within the spectrum that was early Christianity, Paul forged a Christianity that was Jewish to the degree that it forbade idolatry and extramarital sex and was Gentile to the degree that it forbade circumcision, Sabbath, and dietary laws. It was thus both and neither. This broad middle was a highly significant adaptation that Paul reached, for it is likely that, had Christianity not found an approach at least something like his, it would never have attracted large numbers of Gentile converts. Paul's position here provides further proof of the correctness of Rodney Stark's maxim that successful NRMs 'maintain a *medium* level of *tension* with their surrounding environment; [they] are deviant, but not too deviant'.[153]

Another clear example of advocate adaptation is the use of the Socratic dialogue form as a missionary technique. While Aristo's and Justin's written dialogues may have been intended for Christian readers, Justin's account of his own conversion shows that he, himself, was led to Christianity by such an approach; and it is, further, likely that he intended his dialogue as a sort of model for evangelistic style.

There is one aspect of convert adaptation, however, that Rambo names that we often fail to consider when examining early Christianity, and that is retroversion. Histories of early Christianity almost always proceed from meagre beginnings to substantial membership, yet we would be remiss not to take note of the fact that some – probably, indeed, many – people who became Christians in the early years later opted out, some sooner, some later. We have some evidence of these people in the discussions of apostasy in early Christian literature, e.g., in the allusion in Heb. 6.1–2: 'not again laying down a foundation of repentance . . . and of faith . . ., of baptisms', etc.; but beyond this we have the witness of some of the people interrogated by Pliny the Younger, who informs Trajan (about 112) about Christians whom he was investigating in Bithynia, that some of the people brought in claimed to have been Christians formerly but to have left the movement (*deseo*) 'some three years ago, some many years ago, many a one even twenty years ago' (*Epp.* 10 [*ad Traj.*] 96.6).

Finally we also have abundant evidence that Christianity, in all its forms, made good use of *encapsulation*. Christians met together regularly on Sunday (Rev. 1.10) for meals (I Cor. 11.20) and for prayers and hymns (Col. 3.16) – here we see three of Rambo's 4 Rs, ritual, rhetoric and roles; and that Christians promoted relationships within the movement is clear from the terms 'brother' and 'sister'. The official offices that Christianity developed – apostle, evangelist, bishop, elder, deacon – also created encapsulating roles, as did the unofficial offices, e.g., the charismatic competencies of I Corinthians 12.

Of *commitment* and *consequences* it seems unnecessary to write further, as we noted above.

Because of the dearth of sources for conversion to Christianity's competitor NRMs, we are much less well informed about the reasons for their success; but surely the same convert factors of context, crisis and quest, as well as of convert adaptation, worked in favour of the Isis religion and of the mysteries just as well as in favour of Christianity. What we cannot know is the degree to which those religious movements used advocates, and how successfully, i.e., how well the advocates adapted, and more especially what appeals they used and how effective they were in presenting the appeals. Except for Mithraism, the religions with which Christianity was competing may have been weaker than Christianity in encapsulation. Obviously they had abundant rituals, but we know nothing of their rhetoric, and the availability of roles may have been limited (except in Mithraism). Further, they may not have developed or promoted relationships much at all. Certainly with the traditional mysteries, like that at Eleusis (which also did not travel), initiates did not form continuing communities of any kind – except that our evidence from Italy is that initiates into the Dionysiac mysteries did regularly meet together, for which (among other things) they were persecuted (Livy 39.8–19). The iconographic evidence of initiations and of common meals in Mithraism, however – as well as the architectural style of their cave-sanctuaries – implies continuing worshipping communities.

Commitment was also doubtless strong in Mithraism because of the progressive degrees of initiation, and the evidence of *Metamorphoses* 11 is that initiates into the mysteries of Isis and of Osiris were deeply committed, although we should be careful not to generalize this at-least-quasi-fictional evidence. The priests who castrated themselves in the worship of the Great Mother and of the Syrian Goddess (Lucian, *De Dea Syria*) also committed themselves irrevocably (*Dea Syr.* 53), but the same cannot be said for the other devotees of these and similar goddesses.

Here also we need to reconsider the notion that Christianity was exclusive and that none of its competitors was. Making this contrast vastly oversimplifies the real situation. Of course most if not all devotees of Mithras or of Isis participated to a lesser or greater degree in public ceremonies, and these people we may call adherents in Nock's sense. They *could* have worshipped one deity one day and another the next, but that may well not have been the case. It is doubtless generally true that everyone except Christians and Jews participated at least to some degree in the civic cults where they lived, and that means also to some degree in the imperial cult everywhere. None of the participants in Christianity's competitor NRMs was theologically mono-theistic. *Nevertheless*, they were often henotheistic in practice. That was surely the case for the initiates into the Mithraic and the Isiac mysteries and for the self-emasculated priests of the several goddesses, and it may have been true for many others as well – witness the 'adherents' of the Dionysiac mystery in Italy who endured harsh persecution in the second century BCE. And are we to imagine that all the various functionaries listed by Apuleius in *Metamorphoses* 11 who participated in the Isis procession then went off on other days and behaved similarly in the train of other gods and goddesses? Reason dictates that they probably did not. They may have participated in the public cults, but their devotion was to Isis. Thus *except for the monotheism and the strict exclusivity* of Christianity, converts to the Isis religion, certainly to the Isis mysteries, to Mithraism, and to certain of the other mysteries, in any case, were doubt-less as committed to their faiths as were Christians to theirs. On the whole, however, Christianity may well have done better at encapsulation than did any of its competitors.

7. Summary

Analyses of conversion by modern sociologists, especially that of Lewis Rambo, have helped us to answer our question, Why did Gentiles become Christians? The short answer is that all elements of conversion were present. It is not merely that Christianity provided satisfactory answers to questions that Gentiles were asking (so Nock), although that is certainly true. And it is not merely that Christianity offered a solid alternative to the shallowness and indefiniteness of Gentile religion (so MacMullen). While there is some truth to MacMullen's position, it is rather prejudicial, especially with regard to the mysteries and the religion of Isis, which both called for commitment and appealed to Gentile longings. We have seen that the factors leading to conversion to Christianity were little different from those leading to conversion to the other NRMs, except for the fact that Christianity may have excelled in its missionary effort (advocacy) and in its modes of encapsulation. Probably, however – especially in view of the uncertainty of these tentative conclusions – the possible superiority of Christianity in advocacy and in encapsulation does not adequately explain why Christianity *triumphed*. That topic must be the subject of the next chapter. At this stage we rest content to have gained clarity regarding what it was about early Christianity itself and what it was about the situation of its converts that caused Gentiles to join the movement. We have seen both that there were abundant personal and social factors that provided fertile ground for a new religion like Christianity and that the Christian movement was simply highly successful – sometimes perhaps by chance – in doing all the right things to promote and to solidify conversion. While these same factors also operated for the other NRMs, perhaps they were not quite as adept as Christianity in recruiting and holding converts.

III

Why Did Christianity Succeed in the Roman Empire?

'A religious portfolio can serve well enough when full-service religious firms are missing. But history suggests that when non-exclusive faiths are challenged by exclusive competitors, in a relatively unregulated market, the exclusive firms win. They win because they are the better bargain, despite their higher costs.'

(Rodney Stark)

1. The problem

In the previous chapter we analysed Gentile conversion to Christianity in the early decades, and we found that Christianity attracted converts because it appeared on the scene at the right time and did all the right things – in its encounter with people in a situation of distress or who were seekers, in its interaction with these people, and in its promotion of commitment among and successful encapsulation of new members. At the same time, of course, these very same factors contributed to the ultimate success of Christianity within the Roman Empire; for it was the growth of Gentile converts that gave Christianity that success. In analysing Gentile conversion to Christianity, however, we were not able to shed much light on Christianity's ultimate triumph, because we saw that other NRMs of the day, especially the religions of Isis and of Mithras, seemed also to be successful at gaining converts in the Greco-Roman world. It is appropriate now, then, to ask the next question – that is, Why did *Christianity* succeed and not one of the other NRMs? In order to attempt to answer this question, we again pass over theological answers, which can only be believed and cannot be tested, and seek answers related to the society and the social movements of the day. What *social and sociological factors* were at work that abetted Christianity's success?

2. A. D. Nock's proposals

In his essay on early Gentile Christianity, Nock first laid out a number of ways in which early Christianity was similar to its competitors (some kind of saviour, something like baptism and eucharist, and a church order),[1] and he then briefly listed the reasons 'why Christianity won'.[2] First of all it 'satisfied both the religious and the philosophic instincts of the time'; and it also 'offered a cultus in which the individual found his own personal needs and the desire for brotherhood in worship satisfied'. Further, it was superior to its competitors 'in that the Saviour was not merely a figure of unique attraction, but also a recent historical figure invested with deity – not a mythological personage encumbered with legends which to many thinking men were positively offensive'. Thus 'Mithras was and remained Persian: Jesus was universal'. Further, 'the salvation involved was a salvation from forces of moral evil', having 'a common-sense practical ethics', and 'the cultus itself was simple and free from primitive ritual survivals in need of allegorical explanation'. 'Again, the new faith satisfied the desire of contemporary mystical faith for *gnosis*, . . . combining with this a personal conception of God often lacking' in its competitors' theologies. Christianity also 'gave a dogmatic philosophy of the universe'; 'and it had a sacred Book which . . . compared and compares favourably with the other religious literature of the time'.

In those respects 'Christianity could do what other rivals claimed, and could do it better'. Beyond such excelling competition with its rivals, however, Christianity had certain unique advantages. 'It combined belief in God's perfect justice with the conviction that He loved the sinner even in his sin and desired his salvation.' Consequently 'it freed from fear'. Furthermore, Christianity's 'exclusiveness' was an advantage; and 'the monarchic episcopate gave [it] a unity and a purpose which other religions of the time lacked'. Also, 'once Christianity had made considerable headway' its sheer numbers would show it to be more powerful. Finally, 'Christian brotherhood and Christian assertion of the value of each individual soul had great attraction' in a world in which all people were hardly equal.

With all these advantages, Christianity was sure to succeed! And yet, many of the advantages do not prove true, and some may be little more than wishful thinking. Let us take them up in order.

Christianity certainly satisfied the 'religious instincts' of many persons in the Roman Empire, otherwise it would not have won converts; but one could say the same of Mithraism and of the Isis religion. They also won converts. Nock's distinction, further, between the Christian saviour, a historical person elevated to deity, and the mythical, albeit unique saviours of the other religions is not clear. Many early Christians, we may recall – Gnostics, Arius' opponent Alexander – did not consider the humanity of Christ at all important; and even for what we may loosely call the mainstream, i.e., everyone between Gnosticism and Arianism, it is highly likely that what was most important about Christ was his divine, not his human status. We may recall, e.g., the miraculous events in the Apocryphal Acts of the Apostles, where it is Christ's supernatural powers, not his incarnation, that are of prime importance. When Nock then reminds us that even intelligent pagans were offended by the 'legends' told of non-Christian deities, he almost seeks deliberately to confuse; for, on the one hand, the offence lay primarily in myths about Zeus, in which Zeus behaved immorally or even absurdly, and not in myths related to the saviour gods. Hence the famous Stoic allegorizing of those myths. On the other hand, thinking pagans – we think especially of Celsus and Porphyry – had plenty of criticisms of Christianity, which they considered an affront to good sense. And we should remember,

further, Paul's tortured attempt in I Corinthians 15 to explain
the resurrection of the body, which recollection reminds us that
Christianity had its own myths that were in constant need of
explanation.

Just what Nock intends by stating that Christ was universal
while Mithras remained Persian is not clear. Mithras may have
been Persian in origin, just as Christ was Jewish; but the
followers of both certainly experienced them as universal
saviours. In any case the competing deity to mention in connection with Christ's universalism should have been Isis, not
Mithras, for it was Isis who claimed to be the sole goddess who
embodied the best qualities of other goddesses, who claimed to
be the creatrix of all that was good for people, and who offered
a nurturing care that would protect her followers at all times.
Her aretalogies, found at several places around the Mediterranean, make these attributes clear, as we see from the following lines from the inscription from Cyme.

I am Isis, the mistress (ἡ τύραννος) of every land.
. . .
I laid down laws for people, and I legislated what no one is
    able to emend.
. . .
I separated earth from sky.
I showed the paths of the stars.
I ordered the course of sun and moon.
. . .
I made the right strong.
I brought woman and man together.
. . .
I destroyed the rule (ἀρχάς) of tyrants.
I stopped murders.
. . .
I made the right stronger than gold and silver.
. . .
I assigned languages to Greeks and barbarians.
. . .

I legislated showing mercy to suppliants.
. . .
I calm the sea and make it swell.
I am in the rays of the sun.
. . .
I conquer what is fated.
What is fated obeys me.

People in Greco-Roman society could hardly have considered Christ's claims more universal – or more appealing – than these.

Returning to Nock's argument; for him to claim that Christianity had no embarrassing myths is analogous to claiming that its religious practices contained no 'primitive ritual survivals in need of allegorical explanation'; but isn't Romans 6 an allegorical explanation of baptism? If in going under the water we die with Christ, and if in coming out of the water we rise to the hope of new life with him, surely we have understood the baptism allegorically? How different is this from Lucius' saying, in describing his first initiation, that he approached Persephone's door (*Proserpinae limen*; *Metam.* 11.23)? The mention of Celsus and Porphyry, further, reminds us that Nock's claim about Christianity's answering philosophical yearnings may well be mistaken since, for all that third-century Christian theology reached a rapprochement with Platonism, it hardly convinced pagan philosophers of the correctness of its approach.[3]

When Nock then proposes that Christianity's success was due in part to its superior ability to meet people's personal needs and to satisfy their desire for brotherhood, he seems to be overlooking most of what we know about worshippers of Isis and members of Mithraic cells. At the least, we would have to say that the Isis religion met personal needs and that Mithraism promoted brotherhood; and it would be reasonable to assume that, in ways for which the evidence is lacking, both religions did both.[4] And proposing that Christianity's competitors did not save their adherents from 'forces of moral evil' and that they did not have 'a common-sense practical ethics' strikes the reader as almost disingenuous; for surely Isis saved Lucius to a new kind of life, devoted to her, from his old self-indulgence. Even though, it is worth repeating, the *Metamorphoses* is a fiction, still Book 11 carries a weighty verisimilitude. Nock's judgment on the ethics of the Isis religion and of Mithraism, further, is unjustified, since our knowledge of their ethical teachings is so woefully lacking.[5]

Nock's points about Christianity's offering a *gnosis* and a dogmatic philosophy of the universe could almost surely be made about the Isis religion and of Mithraism as well; and his mentioning the Christian sacred books is also amiss, since the Isis religion in any case had fixed sacred texts (a point to which we shall return at the end of the chapter); probably the Mithraists as well.[6]

When we then turn to Nock's unique characteristics of Christianity that led to its success, we hardly advance further. Nock may well be right that the Christian doctrine of God's love of sinners was an important factor in Christianity's success; yet, that would be difficult to demonstrate. And the Isis religion surely freed from fear just as much as did Christianity. Christianity, the Isis religion, and the mysteries generally offered their adherents freedom from the fear of either annihilation or a miserable existence after death. (This hope for a better existence after death seems, in the case of Mithraism alone, to have been late and insignificant.)[7] Christian exclusiveness surely did abet the growth of Christianity in that it created a more cohesive movement than any of the others. This exclusiveness will have 'raised the stakes' for membership, keeping out less committed members and increasing the commitment of those who came in. We have already observed the advantage of committed conversion in the previous chapter, and we shall yet have occasion to note that others continue to propose it as one of the reasons for Christianity's success. Whether the ecclesiastical organization that was emerging during the period that we are considering here was a factor is more difficult to say. Mithraism, at least, seems to have had a very hierarchical and rigid structure.

That Christianity's overwhelming numbers, once it gained the advantage, were a further asset goes without saying, but is hardly relevant as one of the factors leading to that advantage. The theology of brotherhood is perhaps a more telling point, but, as in the case of the theology of God's love of sinners, that it was effective in Christianity's growth would be very difficult to demonstrate. What can be demonstrated is that Christians excelled at caring for their own – a point to which we shall return. Doubtless such care was in some way related to the theology of brotherhood; a number of New Testament injunctions come readily to mind.

In the end, it appears that while Nock's effort to show why Christianity triumphed could hardly be called a failure, it has not moved us very far forward. We seem to be left only with the theological points of God's love of sinners and the brotherhood of all believers, as well as with the exclusiveness of membership. The theological points will hardly have led to success in and of themselves, but only as Christians demonstrated the truth of those theological points in practice. There is no doubt that many did so, and we shall take up this point again in detail below. Exclusiveness also helped. Could these factors alone have led to Christianity's ultimate conquest of the Roman world? That is not inconceivable, but it behooves us to look further.

3. Rodney Stark's proposals

A well-known sociologist of religion, Rodney Stark, recently published a volume of essays aimed at helping to explain how Christianity took over the Roman Empire,[8] the very topic of this chapter, and it should be quite useful now to proceed with an evaluation of that work. The book has received quite a good press,[9] and it has already found its way into the work of at least one historian of the period, where it has been used to good advantage.[10]

In order to evaluate Stark's contribution to the subject of the growth of early Christianity, we need to look at the evidence that he presents in each chapter of the book, since each one was originally an independent study that looked at one or another societal factor that may have abetted Christianity's success; although some issues, e.g., Jews and women, turn up in more than one place. Before setting out on that course, however, we certainly want to note the degree to which Stark has immersed himself in the literature appropriate to this field, both ancient and modern. He has read all the right sources, and this alone is quite an impressive accomplishment for someone with no background or training in the study of early Christianity or of Roman antiquity.

A. General societal factors

In the first chapter of his book, 'Conversion and Christian Growth',[11] Stark guesses that there may have been 1000 Christians in the year 40 and then applies a 40% growth rate from that date up until the year 350, at which time – given an educated guess as to the total population of the Roman Empire, which he takes from modern Roman historians – Christians would have been in the majority![12] Small wonder that the emperor Constantine, then, turned to Christianity in 313. Stark is fully aware that his figures are *'estimates*, not recorded fact',[13] but he has sought to show that a Christian growth rate comparable to that of the Mormon Church in the United States since its inception (approximately 40%) would have produced such a large proportion of the population of the Empire in 300 years 'without miracles or conversions en masse'.[14] However soft all the figures may be – the number of Christians in 40, the population of the Empire, and the growth rate – the study is still credible in that it shows the possibility that Christianity could have grown *in the same way* as other religious movements today – via individual evangelizing and networks. We historians should have known as much all along. Wayne Meeks had already proposed it,[15] and our discussion in the last chapter also emphasized the importance of normal conversion processes in the rise of early Christianity. Thus it is very unlikely that Christianity grew because the apostles and others preached to large crowds. When Paul, after all, finally got to the Colosseum it was to face lions, not to preach, like an early-day Billy Graham, to a friendly crowd that had come to hear him.

Stark's solid work in the modern sociological study of religion seems also to have shown something about early Christianity that we could not demonstrate from the historical resources at our disposal, namely that it is not necessary to assume miraculous elements in order to explain Christianity's success in the Greco-Roman world after the time of Jesus. At this point, of course, we have only the *theoretical possibility* of such growth as Stark posits: *If* Christianity grew at the same rate as the Mormon church in the United States in recent decades, it would have triumphed by Constantine's time. Stark then adduces evidence that makes it reasonable to assume such growth.

Stark cites an objection to his assumption that early Christianity grew through networks, an assumption based on the fact that one can observe growth of NRMs in that way today. Since, in the preceding chapter, we have proposed agreeing with this network theory, it is proper that we pay attention to the objection here. The objection was that of Ronald Hock, presented orally to the first oral presentation of Stark's paper on the mission to the Jews (cf. immediately below). Hock pointed out that ancient networks would have been different from modern ones in that they 'were centred in aristocratic households [and therefore] included more than family and friends'.[16] This is, however, no criticism of the thesis that early Christianity spread through networks, for it simply posits more points of contact within a network than would be the case in a modern Western setting; and, as we have had occasion to note before and as a reviewer of Stark's book makes clear in this case, 'it appears that Paul's own mission was targeted in the first instance to more well-to-do members of society who offered a wider network of potential contacts than more disenfranchised members.'[17] Other ancient NRMs, of course, probably grew in the same way; thus Wolf Liebeschuetz concludes from the 'substantial proportion of slaves' mentioned among the Mithraic inscriptions that 'many (of course not all) of the earlier Mithraic groups were based on a household' (*sic*).[18]

In his next chapter Stark argues that Christianity would have appealed to 'the more, rather than the less, privileged classes',[19] a statement that is probably more or less true, if one thinks of privileged classes in terms of modern Western society instead of in terms of status, as would normally have been the case in antiquity. Certainly early Christianity did appeal to quite a few persons of means (as Wayne Meeks had earlier pointed out).[20] Stark's discussion here, interestingly, is entirely theoretical, being based not on ancient evidence, but on his studies of modern NRMs that show that persons of means are more inclined to adopt exotic new religions ('cults' in his terminology) than are other persons. Yet even if Stark is correct about the class appeal of early Christianity, that fact does not help us to understand why Christianity triumphed, since the same would have been true for the religion of Isis and for Mithraism as well. Above we noted evidence indicating that converts to Mithraism and to Christianity were about equal in status.[21]

B. Massive Jewish conversions

With 'The Mission to the Jews: Why It Probably Succeeded',[22] Stark gets into trouble, primarily because he has not quite understood the phenomenon that we call 'Hellenistic Judaism'. He mistakenly thinks that Hellenized Jews of the Roman period were comparable to emancipated Jews in the United States and Europe in the nineteenth century,[23] but this is not the case. He also thinks that these Hellenized Jews were the people most likely to become Christians,[24] and that they were in fact the *main source of converts to Christianity* until into the Byzantine period. We need to look at this evidence and at Stark's arguments in some detail.

When, beginning in the late eighteenth century, Jews first in the United States and then in Western Europe were granted the rights of full citizenship, this led many to assimilate to the societies of the national states where they lived. This assimilative tendency not only produced Reform Judaism,[25] in which pipe organs were placed in synagogue buildings and in which many Jews thought of themselves as just like other Germans except that they went to 'church' on Saturday rather than on Sunday, but it also produced true assimilation – that is, a situation in which many Jews thought of themselves primarily as Germans (or as Americans or some other Western nationality) and as Jews only by ancestry. In this situation, Jewish soldiers fought in the German army during World War I, and those who survived the war were often quite proud of their war record and considered themselves good and loyal Germans. One can see evidence of these people and of their attitude today in the displays at Auschwitz (the great irony of the Holocaust), and this author is personally acquainted with the daughter of one such soldier, who reports that her mother only with difficulty persuaded her father to get the family out of Munich in the late 1930s.

In this situation, further, at least a few well-known European Jews did become Christians, thus abandoning their Judaism and becoming totally identified with the dominant society. The best-known such is probably the composer Felix Mendelssohn; but several members of a prominent English family, the Montefiores, became Christians, and one became an Anglican bishop. There were other less prominent persons who also became Christians.[26]

In the Roman period there were doubtless a few Jews who went so far in their assimilation. We have no idea how many such there may have been because, of course, they disappear from any possible record that we have of Jews. We do, however, know of one famous (or infamous, depending on our point of view) case, that of Tiberius Julius Alexander, the nephew of Philo, to whom Stark mistakenly refers as a model of the tendency to accommodate.[27] This Tiberius Julius was the Roman procurator of Judaea in 46–48 and the governor of

Egypt in 66–69, during which time he had to suppress a Jewish revolt in Alexandria. He did so in typically brutal Roman fashion. At the end of his Egyptian governorship he became the second-in-command to the Roman general Titus, who was laying siege to Jerusalem at the time.[28] Were there other Jews who, if not so famous, nevertheless renounced their Jewish heritage and assimilated to an equal degree? Of course there were. Was such assimilation normal for Hellenistic Jews? Decidedly not; were such the case, literary opposition to such apostasy would have survived. But we should note that Jews who really wanted to assimilate, even if there were much larger numbers of them than we think, did not become Christians. If they assimilated, they did so to the *dominant society*, as was the case with Tiberius Julius Alexander, Felix Mendelssohn, and all other such persons. To have become a Christian in the Roman period would hardly have been a social advantage, since Christians were often held in ill repute.[29]

Stark's main example of a Jew in the Roman period who accommodated to the dominant society and who thus typifies the type of Jew to whom the Christian alternative would have appealed is the aforementioned Philo.[30] Stark has chosen the wrong example. He writes, 'Not only were the Hellenized Jews socially marginal, they were also relatively worldly, accommodated, and secular. The example of Philo is compelling.'[31] Nothing could be farther from the truth. Philo, to be sure, was worldly. John Barclay summarizes, 'As an adult he swims in the mainstream of Alexandrian cultural life. He mingles with the crowd at sporting events of all kinds – boxing, wrestling and pancratist contests as well as chariot races . . . Similarly, he attends the theatre to watch plays, dances and puppet shows, and knows all about . . . elaborate private banquets.'[32] This worldliness did not mean, however, contrary to what Stark apparently thinks, that Philo was not Jewish or not religious. The Jewish religion did not then and does not now require some kind of monastic asceticism, and those 'worldly' pursuits of Philo's in no way separated him from the Jewish people or from his God, to whom – as we learn from almost every page of his voluminous writings – he was devoted with his whole being. This worldliness is not to be equated with secularity in the modern sense, a life-style that was hardly known in antiquity and that would have seemed abhorrent to Philo.

Stark seems to think that Philo's explaining the Jewish law in terms of Greek, largely Platonic philosophy and his allegorizing of many of the narratives in the Bible represent 'a turn toward worldliness and away from other-worldliness',[33] but that is not the case at all. Not only, as we have just noted, does the Jewish religion not require 'other-worldliness', but Philo's Platonizing explanations are in fact often more other-worldly than the biblical originals. One example will prove both points, i.e., that Philo is given to considerable otherworldliness and that his worldliness is not the same as secularism. In *de Migratione Abrahami* 89–93 Philo strongly criticizes those Alexandrian Jews who, because they share his allegorical interpretation of the Torah, have given up practice (Sabbath, dietary laws, and the like). Simply recognizing the real (allegorical) meaning of the laws, according to Philo, does not relieve one of the obligation to follow them in their literal sense, although the allegorical meaning is indeed the true meaning. Thus the Sabbath is meant to teach 'the power of that which concerns ungenerated being and the inactivity of that which concerns generated being' (*Mig. Abr.* 91). He argues further (*Mig. Abr.* 93), 'We should think of the literal observance as like the body and the allegorical meaning as the soul: just as we ought to take care of the body, since it is the home of the soul, so we ought to pay heed to the letter of the law.' Ungenerated being and soul should be other-worldly enough for anyone; yet Philo scores his acquaintances for their lack of observance.

Stark proposes three separate appeals that Christianity may have held for Hellenized Jews. They are the appeal of a cult to disaffected but prosperous Jews;[34] the appeal of the situation of the 'God-fearers', those Gentiles known from the book of Acts in the New Testament and hardly anywhere else who were attracted to Jewish religion and life but who demurred at giving up a centimetre of flesh and converting, but whose life-style nevertheless appealed to many Hellenized Jews; and the appeal of being both Jewish and Hellenic at the same time.[35]

The first appeal assumes that Hellenized Jews were 'socially marginal';[36] yet, since Stark's main example is Philo, we see that this categorization is incorrect. Philo was a pillar of his society and was picked to lead a delegation to the emperor after a pogrom in Alexandria.[37] Stark's modern analogy, disaffected Jews in the United States today who join such movements as Hare Krishna, actually argues against his proposed second and third appeals, which require 'cultural continuity'.[38]

Stark's characterization of the appeal of the situation of the God-fearers is puzzling. He writes, 'For Hellenized Jews who had social and intellectual problems with the Law, the God-Fearers could easily have been a very tempting model of an alternative, fully Greek Judaism . . . But the God-Fearers were not a movement. The Christians were.'[39] Now, in the first place, Jews who had social and intellectual problems with the Torah simply had not to practise; they did not have to join anything, movement or otherwise. The non-observant Alexandrian Jews whom Philo scolds (above) are just such. In the second place, however, it is difficult to understand why the existence of the God-fearers (to the degree that they did exist) would have encouraged any Jews to give up Jewish practice. If I were finding that outsiders were manifesting interest, sometimes considerable, in my religion, would I not be more inclined to be *proud* of my religion?

The third presumed appeal, that Christianity offered Jews the opportunity to be both Jewish and Hellenic, is a non-starter. Of course, Christianity outside Palestine did rapidly become, in a sense, both; but why would such a despised religion appeal to Hellenized Jews, who were already by definition what Stark thinks they wanted to become? Jews, not only in the Dispersion but also in the Jewish homeland, could be just as Hellenized or not as they wished. Happy in their social situation, why would they want to convert to Christianity?

We have a failure here of two types. One is misunderstanding the evidence and the other is applying models that work in the

United States in the twentieth century to first–fifth century Alexandria and elsewhere. Here the issue of commensurability arises. Sometimes models that work here and now can enlighten situations long ago and far, far away, and sometimes they are useless. What a good historical sociologist will do, of course, is first analyse the evidence carefully and then formulate new models that fit the evidence,[40] or perhaps apply existing models that seem to fit, even though they may need a little 'tinkering' to fit exactly.[41] Stark has very little evidence here to support his position, and he has largely misunderstood the evidence that he has. By ascribing universal validity to his previously-derived models, he has used them as lenses for viewing antiquity and has consequently seen antiquity in terms of the models. This is to put the cart before the horse.

It is always the fate of productive scholarship, of course, to be surpassed by yet another contribution; and yet it is particularly unfortunate that Stark could not have known the recent work of John Barclay, which has the cart in the right place. Barclay provides extensive analysis of the evidence and creates a model to go with the evidence. He proposes that one must consider three paradigms side by side – those of assimilation (social integration), acculturation (language/education), and accommodation (use of acculturation).[42] These paradigms reveal spectra, the first running from 'social life confined to the Jewish community' to 'abandonment of key Jewish social distinctives' and the second from 'no facility in Greek' to 'scholarly expertise'. Thus it would be possible to be highly acculturated – speaking excellent Greek and knowing Homer and the playwrights well – without being assimilated in the least. In other words, such a highly educated (in the Greek sense) Jew *could* remain immersed in Jewish social life and have no contact with any Gentiles. Philo, by and large, was such a person. On the other hand, one could be highly assimilated – say, by marriage or because of experience in the military – and yet have little acculturation, e.g., no knowledge of Greek literature and culture.

Barclay's paradigm of accommodation is his most interesting. Here the spectrum runs from antagonism to Greco-Roman culture to submersion of Jewish cultural uniqueness. Of course, someone who employed Hellenic culture to accommodate at the high end of the spectrum would also rank high on the assimilation paradigm, but what comes as a bit of a surprise is that the low end of the spectrum *also* involves a form of accommodation, but an oppositional rather than an integrative form. Barclay offers several literary works as examples of oppositional accommodation in Egypt alone,[43] from among which we may note only the most readily known, the Wisdom of Solomon.[44] Written in Alexandria around the turn of the millennium in very good Greek, this work is capable of appropriating Hellenic philosophical motifs. Here we find for the first time in Judaic literature *athanasia*, immortality, in Wis. 3.4; and we find the Wisdom of God described in Middle-Platonic terms as 'a pure emanation of the glory of the Almighty . . ., for she is a reflection of eternal light, a spotless mirror of the working of God, and an image of his goodness' (Wis. 7.25–26). Yet the accommodation here, the use of Greek culture, is strictly oppositional, as witness the long tirade against idolatry in 13.1–15.7.[45] Barclay is able to locate different literary works and other pieces of evidence at different places along these three paradigms. His is now by far the best model of Jewish life in the Roman Diaspora that we have, and he has developed it on the basis of the evidence.

We noted above that one of Stark's proposals is that Christianity grew through networks rather than by public sermons and demonstrations – surely correct; but he also thought that the most likely networks were provided by other Jews.[46] The idea seems reasonable as long as one ignores the evidence of Gentile conversions. Thus Michael White writes, 'Such networks may or may not have included Jews within a given locale or house church.'[47] In fact there is little evidence of Jewish conversion to Christianity after the formation of the first Christian congregations in the Jewish homeland, whereas there is quite a bit of evidence that early Christian congregations elsewhere were at least predominantly Gentile.[48] To mention only two examples: Paul's letter to the Galatians is prompted by the attempt of some unnamed persons to convert the new Galatian Christians, who obviously could not have been Jews, to Judaism; and about fifty years later Pliny, the governor of Bithynia and Pontus, writes to the emperor that since he had begun persecuting Christians, 'the temples, which have been almost deserted, are beginning to be frequented once more' (*Epistles* 10 [*to Trajan*] 96.10). It was not conversions of Jews to Christianity that had taken people away from the Bithynian temples.

In at least one place Stark has read one of his modern sources incorrectly.[49] He states that MacLennan and Kraabel 'tell us that the archaeological evidence fails to show much Gentile presence around the synagogues in the Jewish settlements in the diaspora. But they also tells (*sic*) us that this is where the churches were!'[50] Unfortunately the only church mentioned in the article to which he refers is the one built on the site of a destroyed synagogue in Stobi in the fifth century. In the earlier version of this chapter, Stark wrote the same thing but referred to an earlier article by Kraabel.[51] This former article, however, includes the same information about Stobi. MacLennan and Kraabel state, 'Diaspora synagogue contact with Christians was rare.'[52]

The physical evidence that Stark cites as support for his position shows only contact,[53] from which we might conclude many things. Churches, when church buildings began to be built, were more likely to be built on the sites of abandoned or destroyed Mithraea, the most notable examples being St Peter's basilica and the church of San Clemente, both in Rome.[54] Michael White's monumental study of the architectural development of meeting places of non-traditional religions in the Roman world, a work that Stark knows and otherwise cites, emphasizes the situation in the Mesopotamian city of Dura Europos, where a synagogue, a church, a Mithraeum, and a 'private sanctuary to an unnamed god' were all close to one another.[55] Surely the only thing that one can infer about conversions to Christianity in the light of such evidence is that early Christians had varied religious backgrounds.

Stark's chapter entitled 'Christianizing the Urban Empire: A Quantitative Approach' also maintains the thesis that most early converts to Christianity came from Judaism.[56] By consulting various histories and atlases Stark determines the relative size of cities in the empire, in what century those cities first had a Jewish congregation, and in what century they first had a Christian congregation. Then, employing a number of statistical analyses, he finds that the larger the city, the more likely it was to have a Christian congregation early,[57] thus supporting the findings of historians of early Christianity,[58] whom he cites. He also finds a strong positive correlation between nearness to Jerusalem and the early establishment of Christianity in a city, and between prior Jewish presence in a city and the establishment of a Christian congregation there.[59] A corollary of the finding about nearness to Jerusalem is the finding that the nearer a city was to Rome (with the exception of Rome itself), the less likely it was to have a Christian congregation early.

Since Christianity spread from Jerusalem out, the findings about distance are not surprising; and Rome as an exception is also not surprising, since people migrated from all over the empire to the great city of Rome itself. Because, however, we are remarkably uninformed about the spread of Christianity east into eastern Syria and Mesopotamia, the point about distance from Rome probably has little significance. Stark mistakenly thinks that the farther a city was from Rome, 'the less [would have been] the local impact of Roman policy' – that is, the farther from Rome the less 'Romanization'.[60] It thus appears to him that Christianity found a foothold in less Romanized cities early. Jerusalem and Antioch, however, were just as much under Roman control as were Ephesus and Sardis, so that distance from Jerusalem remains the only finding of relevance here.[61]

Stark's finding about the prior establishment of Judaism in a city is misleading for two reasons. First, Jews were simply everywhere; second, we have abundant evidence of non-Jewish Christian congregations from the first generation on. About the time that Christianity began, Philo wrote (*Leg. alleg.*

281–2) that there were Jews in Egypt, Phoenicia, Syria, Pamphilia, Cilicia, most of Asia 'as far as Bithynia' and the 'remote corners of Pontus', Europe, Thessaly, Boeotia, Macedonia, Aetolia, Attica, Argos, Corinth, 'the best parts of Peloponnese', Euboea, Cyprus and Crete. Mary Smallwood gives a still more extensive list based on information from Josephus, I and II Maccabees, and other ancient sources.[62] In short, there was hardly any place in the eastern Roman Empire where Christianity could expand where there were not Jews already. Therefore, the relevance of prior presence of Jews for the expansion of Christianity loses any statistical significance.

Early Christian literature, furthermore, is filled with evidence of Gentile Christianity (cf. above, in the discussion of Stark's chapter on the mission to the Jews). Originally, of course, all Christians were Jews; but as Christianity spread, while there were Jewish conversions (Paul's letter to the Romans gives evidence of Jewish Christianity in Rome), Christianity rapidly became predominantly Gentile. When in the mid-second century Justin wrote his *Dialogue with Trypho the Jew*, Jews were clearly other, albeit still persons with whom one might have a friendly argument over the meaning of scripture.[63] Justin had been reared in Sebaste (Samaria) and had lived in Ephesus before moving to Rome.

Christianity did not win most of its converts in the Greco-Roman world from among the Jewish population, and so massive Jewish conversions cannot explain Christianity's ultimate success. In fact, Stark himself finally disproves the point about Jewish conversions, although he does not realize that he has done so. We shall see that evidence shortly.

C. Appeals to Gentiles

In his chapter on 'Epidemics, Networks, and Conversion', Stark advances three principles.[64] The first is that Christianity offered a better explanation of the terrible plagues that ravaged the Roman world in the second and third centuries than did pagan religions; the second is that Christians, because of their theologically driven care for one another at these times, had a higher survival rate than did pagans; and the third is that, because of Christian care for their *pagan* neighbors during such times, whose other friends and neighbours may have perished, 'very substantial numbers of pagans [i.e., among the survivors] would have been shifted from mainly pagan to mainly Christian social networks'.[65] The first point is correct to a degree, and Stark cites the best sources, e.g., Cyprian, bishop of Carthage.[66] Also, that Christians cared for the sick when other healthy people left town if they could, and that this gave Christianity more prestige, are in the one case certain and in the other likely, and this same point was made a number of years ago by Peter Brown.[67] That pagans who survived the epidemics were drawn into the Christian orbit is, further, a reasonable inference.

All that is demonstrable here, however, is the Christian theology and the fact that Christians cared for the sick – including, at least occasionally, non-Christians – when others would not do so. Did the Christian theology of facing death bravely because of the belief in heavenly reward influence persons to become Christians? Perhaps some; but most of Christianity's competitors, from the oldest mystery religions to the Isis-Sarapis religion, also offered the hope of some kind of better existence beyond death than miserable Hades. Thus, other things being equal, all those religions might have been expected to profit equally from epidemics. That Christian care for the pagan sick – to the extent that such happened (and most of the evidence concerns care for other Christians)[68] – would have brought converts in by one way or another is a reasonable inference but impossible to prove. When Stark then adds, however, the issue of differential mortality,[69] he surely has a point. On average, Christians must have had a higher survival rate because of their caring for their own sick; so, even if the epidemics resulted in *no* conversions to Christianity, after each plague the Christian proportion of the general population would have risen.

In trying to guess the degree to which Christian theology and Christian care of the sick during times of pestilence would have led to pagan conversions to Christianity, Stark has unfortunately overlooked the degree to which Christians were widely hated by pagans.[70] Analysing 'Popular Reactions against Christianity' a number of years ago, E. C. Colwell noted that both in the Gospels and in Acts 'it is the mob that strikes first; official action becomes necessary to preserve the peace and restrain disorder'.[71] We may recall especially Tertullian's famous statement that, whenever there was any difficulty, the cry was, '*Christianos ad leonem*' (*Apol.* 40.2). In fact, quite contrary to what Stark would have us believe, 'the Christians as "atheists" in the opinion of the pagan world were repeatedly accused of angering the gods and thus *causing* the disastrous public calamities'.[72] As causes for pagan hostility, George Oborn cites disruption of the family,[73] Christian interference with pagan temples (destroying idols, and the like),[74] the Christian desire 'to keep the believers from all contact and association with pagans whether in business or pleasure',[75] and Christian economic competition,[76] comprising both greater industriousness and competitive businesses. (Hippolytus refers, e.g., to a Christian bank.)[77] Tacitus, finally (*Annals* 15.44), refers to 'those who were called Christians by the mob and were hated for their crimes'.[78] Did Christian care for the sick (mostly other Christians) during the second- and third-century times of pestilence offset this negative attitude toward Christians entirely? That is possible but seems unlikely, and in any case there are no statistics.

On the other hand, both Colwell and Oborn note that, beginning with the reign of the Emperor Decius (mid-third century), the popular and popularly inspired persecution of Christians ceased and that persecution thenceforth was initiated by the highest authorities.[79] This change might reflect the kind of effect that Stark thinks Christianity had on the pagan population, yet there is no direct evidence that such is the case, and it is more likely (as we might infer from Stark's first analysis, about Christian growth) that by around 250 a near majority of the population was Christian. Such a population would be unlikely to stir up persecutions of Christians.

This chapter oddly, especially since it immediately follows the chapter on the 'Mission to the Jews', mentions no Jewish conversions and seems to imply that the great growth of Christianity came not from Jewish, but from pagan conversions. Stark appears to have overlooked this inconsistency.

Stark's chapter on 'Urban Chaos and Crisis: The Case of Antioch' is a marvellous accomplishment.[80] Here Stark makes us feel the urban crowding, the flies and mosquitoes, the open sewer drains in the narrow streets, the frequent devastation of fire and earthquake, the pollution of water supplies, the constant threat from night-time crime on the streets, and all the other nuisances and agonies of urban life in the early Roman Empire. He makes those of us who long for time machines so that we could personally visit the antiquity that we so lovingly study realize that we would not actually want to go there. If an earthquake didn't get us, we would surely suddenly sicken and die from the polluted environment and water. Given this 'chronic urban misery', Stark proposes, it is no wonder that Christianity grew rapidly, inasmuch as it offered salvation out of this life.[81] 'People living in such circumstances must often have despaired,' Stark writes.[82] 'Surely it would not be strange for them to have concluded that the end of days drew near. And surely too they must often have longed for relief, for hope, indeed for salvation.' Stark correctly notes that historians have normally failed to comment on these aspects of ancient life,[83] and he is to be congratulated on his industriousness in ferreting out facts that we have normally overlooked. As for such chronic urban misery's abetting the growth of Christianity, however, we unfortunately have to pronounce a *non sequitur*.

The main problem is that, while for upper-middle-class white American males living in the latter part of the twentieth century (as do Rodney Stark and the present writer) in the Pacific Northwest of the United States ancient urban life would have been something of a horror, the ancients, not knowing what they were missing, were not horrified by urban life and in fact continually flocked to the cities by the hundreds of thousands, a fact of which Stark is aware![84] Infant mortality was high, but those who survived will have developed immunities to many of the germs and bacteria that would get Stark and this writer at once.

One reason for ancients' finding urban life pleasing – perhaps second after economic opportunity – hinges on an aspect of ancient urban life of which Stark is aware but to the meaning of which he seems immune. He calculates that, on average, approximately 40% of ancient urban space was devoted to public buildings,[85] and he thus correctly notes that 'the typical residents of Greco-Roman cities spent their lives mainly in public places and that the average "domicile must have served only as a place to sleep and store possessions"'.[86] What Stark sees here is deprivation: no indoor plumbing, no private study with its book-lined walls, no television or VCR, no stereo, no three-car garage. The ancients will have viewed the matter differently, however. They will have accepted that living areas were small and cramped and will have rejoiced in the splendid public buildings, richly painted, in the many statues and other works of art, in the baths, in the theatres, in the amphitheatres with their spectacles, in the odeia with their concerts, and in the many religious festivals of the year with their free food.[87] For men, furthermore, the city offered a variety of sexual partners, Greco-Roman morality in the matter of sex being quite differ- ent from the Jewish and Christian version. Furthermore, as Stark has already confirmed in his chapter on the class basis of early Christianity, Christianity did not appeal primarily to the lower classes, thus to those in the most cramped living quarters. Christian churches were house based. Some people living in the cramped *insulae* may have attended services in those house churches, but – except for the slaves of Christian householders, who normally had to go along with the religion of the master – Christians were predominantly from those classes that felt the pain of cities less than the lower classes. Even they, however, may not have felt the pain as much as Stark supposes, since

John Stambaugh observes that, for Rome at least, 'the poorest immigrant from Egypt could watch the processions and stroll through the fora, enjoying the spectacular panorama of the city just as readily as a senator or an emperor'.[88]

The emerging 'Christian class' would thus not have been made up of people who were subject to routine despair, nor would their circumstances have made them think that 'the end' was near, as Stark proposes (above). The concept of the end, in any case, already implies Christian teaching, and convincing people that the end was coming was a stock part of early Christian preaching, as we see from many passages in the New Testament. Readers of this volume will be well aware that, even today, Christian preachers convince followers that the end is near without the followers' having experienced the chronic urban misery of ancient Antioch.

Doubtless many people longed for relief and hope, and they may also have longed for salvation. The author of a work on which Stark relies has canvassed inscriptions and concluded that pagans prayed most often for health, second for beauty, and third for progeny. There are also frequent prayers for protection from natural disasters, for freedom from slavery, for preservation of wealth, and 'for relief from tax payments'.[89] There is therefore some overlap in this list with the kinds of anxieties that we may associate with chronic urban misery, but it would seem difficult to subsume requests for beauty, for offspring, and for relief from taxes under such a heading. We should also note the high degree to which prayers to pagan deities for health were answered. The shrines of Asclepius collected numerous votives in the shape of healed body parts, and non-Christian healers were abundant, sometimes famous, but surely as effective as the Christian ones.[90]

In any case, there is no evidence in early Christian literature that the longings that led people to become Christians were prompted by urban misery; so we need to remind ourselves just what it was that Christianity did offer. It did not offer cleaner or safer streets, better sanitation, or freedom from earthquake, fire, famine and pestilence. What it offered was eternal life. This is so patently obvious that it hardly needs demonstration, but we may note in the New Testament Rom. 6.23, which can still be read on many highway billboards in the United States, 'The gift of God is eternal life in Christ Jesus our Lord.'

Was it chronic urban misery that rendered people susceptible to the appeal of eternal life? In some cases it may have been, but there is also something to be said for a general malaise in the age that had been brought about by the conquests of Alexander three centuries earlier. After Alexander, the Mediterranean world was never again a group of small communities. From then on internationalism prevailed, along with which went an inevitable individualism, inasmuch as individuals were cut loose from the stability of traditional communities. It was this situation that opened up the possibility of the internationalism of the gods, so that one could worship Isis, Mithras, or Christ wherever one went – a situation that had hardly existed before Alexander's time. Ancient historians of a few years previous have sought to express this malaise with terms like 'failure of nerve' and 'anxiety' – terms that Stark, following MacMullen, dismisses.[91]

The causes of conversion are complex, as we detailed in the previous chapter. Doubtless urban misery had something to do with some peoples' conversions to Christianity, as well as to other salvation cults (like the Isis religion), and Stark deserves applause for bringing this factor to attention. But it did not provide a universal nudge in the direction of Christianity.

Stark's chapter on 'The Role of Women in Christian Growth' is one of the most helpful in the entire book. First, Stark mentions two factors that will have given Christianity a considerably larger proportion of women than that in the empire generally. Those factors are the prohibition among Christians of infanticide,[92] of which girl babies were the primary victims, and the higher proportion of female converts.[93] The two factors will have worked together to increase the proportion of female Christians even more.[94] Stark then seeks to show that higher status for women and a greater proportion of women go together in early Christianity,[95] which situation he connects to the conversion of non-Christian husbands.[96] Only the last point is debatable.

Regarding marriage between Christian women and pagan men, Stark correctly observes that, 'in truth, there is no abundance of direct evidence that inter-marriages between Christian women and pagan men were widespread',[97] and the truth is that much evidence argues against such a phenomenon.[98] Yet the fact remains that probably many married women became Christians. This does not necessarily imply secondary conversions of husbands, however, for 'in the first two centuries of its history Christianity broke up many homes. Many a pagan first heard of Christianity as the disintegrating force that had wrecked a neighbor's home.'[99] Oborn noted that when one member of a marriage converted to Christianity, 'it interfered positively with the economic structure of the group'. Such a division in the family also 'disrupted the family cult', an assumed part of everyday life in antiquity. Citing Tertullian, *Apol.* 3 and *Ad nationes* 1.4, and Arnobius, *Adversus nationes* 2.5, Oborn concluded that it was 'small wonder . . . that pagan husbands not uncommonly disowned their Christian wives'.[100] The evidence, therefore, hardly supports Christian growth through such secondary conversions.

Also regarding this chapter, Stark's proposals need to be up-dated by the recent work of Torjesen, which shows that Christian women's status in the church declined 'somewhere around the beginning of the third century'.[101] What brought about this change was the beginning of considerable numbers of conversions of 'the municipal ruling elites', who assumed leadership roles within the churches and brought with them their normal assumption that women belonged in private space while men controlled public space, into which Christianity was at this time moving energetically.[102] Before this time, Christianity was primarily a household phenomenon, all churches being house churches;[103] and there women had traditional leadership roles. It is in this earlier setting that Stark's examples of Christian women's leadership (taken mostly from Paul's letters) belong.[104] Thus the higher status of women within Christianity can be used to explain the growth of Christianity for only the first two-hundred years, after which time women retreated in importance in Christianity. But the status and pre-ponderance of women during those two hundred years may well have given Christianity the lead that it needed.

Judith Lieu has recently offered some cautions about the tendency of male scholars to assume that Christianity (and Judaism) attracted a heavy proportion of female converts.[105] 'Much of the supposed evidence of the significance of women in early Christianity,' she points out, 'is rather of women as a topic of concern in the early Church', as is often the case in the modern scholarly discussion, e.g., of Paul's discussion of marriage and related topics in I Corinthians 11–14.[106] Lieu enters into evidence the conversion of prostitutes in early Christian and in early rabbinic literature. 'Interestingly,' she notes, 'prostitutes drop out of Christian accounts of conversion after the Synoptic Gospels, further confirmation that they say more about our authors' views on women than about social reality.' Thus, 'the evidence often cited for the attraction of women to Judaism or Christianity is not this; they are sources for different political agenda'.[107] Rather than a special appeal of Christianity and Judaism to pagan women, Lieu sees rather 'that in some parts of the Empire influential women were able to use religion, including non-civic religion, to negotiate a role for themselves in society'. She sees women in the early empire 'seeking a social framework for . . . independence . . ., and finding it in the growing ambiguities that were breaking down the public/private divide, *ambiguities that were inevitably characteristic of these new religious movements*'.[108] In the last analysis, then, the numbers of women converts in Judaism and Christianity during the time that we are considering was not so much the result of those religious movements' appealing especially to women, but rather of the movements' amenability to women's purposes! 'It does no service either to historical reconstruction or to the political agenda to deny that women too were able to use and therefore to shape Judaism and Christianity as vehicles of their own identity.'[109]

Lieu has made two points here that she does not entirely harmonize: first, that there were not as many female converts to Christianity and Judaism as the ancient literature would lead us to believe; and, that women joined Jewish and Christian groups because those religious movements gave women opportunities to realize their identities. There is no reason to dispute the former point; and the second is in fact not disharmonious with Stark's and Torjesen's findings that early Christianity – at least through the first two centuries – offered women status opportunity, thus increasing the numbers of female converts, however many of those there were. We cannot take a census of ancient congregations, and certainly suggesting proportions of male and female converts is precarious; but Stark's reasons seem to stand. The prohibition of infanticide and the opportunity for status will have increased the female component in Christianity – and in Judaism, as well, to the degree that Jewish congregations were seeking converts – beyond what it otherwise would have been. This will have been true in both gnostic and catholic circles (as those identities emerged).

Stark's chapter on 'The Martyrs: Sacrifice as Rational Choice' of course presents rational choice theory.[110] While most historians of all stripes, and many sociologists as well, are quite leery of this theory, it needs to be given its due. In this case, Stark employs the theory first to rebut the traditional theory of social scientists that willing martyrs must be crazy or masochists; and in this he is surely correct. We have only to read Ignatius' letter to the Roman Christians, in which he asks them not to intervene with the authorities and to let him die the martyr's death to which he has been condemned, to see the reasoning. Ignatius wrote, 'Suffer me to be the food of wild beasts, which are the means of making my way to God. God's wheat I am, and by the teeth of wild beasts I am to be ground that I may prove Christ's pure bread.'[111] From this appeal we learn two things. The first is that Ignatius sincerely believes that when he dies he will go to be with God. Other early Christians wrote essentially the same thing (cf. Paul in Phil. 1.21–24), and this confirms the point about eternal life made above. It is sometimes difficult for us modern scholars to accept that early Christians truly believed that when they died they would live with God for eternity, but that is what they believed. When people are entirely convinced of such a belief, death holds little terror. Admittedly, perhaps not all Christians were equally convinced, but they were not the ones voluntarily suffering martyrdom.[112] Second, for Christian leaders like Ignatius to have backed down in such circumstances would have shown cowardice and would have weakened the faith of many believers. They had little choice but to go willingly, otherwise they deconfirmed their own doctrine. Stark writes, 'By voluntarily accepting torture and death rather than defecting, a person sets the highest imaginable value upon a religion and communicates that value to others.'[113] The promise of eternal life is what Stark calls a 'compensator', i.e., 'a sort of substitute for desired rewards' that 'cannot be had, here and now, by anyone'.[114]

Further to support the rational choice theory, Stark argues that Christians in fact experienced rewards in this life for their Christian commitment. He lists 'an immense, shared emotional satisfaction', financial aid and nursing care, a 'secure family life', a lessening of tensions between social classes, and possibly longer life.[115] These concrete rewards will have functioned to abet the veracity of the compensator. Doubtless many Christians experienced these rewards, but whether the rewards motivated either martyrdom or conversion to Christianity must remain an open question, in view of the uniform emphasis on the reward – or compensator – of eternal life. Such rewards, however, surely motivated people to remain Christians and not to drop out – a possibility that, as we noted in the last chapter, was probably more often realized than we may have been wont to think.

In his penultimate chapter, 'Opportunity and Organization',[116] Stark makes two points. The first is that paganism was declining as an effective social force and that Christianity was able to take advantage of that decline.[117] The second is that Christianity, as an exclusive movement, built a greater cohesiveness than did paganism.[118]

The former explanation is as old as Christianity itself (cf. I Cor. 8.5–6) and is in part true; yet Stark, without realizing it, reveals the weakness of the argument, for he brings in the Isis religion as a comparator.[119] After looking briefly at the evidence for the spread of this religion, he writes, 'I can report a highly significant correlation of .67 between the expansion of Isis and the expansion of Christianity. Where Isis went, Christianity followed.' But if Isis, like Christ, was filling the gap left by the older local gods who were in decline, then the contrast is obviously not between Christianity and paganism, but between old and new religions, of which Christianity was only one. The problem then becomes how to explain the triumph of Christianity over the Isis religion, a topic that Stark does not address and the question that requires an answer.

In view of Stark's earlier contention that Christianity went where there were Jews and that most early Christians were Jews, his correlation between the presence of the Isis religion and the establishment of Christianity is astounding, for it is very nearly identical with the correlation that he found between synagogues and the establishment of Christianity (.69).[120] Thus Stark appears here to have unwittingly disproved his earlier theory about Jewish conversions to Christianity. Given the closeness of the two comparators, we might ask, Were most devotees of the Isis religion Jews? Alternatively, were most converts to Christianity worshippers of Isis and not Jews? The answer to both questions is likely to be no. What we see with the Isis correlation is that both Christianity and the Isis religion found most of their converts in urban areas, where many pagans were attracted to new religions – for a great variety of reasons, some of which Stark has confirmed or discovered. Like Christianity, of course, the Isis religion offered – at least to those who were initiated into the mysteries, which did not include all worshippers of Isis – hope for a better existence after death. Isis was also, like Christ, a very benevolent and caring deity.[121]

Stark's point about Christianity's filling the vacuum left by a declining paganism does not help us to understand Christ-

ianity's triumph over its competitors; but Christianity doubtless was a more cohesive movement than pagan religion generally and the Isis cult in particular – a point to which we shall
return.

D. Summary of the discussion with Stark

The fact that Stark has failed in his attempt to make certain
points about early Christianity should not obscure the fact
that his approach has underscored other points previously
made (Christianity was not primarily a lower-class movement,
Christianity offered benefits that made joining the movement a
reasonable choice, Christian care for the sick and needy contributed to growth, Christianity filled a need in the society of
the early Roman empire, most conversions came through networks, the place of women in Christianity abetted its growth)
and has brought at least two others to the surface for the first
time (Christianity could have grown to take over the empire
without miraculous or dramatic activity, Christianity was more
cohesive than its competitors). While all these social factors
were important in the growth of Christianity, only the care for
the ill, the (early) status and role of women and greater cohesiveness can bid to explain Christianity's triumph. Before
returning to the subject of cohesiveness, we need also to examine other possible factors in Christianity's success.

4. Further possibilities

A. Anthony Blasi's proposals

Already in 1989, the sociologist Anthony Blasi had published a
preliminary analysis of early Christianity as a social movement,
at the end of which he briefly listed 'predisposing factors' that
led people to become Christians.

The first of these factors was Jesus himself, and Blasi understands Jesus as such a predisposing factor in two ways.[122] First,

while Jesus inspired a following, he did not create an organization; thus he 'made early Christianity diffuse, and thereby contributed toward its durability. It was precisely because Jesus
was not a founder that he could inspire subsequent foundings
by such people as James, Peter, and Paul.' Second, Jesus passed
on his 'value sensitivity' to succeeding Christians, so that 'the
example of *his* value sensitivity would come to mind whenever
his followers had to settle value questions themselves'.

Blasi's second aspect of Jesus' having been a predisposing
factor in the success of Christianity is open to serious question,
since the nearest that one can come to showing that the historical Jesus influenced later Christian value judgments is that later
Christian writers quote the love command; but they do so in
different ways, and the command becomes ossified by the third
generation, at the latest.[123]

That early Christianity was diffuse in its form, however
(which is Blasi's meaning), probably did contribute to its success. Another way of putting that is to say that early Christianity
was more adaptable than were its competitors. Aside from the
fact that there were Jewish Christians and Gentile Christians in
the first decades, Gentile Christianity displayed many faces.
There were Pauline Christianity, Johannine Christianity, the
Christianity that took root in Corinth that Paul opposed, the
Christianity of 'Jezebel' and of the 'Nicolaitans' that the author
of Revelation opposed, and by the end of the first century
several forms of gnostic Christianity – to name only the most
obvious varieties. While some persons – the Jerusalem leaders
during Paul's time and perhaps until the war with Rome, Paul
himself, the author of the *Didache* – *tried* to impose uniformity
on this conglomeration of Christianities, success was elusive
(and has not arrived to this day). This kind of rampant adaptability of the new social organism that we call Christianity may
well have been much greater than the adaptability of which
Mithraism and the Isis religion were capable. We could be more
certain of that comparison if we knew more about the other
religions; but the iconography, in any case, of Mithraism
throughout the vast reaches of the empire and over several

centuries is remarkably consistent, even if there is no fixed sequence for the several mythical events portrayed (Mithras' birth from a rock, Mithras' killing the bull, Mithras' dragging the bull to his cave, etc.).[124] And, if Apuleius is a reliable guide, the process of being initiated into either the Isis or the Osiris mystery was quite similar in different places.

To be sure, Mithraism and the Isis religion had certainly adapted. Mithraism was a pre-eminently Roman, not an Iranian religion; and the Isis who is portrayed in Greco-Roman statuary is hardly traditionally Egyptian. But the issue is the *degree* of adaptability. Lack of uniformity *seems* to have been much greater in Christianity than in Mithraism and in the Isis religion, based on the evidence available to us.[125] Thus to the degree that Christianity could be 'all things to all people' (I Cor. 9.22) it could succeed in attracting followers beyond the ability of its competitors.

Much earlier, Harnack had also emphasized Christianity's adaptive ability. The reasons for Christianity's success, he wrote,

> on the one hand, were native to the very essence of the new religion (as vital monotheism and as evangel). On the other hand, they lay in its versatility and amazing powers of adaptation. To say that the victory of Christianity was a victory of Christ is true; but it is also true to say that Christianity simply supplied the form in which syncretistic monotheism won the day.[126]

There can be little doubt that Christianity's excellent adaptability to the societies in which it took root, an adaptability that continues to this day, was a major cause of its ultimate success.

Blasi's second predisposing factor, after Jesus, is 'status inequalities which threatened social relationships',[127] by which he means disparities of wealth and status within households that 'threatened to divide people'. Since Christianity created communities that emphasized equality of all members and de-emphasized traditional wealth and status, it provided a home (according to Blasi) for those who felt cut off by status inequality. Unfortunately for this proposal, however, Blasi had earlier noted the quarrels in the early church in Corinth that he had attributed, following Gerd Theissen, to status and wealth inequality in the congregation.[128] The artificial equality of a Christian congregation thus appears to have been more an ideal than a reality (I Cor. 11.17–34).

Finally, as a factor predisposing the success of Christianity, Blasi mentions 'cultural plurality'.[129] Here Blasi's examples may be less instructive than the principle, for he mentions 1. Latins in Corinth (whose status was high but who 'could not claim any cultural superiority over Greek culture'), 2. Greeks in Rome, 3. Hellenist God-fearers in synagogues, and 4. Greek-language ethnic groups in Jerusalem, the targets of Stephen's evangelistic activity. Whatever one may think of these examples – and they would all be difficult to substantiate – what Blasi has touched on here is the tendency towards loss of local social and cultural solidarity in the internationalism and mobility of the early empire, as we discussed above (p. 153). Surely that did abet the recruiting efforts of the NRMs, but Christianity would not have benefited from this situation any more than would have the religions of Isis and of Mithras.

B. Robert Grant's proposal

First in his chapter on 'Christian Devotion to the Monarchy' in his *Early Christianity and Society*,[130] and then in considerably more detail in his *Augustus to Constantine*, Robert Grant has argued that a main element in Christianity's ultimate success is that, in spite of persecutions, it kept hammering away at the emperor that it was a loyal movement devoted to the welfare of both emperor and empire and that it was deserving of the justice appropriate to the empire. Grant appeals primarily to the Apologists. Justin, for example, 'insists that Christians pay taxes and tribute to Roman tax collectors everywhere, as Jesus taught them to do. Though they worship God alone, they rejoice in loyal service to the emperors.' In keeping with this attitude, 'they not only acknowledge the authority of the state but also pray that the imperial power may be accompanied by "disciplined reason"'.[131] Athenagoras, further, 'tried to show that Christians were trinitarian monotheists who exhibited a high morality and shared in the best of Graeco-Roman literary culture'.[132] While Grant recognizes that the Apologists may have been 'excessively optimistic when they appealed to Roman justice and to what they viewed as the best elements of Graeco-Roman culture', still 'it may also be that they were justified in doing so and that the final victory of Christianity was largely due to Roman acceptance of their claims'. Thus, 'during the first three centuries many Roman administrators recognized the validity of the Christian goal, and finally it was accepted by the emperor himself'.[133]

Reasonable as this approach is, what little evidence we have about the Emperor Constantine's ultimate embracing of Christianity does not support the notion that he did so because he accepted the Apologists' appeals. His endorsing of Christianity was more likely a political step. Thus Stark,[134] in reliance on Shirley Jackson Case.[135]

C. Early Christianity as a form of transnational civil society

Let us return to the issue of Christian cohesiveness that Stark brought to our attention above. We gain a new perspective on this cohesiveness when we look at one of the more interesting discussions under way in contemporary sociology, that concerning what are called institutions of transnational civil society. This sociological discussion grows out of concerns about national security, since 'in a world of rapid communication, global and local processes can move money and products, images and people, guns and drugs, diseases and pollution, across increasingly porous and irrelevant state frontiers'.[136] When individual states, then, can no longer preserve the world's peace and security, at least a portion of the mantle falls on international non-governmental organizations (NGOs).

Perhaps, since governments cannot provide transnational civil society, a congeries of NGOs can do so – so runs the theory. A number of sociologists think that religion, while it may some-times promote or abet conflict, can help to serve this function of transnational civilizer. For that to happen, 'the religious forma-tions and movements that inhabit transnational civil society [would have to] engage in the persuasion and collective action of world politics'.[137] In this function, one could 'imagine them as transparent plastic overlays, alternative meaning systems superimposed upon the meaning system of political maps'.[138] An example:

Ousmane Kane examined Sufi *turuq* (orders; singular *tariqa*) in west Africa. These *turuq*,

> which contributed a great deal to the spread of Islam in black Africa, make tension less likely, while their absence actually makes it more likely. They perform many of the survival functions – providing community, shelter for the needy, medical support, economic networks – that family or state performs in other societies, and they do so without regard to state borders. Thus they create networks of trust and routines of peaceable interaction that contrast with the experience of distrust, conflict, and violence between ethnic communities that has afflicted some African states.[139]

These *turuq* have thus operated 'in a space that corresponds not to the political map of the colonial and, later on, the post-colonial state, but to a sacred geography created by pilgrimage routes and centres'.[140]

A recent report by the Associated Press, further, details how NGOs operate and what their influence is.

> Thousands of nonprofit, non-governmental organizations – the NGOs – distribute more aid than the World Bank, wield greater power than some governments and readily put their employees at incredible risk . . . NGOs have played key roles in negotiating trade and environmental treaties and now sit in on government and corporate decision-making . . . They

tread into some of the world's hottest trouble spots and biggest disasters – Kosovo, Honduras, Bosnia, Somalia, Chechnya, Afghanistan – often suffering more casualties than the government agents and soldiers they precede . . . In addition to dispensing charity, NGOs take surveys, dig wells, fix bad teeth, stop epidemics, house refugees, protect natural resources, lend money, sue polluters and sometimes demonstrate against governments.[141]

Such is exactly, of course, what early Christianity did, as Rodney Stark and Peter Brown before him have indicated. It may be worthwhile here to recall some of Brown's evidence.

During public emergencies, such as plague or rioting, the Christian clergy were shown to be the only united group in the town, able to look after the burial of the dead and to organize food-supplies. In Rome, the Church was supporting fifteen hundred poor and widows by 250. The churches of Rome and Carthage were able to send large sums of money to Africa and Cappadocia, to ransom Christian captives after barbarian raids in 254 and 256. Two generations previously, the Roman state, faced by similar problems after an invasion, had washed its hands of the poorer provincials . . . Plainly, to be a Christian in 250 brought more protection from one's fellows than to be a *civis romanus*.[142]

While Brown writes here of the third century, we readily recall that the tendency in the direction of a transnational civil society reaches back as far as the Apostolic Council (Acts 15; Galatians 2) and Paul's attempt to raise an offering from his Gentile churches for the 'poor' in Jerusalem (Gal. 2.10; II Corinthians 8–9). To be sure, the capital of that original transnational society was Jerusalem, and the society included both Jewish and Gentile Christians, whereas after a few decades the Jewish Christians were moved out of the growing Gentile consciousness of the unity of the church. Justin (*Dial.* 47–48) marks a mid-point in this exclusion when he describes some Jewish Christians whom he considers acceptable (ἀποδέχομαι) and others whom he considers unacceptable. And, furthermore, around this time (cf. Irenaeus) gnostic Christians in general became unacceptable to the catholic church. Aside from those exclusions, however, emerging Christianity cultivated a transnational civil society continuously.

A further example of this tendency is the letter that we call I Clement. The author of this epistle, while not writing as an apostle, nevertheless writes in the tradition of Paul, addressing the church at Corinth about matters internal to it and offering advice and counsel. As far as we can tell, there was nothing like this kind of international involvement among Christianity's competitors. This is not to say that there was not uniformity across the empire in the religion and especially in the worship of Mithras, and that there was not contact, as well as movement from one congregation to another.[143] The individual congregations, however, seem to have remained independent and autonomous, not acting in any coordinated effort with other congregations.

This statement may be debated. Thus a recent handbook of Roman religion cites, as possible evidence of Mithraic transnational cooperation, the inscription (properly, dipinto) from the Mithraeum under the church of Santa Prisca in Rome that proclaims, 'Hail to the Fathers from East and West.'[144] The authors of the handbook take this statement of praise to imply visits of Mithraic Fathers from one congregation to another. The full text, however, (written around drawings of persons in the several Mithraic grades) shows the inadequacy of this interpretation:

Hail [to the Fathers] from east to west under the protection of Saturn. Hail to the Sun-runners under the protection of Sun. Hail to the Persians under the protection of Moon. Hail to the Lions under the protection of Jupiter. Hail to the Soldiers under the protection of Mars. Hail to the Male brides (Nymphi) under the protection [of Venus]. [Hail to the Ravens under the protection of Mercury.][145]

The text is simply a blessing on the several grades within the order, worldwide; it does not include a greeting to Fathers, members of the supreme grade, who were visiting from other congregations.

Again, one might note that Apuleius' Lucius travels from his home Isiac congregation in Corinth to Rome and there becomes affiliated with the local congregation (*Metam.* 11.29). Precisely here, however, we see the difference from Christianity; for Lucius must be initiated again in Rome (*rursum sacris initiare*), a requirement that was manifestly *not* laid on Christians visiting or migrating from one congregation to another! Thus, for all the international *conformity* that doubtless existed in Mithraism and in the religion of Isis and Sarapis, the kind of international *involvement* of Christian congregations with one another that we know from Paul's time forward seems to have been unique to Christianity.

Peter Brown, again, observed that a Christian's

> literature, his beliefs, his art and his jargon were extraordinarily uniform, whether he lived in Rome, Lyons, Carthage or Smyrna. The Christians were immigrants at heart – ideological *déracinés*, separated from their environment by a belief which they knew they shared with little groups all over the empire. At a time when so many local barriers were being painfully and obscurely eroded, the Christians had already taken the step of calling themselves a 'non-nation'.[146]

The fictitious Isis devotee Lucius, who at the end of Apuleius' novel is promised glory as an advocate (*in foro reddere*), and the soldier members of Mithraic cells would not have been able to relate to that kind of internationalism. Christianity created a transnational civil society that showed itself more adept at handling crises than were the authorities, and there can be little doubt that this development was a major factor in Christianity's ultimate success.

It is possible that the Christian production of literature abetted both the formation of Christian transnational civil society and Christianity's triumph over its competitors, but that is somewhat less than certain. The splendidly thorough recent study by Harry Gamble of early Christian books draws attention again to this aspect of early Christianity, which older scholars had also noted at different times.[147] Gamble cites, as examples of the rapid spread of Christian literature, the presence in Egypt of manuscripts, shortly after the known or likely time of composition, of Irenaeus' *Against Heresies*, of Hermas, and of the Fourth Gospel. Gamble lays emphasis on the express intent of some early Christian literature that it be disseminated, e.g., statements in Hermas, *Visions* 2 about copying and reading the book and in Polycarp, Philippians 13 about the circulation of Ignatius' letters; and also John 21, which – unlike the rest of the Gospel – is 'book conscious', referring as it does (similarly to the prologue of Luke), to such things as 'the reliability of the author and his traditions' and 'the explicit awareness of producing one book among many others'.[148]

Yet, the Isis religion certainly had sacred books, which were doubtless the same everywhere, and Mithraism may have had such, as well, although none have survived. When Lucius, after being saved from his asinine state, attended his first religious service in an Isis temple, one of the *Pastophores* read from a book (*de libro, de litteris . . . praefari*). Since the priest's prayer concerned the '*princeps magnus* and the Senate, the Equites and the whole Roman people' (Apuleius, *Metam.* 11.17), and since the prayer was understandable to the congregation, we may be certain that this book was not done in hieroglyphs, as were the books later used to direct Lucius in his initiation (*libri litteris ignorabilibus praenotati*; *Metam.* 11.22).

It seems incautious, therefore, to conclude that literary production, *in and of itself*, was a significant factor in Christianity's success. That Christian literature, however, greatly abetted the formation of a Christian transnational civil society, and that this social form greatly abetted the success of Christianity can hardly be doubted.

5. Summary

We have reached the end of our analysis. What have we discovered?

Surely one thing of which we can be most certain is that no single factor led to Christianity's triumph over all the alternative religious movements in the Roman Empire; rather, the causes were many, and we should probably not attribute the same weight to each in every locale. Furthermore, much remains beyond our grasp, dependent as we are on such fragmentary sources. It is thus surely the case that many different individuals contributed to the growth of Christianity and to its surpassing its rivals in ways that we can never know. There are some matters, however, about which we can be reasonably certain.

First, a number of factors that abetted Christian growth also abetted the growth of other NRMs, so we may not count these factors, important as they were for Christian growth, as explanations for Christianity's ultimate triumph. The Christian gospel and promise of eternal life have to fall into this category, as do also the various benefits, tangible and intangible, that Christianity offered. The other NRMs offered similar benefits and promises, even if they were not exactly the same as the Christian ones. In general, this is to say that the need in Greco-Roman society that Christianity filled was one that the other NRMs also filled, but not necessarily in the same way.

Second, the other NRMs (with one exception) all lacked something that Christianity possessed or were self-limiting in some way, whereas Christianity, by contrast, rejected the limitations elsewhere imposed; and in retrospect we see that those wants or self-limitations among Christianity's competitors would have been fatal to hopes of triumphing, if indeed the adherents entertained such hopes (and we may suspect that most did not). Thus the Eleusinian mysteries were limited to one locale, the religion of Dionysus and that of the Great Mother lacked moral direction, Mithraism admitted no women, and the religion of Jupiter Dolichenus remained an

Eastern phenomenon with primarily military adherents. Noting those flaws in the other religions, we see that, in the last analysis, the only other NRM that might actually have bested Christianity was the religion of Isis which, like Christianity, avoided the flaws that we have just listed. As we round out this analysis, then, our question really comes to concern what Christianity had that the religion of Isis did not have.[149]

Christianity shared with Mithraism one want that may have hindered its advance, and that was the public displays (mostly processions) that all the other NRMs put on in one way or another. Roger Beck refers to the 'external promotion and self-advertisement through exotic public display in which [in contrast to Mithraism] the Isis cult or the cult of the Magna Mater so effectively engaged'.[150] But this one 'deficiency' that Mithraism and Christianity shared did not stop Christianity's ultimate triumph.

Where Christianity was apparently superior to the other NRMs, *including* the religion of Isis, was in its care for the sick (even if that care was primarily directed towards other Christians), in the status and roles that it granted to women, at least in the first two centuries (and here we must include also the abolishing of infanticide), in its cohesiveness expressed in its forming itself into a transnational civil society, and in its constant adaptability. Even the omnipotent and benevolent Isis did not involve herself to such a degree and with such effect in the realia of her worshippers' lives. Had she done so, who could now say what the final outcome would have been?

When we have understood these things, then we should have no hesitation in affirming that Christianity triumphed because it offered a superior product.

Conclusion

Having examined the evidence, the arguments, and the theories that have occupied us in the body of this work, we need now to conclude by formulating succinctly what we have learned. What were those societal and sociological factors that put the Christian movement, by the year 200, squarely on the road to success?

First Jesus, as a charismatic leader of an NRM, launched a movement of devoted followers, at least some of whom later came to the conviction that the movement should be extended to Gentiles. As the inevitable process of routinization began, however, the leaders of the expansion also donned the mantle of Jesus' charisma, so that as organization developed during the first generation, still there was an extension of charismatic leadership. Paul may be our main example of this transitional stage between charisma and its routinization, but we still have evidence of it as late as the time of the *Didache* with its wandering charismatic prophets/apostles. This ability of Jesus' charismatic leadership to outlive him must have given Christianity a thrust that other NRMs of the day lacked.

Christian martyrdoms and miracles probably did not have much to do with the success of the new religion. However widely miracles and martyrdoms have been cited as causes in the growth of Christianity, the evidence is all against miracles having an evangelistic function, and it is only Christian writers who tell us that Christian martyrdoms increased the number of conversions. This does not mean that the willingness of some Christians to face punishment or death for the faith did not gain the admiration of some pagans. Doubtless it did, and such admiration probably led to some conversions. Martyrdoms may have helped to make Christianity stand out from the field of NRMs in the minds of potential converts and may thus have given it an appeal that its competitor movements lacked. But it was not a major impetus toward Gentile conversion.

The actual elements of such conversion doubtless varied from case to case. Rambo's comprehensive model has given us the conceptual framework for contemplating what those elements may have been, but our sources are woefully lacking in details. If we conclude, however, that Christianity excelled at modes of encapsulating new converts—at instructing them; at providing roles, including leadership roles, for them in the new religion; at creating significant relationships within the movement that were absent in the larger society; and at fostering commitments to the movement and to one another—we will surely be close to the truth.

Christianity's success at conversion techniques provided the basis for its ultimate triumph; but some of its practices and social structure also contributed to that success. Chief among these were the unique status of women in Christianity and Christian care for the sick during epidemics. These did much more to increase the number of adherents to Christianity than did martyrdoms. And the fact that, in caring for the sick as well as in meeting other kinds of material needs, Christianity created a transnational civil society gave the religion a social role that no other religious movement of the day approached. When we add to these advantages Christianity's exclusiveness and concomitant greater demands, and also its ready and consistent adaptability, we have a recipe for success.

Finally, we should briefly address the role of Christian theology in the new movement's expansion and triumph. Just as it has been normal to propose that Jesus' message attracted followers, so it has been normal to propose that the Christian kerygma did the same after Jesus' time. We began with Harnack's affirmation of just that. Now on the one hand, there can be no doubt that the Christian proclamation, in whatever form it was presented, was attractive to many, but our problem

here is that we do not know what proclamation we are discussing; for there was not just one. Nowhere has Christianity
been more adaptive—not only in antiquity but throughout its
long history—than in its 'message'. Surely those Christians who
were influential in bringing others in their networks to the new
faith explained that faith in ways that were effective; but we
do not know, in most cases, what they said. Most may have
spoken of Christ's resurrection from the dead, but we cannot
prove that. For Justin and Tatian, the crucial arguments seem to
have been those from the truth of prophecy. Yet even for Paul
we have only the hints that he has given us in his letters, and we
have to recognize that the references that he makes in scattered
places to his earlier preaching are at best incomplete and are
perhaps coloured by the demands of the situations that called
the letters forth.

Nevertheless, we can see the effects of Christian teaching in
the movement's organization and activities, and we can reasonably conclude something about preaching/teaching from those
activities. In Christianity's creation of a transnational civil
society and in the devotion of its leaders to the movement, do
we not see the working out of, however disparate individuals
may have formulated it, one of Jesus' most famous commands:
Love God with all your mind, life, and might; and love your
fellow human beings as yourself? As early Christianity engaged
in those activities that helped to ensure its triumph, it was
attempting to put into effect, so it would seem, some understanding of that command, however distantly related to any
specific activity the command may have been.

So theology certainly played its role in Christianity's triumph; but it hardly explains the triumph (especially since we
know almost nothing of the theology of the Isis religion).
Christian activity and social formation were the primary
factors.

In the context of these reflections, it is instructive to return
here at the end to some comments of Harnack's at the very end
of his *Mission and Expansion of Christianity*, just as we began
with some of his comments at the beginning of that work.

Regarding the causes of Christianity's ultimate dominance in the Roman world, Harnack wrote that

> it baffles us to determine the relative amount of impetus lent by each of the forces which characterized Christianity. We cannot ascertain, *e.g.*, how much was due to its spiritual monotheism, to its preaching of Jesus Christ, to its consciousness of redemption and its hope of immortality, to its active charity and system of social aid, to its discipline and organization, to its syncretistic capacity and contour, or to the skill which it showed during the third century in surpassing the fascinations of any contemporary superstition.[1]

Harnack's list of the factors contributing to Christianity's ultimate success is hardly the same that we have developed here (although there some similarities), but his point remains valid. The triumph of Christianity was the result of a number of factors, but the whole seems to have been greater than the sum of the parts, and it retains an element of the elusive, perhaps we should say of the mysterious. We may perhaps let the matter rest there.

Works Consulted

A *Greek-English Lexicon*, compiled by Henry George Liddell and Robert Scott. Rev. and augmented by Sir Henry Stuart Jones, with the assistance of Roderick McKenzie et al. New ed., Oxford: Clarendon Press 1940, with a revised supplement 1996

Allison, Dale C., *Jesus of Nazareth. Millenarian Prophet*, Minneapolis: Fortress Press 1998

Baab, O. J. 'Marriage', *IDB* 3, 278–87

Babcock, William S., 'MacMullen on Conversion: A Response', *SecCent* 5, 1985–86, 82–9

Bainbridge, William Sims, *Satan's Power. A Deviant Psychotherapy Cult*, Berkeley, Los Angeles and London: University of California Press 1978

— 'The Sociology of Conversion', in *Handbook of Religious Conversion*, ed. H. Newton Malony and Samuel Southard, Birmingham, AL: Religious Education Press 1992, 178–91

Barclay, John M. G., *Jews in the Mediterranean Diaspora from Alexander to Trajan (323 BCE–117 CE)*, Edinburgh: T. & T. Clark 1996

Barker, Eileen, 'Charismatization: The Social Production of "an Ethos Propitious to the Mobilisation of Sentiments"', in *Secularization, Rationalism, and Sectarianism. Essays in Honour of Bryan R. Wilson*, ed. Eileen Barker, James A. Beckford and Karel Dobbelaere, Oxford: Clarendon Press 1993, 181–201

Baron, Salo Wittmayer, *A Social and Religious History of the Jews*, Vol. 2, New York: Columbia University Press ²1952

Barrett, C. K., *A Commentary on the First Epistle to the Corinthians*, London: A. & C. Black and New York: Harper & Row 1968

Beard, Mary, John North and Simon Price (eds), *Religions of Rome*, Vol. 1, *A History*; Vol. 2, *A Sourcebook*, Cambridge: Cambridge University Press 1998

Beck, Roger, 'The Mysteries of Mithras', in *Voluntary Associations in the Graeco-Roman World*, ed. John S. Kloppenborg and Stephen G. Wilson, London and New York: Routledge 1996, 176–85

Benko, Stephen, *Pagan Rome and the Early Christians*, Bloomington:

Indiana University Press 1984

Berger, Peter L., 'Charisma and Religious Innovation. The Social Location of Israelite Prophecy', *ASR* 28, 1963, 940–50

— and Thomas Luckmann, *The Social Construction of Reality. A Treatise in the Sociology of Knowledge*, Garden City, NY: Doubleday 1966

Betz, Hans Dieter, *Galatians. A Commentary on Paul's Letter to the Churches in Galatia*, Hermeneia, Philadelphia: Fortress Press 1979

Blasi, Anthony J., *Early Christianity as a Social Movement*, Toronto Studies in Religion 5, New York, etc.: Peter Lang 1988

Bornkamm, Günther, *Jesus of Nazareth*, trans. Irene and Fraser McLuskey with James M. Robinson, London: Hodder and Stoughton 1960

Brown, Peter, *The World of Late Antiquity AD 150–750*, History of European Civilization Library, New York: Harcourt Brace Jovanovich 1971

Bultmann, Rudolf, *The History of the Synoptic Tradition*, trans. J. Marsh, Oxford: Blackwell and New York: Harper & Row ²1968

— *Theology of the New Testament*, 2 vols, trans. Kendrick Grobel, New York: Charles Scribner's Sons and London: SCM Press 1952, 1955

Burkert, Walter, *Ancient Mystery Cults*, Cambridge, MA, and London: Harvard University Press 1987

Cardman, Francine, 'Women, Ministry, and Church Order in Early Christianity', in *Women & Christian Origins*, ed. Ross Shepard Kraemer and Mary Rose D'Angelo, New York and Oxford: Oxford University Press 1999, 300–29

Case, S. J., 'The Art of Healing in Early Christian Times', *JR* 3, 1923, 238–58

— 'The Acceptance of Christianity by the Roman Emperors', in *Papers of the American Society of Church History*, New York: G. P. Putnam's Sons 1928, 45–64

Clinton, Kevin, *Myth and Cult. The Iconography of the Eleusinian Mysteries*, The Martin P. Nilsson Lectures on Greek Religion, 1990, Skrifter utgivna av Svenska Institutet i Athen, 8°, 11, Stockholm: Paul Åström 1992

Cohen, Shaye J. D., 'Crossing the Boundary and Becoming a Jew', *HTR* 82, 1989, 13–33

— *From the Maccabees to the Mishnah*, Library of Early Christianity, Philadelphia: Westminster Press 1987

Colwell, Ernest Cadman, 'Popular Reactions against Christianity in the Roman Empire', in *Environmental Factors in Christian History*, ed. John Thomas McNeill, Matthew Spinka and Harold R. Willoughby

[S. J. Case Festschrift], Chicago: University of Chicago Press 1939, 53–71

Countryman, L. W., *The Rich Christian in the Church of the Early Empire: Contradictions and Accommodations*, New York and Toronto: The Edwin Mellen Press 1980

Crossan, John Dominic, *The Historical Jesus. The Life of a Mediterranean Jewish Peasant*, San Francisco: HarperSanFrancisco 1991

Cumont, Franz, *The Oriental Religions in Roman Paganism*, with an Introductory Essay by Grant Showerman, New York: Dover Publications 1956

Davidman, Lynn, 'Accommodation and Resistance to Modernity: A Comparison of Two Contemporary Orthodox Jewish Groups', *SA* 51, 1990, 35–51

Dawson, Lorne L., *Comprehending Cults. The Sociology of New Religious Movements*, Toronto, Oxford, New York: Oxford University Press 1993

Dibelius, Martin, *From Tradition to Gospel*, Cambridge: James Clarke and Greenwood, SC: Attic 1971

— *Jesus*, trans. Charles B. Hedrick and Frederick C. Grant, Philadelphia: Westminster Press 1949

Dodds, E. R., *Pagan and Christian in an Age of Anxiety. Some Aspects of Religious Experience from Marcus Aurelius to Constantine*, The Norton Library, New York: W. W. Norton & Company 1965

Edelstein, Emma J., and Ludwig Edelstein, *Asclepius. Collection and Interpretation of the Testimonies*, with a New Introduction by Gary B. Ferngren, Baltimore and London: The Johns Hopkins University Press 1945, 1998

Elliott, J. K. (ed.), *The Apocryphal New Testament. A Collection of Apocryphal Christian Literature in an English Translation*, Oxford: Clarendon Press 1993

Finn, Thomas M., *From Death to Rebirth. Ritual and Conversion in Antiquity*, New York and Mahwah, NJ: Paulist Press 1997

Fredriksen, Paula, 'What You See Is What You Get: Context and Content in Current Research on the Historical Jesus', *Theology Today* 52, 1995, 75–97

— *From Jesus to Christ. The Origins of the New Testament Images of Jesus*, New Haven and London: Yale University Press 1988

Gager, John G., 'Proselytism and Exclusivity in Early Christianity', in *Pushing the Faith. Proselytism and Civility in a Pluralistic World*, ed. Martin E. Marty and Frederick E. Greenspahn, New York: Crossroad 1988, 67–77, 179–80

— 'The Gospels and Jesus: Some Doubts about Method', *JR* 54, 1974, 244–72

— *Kingdom and Community. The Social World of Early Christianity*, Prentice-Hall Studies in Religion, Englewood Cliffs, NJ: Prentice-Hall 1975

Gallagher, Eugene V., 'Conversion and Salvation in the Apocryphal Acts of the Apostles', *SecCent* 8, 1991, 13–29

Gamble, Harry Y., *Books and Readers in the Early Church: A History of Early Christian Texts*, New Haven and London: Yale University Press 1995

Garrett, William R., 'Maligned Mysticism: The Maledicted Career of Troeltsch's Third Type', *SA* 36, 1975, 205–23

Gaventa, Beverly Roberts, 'Conversion in the Bible', in *Handbook of Religious Conversion* (see Bainbridge), 41–54

— *From Darkness to Light. Aspects of Conversion in the New Testament*, OBT 20, Philadelphia: Fortress Press 1986

Goodman, Martin, *Mission and Conversion. Proselytizing in the Religious History of the Roman Empire*, Oxford: Clarendon Press 1994

Gordon, James S., *The Golden Guru. The Strange Journey of Bhagwan Shree Rajneesh*, Lexington, MA: The Stephen Greene Press 1987

Gordon, R. L., 'Mithraism and Roman Society: Social Factors in the Explanation of Religious Change in the Roman Empire', *Religion* 2, 1972, 92–121

Grant, Robert M., *Augustus to Constantine. The Rise and Triumph of Christianity in the Roman World*, San Francisco, etc.: Harper & Row 1970

— *Early Christianity and Society. Seven Studies*, San Francisco etc.: Harper & Row 1977

Green, William Scott, 'Palestinian Holy Men. Charismatic Leadership and Rabbinic Tradition', *ANRW* 2.19.2, 1979, 619–47

Greil, Arthur L., 'Previous Dispositions and Conversion to Perspectives of Social and Religious Movements', *SA* 38, 1977, 115–25

Haenchen, Ernst, *The Acts of the Apostles. A Commentary*, trans. B. Noble et al., Oxford: Blackwell and Philadelphia: Westminster Press 1971

Hare, Douglas R. A., *The Son of Man Tradition*, Minneapolis: Fortress Press 1990

Harnack, Adolf, *The Mission and Expansion of Christianity in the First Three Centuries* [= Vol. 1.], trans. and ed. James Moffatt, Harper Torchbooks, The Cloister Library, reissued New York: Harper & Brothers 1961

— *The Mission and Expansion of Christianity in the First Three*

Centuries, Vol. 2, trans. and ed. James Moffatt, London: Williams and Norgate and New York: G. P. Putnam's Sons 1908

Hengel, Martin, *The Charismatic Leader and His Followers*, trans. James C. G. Greig, ed. John Riches, Edinburgh: T. & T. Clark 1996

Hilhorst, A., 'The Apocryphal Acts as Martyrdom Texts: The Case of the Acts of Andrew', in *The Apocryphal Acts of John*, ed. Jan N. Bremmer, Kampen: Kok Pharos 1995, 1–14

Horsley, Richard A., *Jesus and the Spiral of Violence. Popular Jewish Resistance in Roman Palestine*, San Francisco, etc.: Harper & Row 1987

— and John S. Hanson, *Bandits, Prophets, and Messiahs. Popular Movements in the Time of Jesus*, New Voices in Biblical Studies, Minneapolis, etc.: Winston Press (A Seabury Book) 1985

Jeremias, Joachim, *New Testament Theology. The Proclamation of Jesus*, London: SCM Press and New York: Charles Scribner's Sons 1971

Joshi, Vasant (Swami Satya Vedant), *The Awakened One. The Life and Work of Bhagwan Shree Rajneesh*, San Francisco, etc.: Harper & Row 1982

Kane, Ousmane, 'Muslim Missionaries and African States', in *Transnational Religion and Fading States*, ed. Susanne Hoeber Rudolph and James Piscatori, Boulder, CO: Westview Press 1997, 47–62

Kollmann, Bernd, *Jesus und die Christen als Wundertäter. Studien zu Magie, Medizin und Schamanismus in Antike und Christentum*, FRLANT 170, Göttingen: Vandenhoeck & Ruprecht 1996

Kraabel, A. T., 'The Disappearance of the "God-Fearers"', *Numen* 23, 1981, 113–26

Kraemer, Ross S., 'Jewish Women and Christian Origins: Some Caveats', in *Women & Christian Origins* (see Cardman), 35–49

Lampe, Peter, *Die stadtrömischen Christen in den ersten beiden Jahrhunderten*, WUNT 2. Reihe 18, J. C. B. Mohr (Paul Siebeck): Tübingen 1987

Lane Fox, Robin, *Pagans and Christians*, London: Viking and San Francisco: HarperSanFrancisco 1988

Liebeschuetz, Wolf, 'The Expansion of Mithraism among the Religious Cults of the Second Century', in *Studies in Mithraism. Papers associated with the Mithraic Panel organized on the occasion of the XVIth Congress of the International Association for the History of Religions, Rome 1990*, ed. John R. Hinnells, Rome: "L'Erma" di Bretschneider 1994, 195–216

Lieu, Judith M., 'The "Attraction of Women" in/to Early Judaism and

Christianity: Gender and the Politics of Conversion', *JSNT* 72, 1998, 5–22

Lindholm, Charles, *Charisma*, Cambridge, MA and Oxford: Blackwell 1990

Lofland, John, and Norman Skonovd, 'Conversion Motifs', *JSSR* 20, 1981, 373–85

— 'Patterns of Conversion', in *New Religious Movements: A Perspective for Understanding Society*, ed. Eileen Barker, Studies in Religion and Society 3, New York and Toronto: The Edwin Mellen Press 1982, 1–24

Long, Theodore E., 'Prophecy, Charisma, and Politics: Reinterpreting the Weberian Thesis', in *Prophetic Religions and Politics. Religion and the Political Order*, Vol. 1, ed. Jeffrey K. Hadden and Anson Shupe, A New ERA Book, New York: Paragon House 1986, 3–17

MacDonald, Dennis Ronald, *The Acts of Andrew and The Acts of Andrew and Matthias in the City of the Cannibals*, SBLTT 33, Christian Apocrypha Series 1, Atlanta: Scholars Press 1990

MacDonald, Margaret Y., *Early Christian Women and Pagan Opinion. The Power of the Hysterical Woman*, Cambridge: Cambridge University Press 1996

MacLennan, R. S., and A. T. Kraabel., 'The God-Fearers – A Literary and Theological Invention'. *BAR* 12, 5, September/October 1986, 47–53; reprinted in *Diaspora Jews and Judaism. Essays in Honor of, and in Dialogue with, A. Thomas Kraabel*, ed. J. Andrew Overman and Robert S. MacLennan, South Florida Studies in the History of Judaism 41, Atlanta: Scholars Press 1992, 131–43

MacMullen, Ramsay, *Christianizing the Roman Empire (A. D. 100–400)*, New Haven and London: Yale University Press 1984

— *Paganism in the Roman Empire*, New Haven and London: Yale University Press 1981

Maier, Harry O., Review of *The Rise of Christianity. A Sociologist Reconsiders History*, by Rodney Stark, *JTS* 49, 1998, 328–35

Malina, Bruce J., 'Jesus as Charismatic Leader?' *BTB* 14, 1984, 55–62

Malony, H. Newton, 'The Psychology of Proselytism', in *Pushing the Faith* (see Gager), 125–42, 184–6

Mann, Ted, 'The Crazies – Who Follows Rajneesh and Why', in *The Rajneesh Papers. Studies in a New Religious Movement*, ed. Susan J. Palmer and Arvind Sharma, Delhi: Motilal Banarsidass Publishers Private Limited 1993, 17–45

McCasland, S. Vernon, 'Religious Healing in First-Century Palestine', in *Environmental Factors in Christian History* (see Colwell), 18–34

Meeks, Wayne A., *The First Urban Christians. The Social World of the Apostle Paul*, New Haven and London: Yale University Press 1983

Mehta, Uday, *Modern Godmen in India. A Sociological Appraisal*, Role of Religion in Indian Society Series: Exploratory Studies, Bombay: Popular Prakashan 1993

Meier, John P., 'Jesus in Josephus: A Modest Proposal', *CBQ* 52, 1990, 76–103

— *A Marginal Jew. Rethinking the Historical Jesus*, Vol. 1, *The Roots of the Problem and the Person*, Vol. 2, *Mentor, Message, and Miracles*, Anchor Bible Reference Library, New York, etc.: Doubleday 1991–1994

Meyer, Ben F., 'Jesus: Jesus Christ', *ABD* 3, 773–96

— *The Aims of Jesus*, London: SCM Press 1979

Milne, Hugh, *Bhagwan. The God That Failed*, New York: St Martin's Press 1986

Misset-van de Weg, Magda, '"For the Lord Always Takes Care of His Own". The Purpose of the Wondrous Works and Deeds in the *Acts of Peter*', in *The Apocryphal Acts of Peter. Magic, Miracles and Gnosticism*, ed. Jan N. Bremmer, Studies on the Apocryphal Acts of the Apostles, Leuven: Peeters 1998, 97–110

Nock, A. D., *Conversion. The Old and the New in Religion from Alexander the Great to Augustine of Hippo*, Oxford: Clarendon Press 1933

— 'The Genius of Mithraism', *JRS* 27, 1937, 108–13

— *Early Gentile Christianity and Its Hellenistic Background*, Harper Torchbooks, The Cloister Library, New York, Evanston and London: Harper & Row 1964

Oakes, Len, *Prophetic Charisma. The Psychology of Revolutionary Religious Personalities*, Syracuse, NY: Syracuse University Press 1997

Oborn, George Thomas, 'Economic Factors in the Persecutions of the Christians to A. D. 260', in *Environmental Factors in Christian History* (see Colwell), 131–48

Palmer, Susan J., 'Charisma and Abdication: A Study of the Leadership of Bhagwan Shree Rajneesh', *SA* 49, 1988, 119–35

Pao, David W., 'Physical and Spiritual Restoration: The Role of Healing Miracles in the *Acts of Andrew*', in *The Apocryphal Acts of the Apostles. Harvard Divinity School Studies*, ed. François Bovon, Ann Graham Brock and Christopher R. Matthews, Religions of the World, Cambridge, MA: Harvard University Press 1999, 259–80

Parsons, Talcott, *The Structure of Social Action. A Study in Social Theory with Special Reference to a Group of Recent European Writers*, New York: The Free Press of Glencoe ²1949

Perrin, Norman, *Rediscovering the Teaching of Jesus*, London: SCM Press and New York: Harper & Row 1967
— *The Kingdom of God in the Teaching of Jesus*, New Testament Library, London: SCM Press 1963
Prieur, Jean-Marc, *Acta Andreae. Praefatio–Commentarius* (=Vol. 1); *Textus* (=Vol. 2), Corpus Christianorum, Series Apocryphorum 5, 6, Brepols: Turnhout 1989

Quasten, Johannes, *Patrology*, Vol. 1, *The Beginnings of Patristic Literature*, Westminster, MD: Christian Classics, Inc. 1986

Rambo, Lewis R., 'The Psychology of Conversion', in *Handbook of Religious Conversion* (see Bainbridge), 159–77
— *Understanding Religious Conversion*, New Haven and London: Yale University Press 1993
Rengstorf, Karl Heinrich, 'μανθάνω, κτλ.', *TDNT* 4, 1967, 390–461
Reumann, John, 'Jesus and Christology', in *The New Testament and Its Modern Interpreters*, ed. Eldon Jay Epp and George W. MacRae, The Bible and Its Modern Interpreters 3, Philadelphia: Fortress Press; Atlanta: Scholars Press 1989, 501–64
Richardson, James T., 'Conversion Process in the New Religions', in *Handbook of Religious Conversion* (see Bainbridge), 78–89
Richardson, James T., and Mary Stewart, 'Conversion Process Models and the Jesus Movement', *American Behavioral Scientist* 20, 1977, 819–38
Robbins, Thomas, *Cults, Converts and Charisma: The Sociology of New Religious Movements*, London, etc.: SAGE Publications 1988
Robertson, Archibald and Alfred Plummer, *A Critical and Exegetical Commentary on the First Epistle of St Paul to the Corinthians*, ICC, Edinburgh: T. & T. Clark ²1914
Rudolph, Susanne Hoeber, 'Introduction: Religion, States, and Transnational Civil Society', in *Transnational Religion and Fading States* (see Kane), 1–24
— and James Piscatori, 'Preface', in *Transnational Religion and Fading States* (see Kane), vii–viii

Saldarini, Anthony J., *Matthew's Christian-Jewish Community*, Chicago Studies in the History of Judaism, Chicago and London: University of Chicago Press 1994
Sanders, E. P., *Jesus and Judaism*, London: SCM Press and Philadelphia: Fortress Press 1985
— *Judaism. Practice and Belief 63 BCE–66 CE*, London: SCM Press and Philadelphia: Trinity Press International 1992

— *The Historical Figure of Jesus*, London, etc.: Allen Lane, The Penguin Press 1993

Sanders, Jack T., 'Paul between Jews and Gentiles in Corinth', *JSNT* 65, 1997, 67–83

— *Ethics in the New Testament. Change and Development*, London: SCM Press 1986

— *Schismatics, Sectarians, Dissidents, Deviants. The First One Hundred Years of Jewish-Christian Relations*, London: SCM Press and Valley Forge, PA: Trinity Press International 1993

— *The Jews in Luke-Acts*, London: SCM Press and Philadelphia: Fortress Press 1987

Schäferdiek, Knut, 'The Acts of John', in Schneemelcher-Wilson, *New Testament Apocrypha* (q.v.), Vol. 2, 152–209

Schneemelcher, Wilhelm and R. McL. Wilson, *New Testament Apocrypha, Vol.1, Gospels and Related Writings; Vol.2, Writings related to the Apostles, Apocalypses and Related Subjects*, revised edition, Louisville, KY: Westminster John Knox Press and Cambridge: James Clarke 1991, 1992

Schwarz, Hillel, 'Millenarianism', in *Encyclopedia of Religion*, ed. Mircea Eliade, 1987, vol. 9, 521–32

Schweitzer, Albert, *The Quest of the Historical Jesus. A Critical Study of Its Progress from Reimarus to Wrede*, London: A. & C. Black ³1954

Schweizer, Eduard, *Lordship and Discipleship*, SBT, London: SCM Press 1960

Smallwood, E. Mary, *The Jews under Roman Rule. From Pompey to Diocletian. A Study in Political Relations*, SJLA 20, Leiden: Brill 1976

Smith, Jonathan Z., *Drudgery Divine. On the Comparison of Early Christianities and the Religions of Late Antiquity. Jordan Lectures in Comparative Religion, XIV, School of Oriental and African Studies, University of London*, Chicago: University of Chicago Press 1990

Snow, David A., *Shakubuku. A Study of the Nichiren Shoshu Buddhist Movement in America, 1960–1975*, Cults and Nonconventional Religious Groups, New York and London: Garland Publishing, Inc. 1993

Snow, David A., Louis A. Zurcher, Jr and Sheldon Ekland-Olson, 'Social Networks and Social Movements: A Microstructural Approach to Differential Recruitment', *ASR* 45, 1980, 787–801

Spencer, Martin E., 'What Is Charisma?' *BJS* 24, 1973, 341–54

Stambaugh, John E., 'Greco-Roman Cities', *ABD* 1, 1043–48

— *The Ancient Roman City*, Ancient Society and History, Baltimore and London: Johns Hopkins University Press 1988

Stark, Rodney, 'How New Religions Succeed: A Theoretical Model', in *The Future of New Religious Movements*, ed. David G. Bromley and

Phillip E. Hammond, Macon, GA: Mercer University Press 1987, 11–29

— 'Jewish Conversion and the Rise of Christianity: Rethinking the Received Wisdom', in *Society of Biblical Literature 1986 Seminar Papers*, ed. Kent Harold Richards, SBLSP 25, Atlanta: Scholars Press 1986, 314–29

— *The Rise of Christianity. A Sociologist Reconsiders History*, Princeton: Princeton University Press 1996

— 'A Theory of Revelations', *JSSR* 38, 1999, 287–308

— and William Sims Bainbridge, 'Networks of Faith: Interpersonal Bonds and Recruitment to Cults and Sects', *AJS* 85, 1980, 1376–95

— *A Theory of Religion*, Toronto Studies in Religion 2, New York, etc.: Peter Lang 1987

Strelley, Kate, with Robert D. San Souci, *The Ultimate Game. The Rise and Fall of Bhagwan Shree Rajneesh*, San Francisco, etc.: Harper & Row 1987

Torjesen, Karen Jo, *When Women Were Priests. Women's Leadership in the Early Church and the Scandal of Their Subordination in the Rise of Christianity*, New York: HarperSanFrancisco 1995

Toth, Michael A., *The Theory of the Two Charismas*, Washington, DC: University Press of America 1981

Travisano, Richard V., 'Alternation and Conversion as Qualitatively Different Transformations', in *Social Psychology through Symbolic Interaction*, ed. Gregory P. Stone and Harvey A. Farberman, Waltham, MA and Toronto: Xerox College Publishing 1970, 594–606

Tucker, Robert C., 'The Theory of Charismatic Leadership', *Daedalus* 97, 1968, 731–56

Vermaseren, M. J., *Corpus inscriptionem et monumentorum religionis Mithriacae*, Vol. 2, The Hague: Martinus Nijhoff 1960

— and C. C. van Essen, *The Excavations in the Mithraeum of the Church of Santa Prisca in Rome*, Leiden: E. J. Brill 1965

Vermes, Geza, *Jesus the Jew. A Historian's Reading of the Gospels*, London: SCM Press and Philadelphia: Fortress Press 1973

— *The Religion of Jesus the Jew*, London: SCM Press and Minneapolis: Fortress Press 1993

Wallis, Roy, 'Charisma and Explanation', in *Secularization, Rationalism, and Sectarianism* (see Barker), 167–79

— 'Charisma, Commitment and Control in a New Religious Movement', in *Millennialism and Charisma*, ed. Wallis, Belfast: The Queen's University 1982, 73–140

— 'Religion as Fun? The Rajneesh Movement', in *Sociological Theory, Religion and Collective Action* (see Wallis and Bruce), 191–224

— 'The Social Construction of Charisma', in *Sociological Theory, Religion and Collective Action* (see Wallis and Bruce), 129–54

— *The Elementary Forms of the New Religious Life*, International Library of Sociology, London, etc.: Routledge & Kegan Paul 1984

— with Steve Bruce, 'Charisma, Tradition, Paisley and the Prophets', in *Sociological Theory, Religion and Collective Action*, by Wallis and Bruce, Belfast: The Queen's University 1986, 83–113

Weber, Max, *Economy and Society. An Outline of Interpretive Sociology*, 3 vols., ed. Guenther Roth and Claus Wittich, trans. E. Fischoff et al., New York: Bedminster Press 1968

Weder, Hans, 'Disciple, Discipleship', trans. Dennis Martin, *ABD* 2, 207–10

White, L. Michael, 'Adolf Harnack and the "Expansion" of Early Christianity: A Reappraisal of Social History', *SecCent* 5, 1985/1986, 97–127

— 'Urban Development and Social Change in Imperial Ephesos', in *Ephesos Metropolis of Asia. An Interdisciplinary Approach to Its Archaeology, Religion, and Culture*, ed. Helmut Koester, HTS 41, Valley Forge, PA: Trinity Press International 1995, 27–79

— *Building God's House in the Roman World. Architectural Adaptation among Pagans, Jews, and Christians*, ASOR Library of Biblical and Near Eastern Archaeology, Baltimore and London: The Johns Hopkins University Press for The American Schools of Oriental Research 1990

Wilken, Robert L., *The Christians as the Romans Saw Them*, New Haven and London: Yale University Press 1984

Williams, Michael Allen, *Rethinking 'Gnosticism'. An Argument for Dismantling a Dubious Category*, Princeton: Princeton University Press 1996

Wilson, Bryan R., *The Noble Savages. The Primitive Origins of Charisma and Its Contemporary Survival*, Quantum Books, Berkeley, Los Angeles, London: University of California Press 1975

Notes

Introduction

1. *Mission and Expansion*, 1, 24.
2. *Mission and Expansion*, 1, 22.
3. *Mission and Expansion*, 2, 317–21.
4. *Augustus to Constantine*, 15–20.
5. *Augustus to Constantine*, 20.
6. *Augustus to Constantine*, 284–311.
7. *Augustus to Constantine*, 304.
8. *Augustus to Constantine*, 18 n. 89.
9. For the evidence cf. Cumont, *Oriental Religions*, 149–50; Liebe-schuetz, 'Expansion of Mithraism', 202.
10. *Ancient Mystery Cults*, 3.
11. *Ancient Mystery Cults*, 22.
12. *Ancient Mystery Cults*, 15–23.
13. *Ancient Mystery Cults*, 23.
14. *Ancient Mystery Cults*, 25.
15. *Taurobolium*.
16. *Ancient Mystery Cults*, 28; emphasis mine.
17. *Ancient Mystery Cults*, 29; emphasis mine.
18. 'Demeter' here instead of 'Eleusis' because, while it has long and widely been assumed that the *Homeric Hymn to Demeter* refers to the Eleusinian mysteries, a recent work by Kevin Clinton argues persuasively that the hymn is related rather to the festival of Thesmophoria (*Myth and Cult*).
19. R. L. Gordon ('Mithraism and Roman Society', 96) also observes that 'all the mysteries' except Mithraism 'presented a theodicy which legitimated the present by offering compensation in the after-life'. The notion of some kind of salvation came only late to Mithraism, and only in the West.
20. *Ancient Mystery Cults*, 30–1.
21. *Ancient Mystery Cults*, 32.
22. *Ancient Mystery Cults*, 42.

23. *Ancient Mystery Cults*, 43.
24. *Ancient Mystery Cults*, 109–10; emphasis mine.
25. *Pagan and Christian*, 132–8.
26. Smith, *Drudgery Divine*, 68.
27. Cf. *Drudgery Divine*, 81.
28. *Drudgery Divine*, 142.
29. *Drudgery Divine*, 143.

I Why Did People Follow Jesus?

1. E.g., Bornkamm, *Jesus of Nazareth*, 147.
2. 'Disciple, Discipleship', 208. The translation of Weder's article, however – both here and elsewhere – is mine from the original German that Professor Weder graciously supplied in response to my request when I found the translation printed in the *ABD* confusing.
3. *Historical Figure*, 123.
4. *Jesus*, 58; emphases mine.
5. *From Jesus to Christ*, 99.
6. *Jesus and Judaism*, 174.
7. *Jesus and Judaism*, 207; cf. his extensive discussion of this point in the chapter on 'The Sinners', 174–211.
8. *Jesus and Judaism*, 178–9.
9. For an even more sceptical view of the attempt to understand Jesus, cf. Gager, 'Gospels and Jesus'.
10. Cf. only Bultmann, *Synoptic Tradition*; Dibelius, *From Tradition to Gospel*.
11. 'Proselytism and Exclusivity', 70.
12. 'μανθάνω, κτλ.'
13. 'μανθάνω, κτλ.', 444.
14. 'μανθάνω, κτλ.', 447.
15. *Lordship and Discipleship*, 13.
16. *Lordship and Discipleship*, 14.
17. 'Disciple, Discipleship', 207.
18. *Jesus of Nazareth*, 144–5.
19. *Jesus of Nazareth*, 148.
20. *Historical Figure*, 119.
21. *Historical Figure*, 119–20.
22. 'μανθάνω, κτλ.', 445–6.
23. *Jesus*, 58.
24. Above, p. 12.
25. So Crossan, *Historical Jesus*.
26. *Jesus of Nazareth*, 145–6.
27. The original German publication date of the work that came to be

called *The Charismatic Leader and His Followers* in English translation.

28. *Charismatic Leader*, 3–15.
29. *Charismatic Leader*, 34. Oddly Bruce J. Malina ('Jesus as Charismatic Leader?') has sought to show that, according to Weber's principles, Jesus was *not* a charismatic leader. While Malina refers to Weber, he seems not to have noted that Jesus is one of Weber's main examples for the charisma of authority in *Economy and Society* and that Weber frequently elsewhere refers to Jesus as a charismatic figure.
30. *Charismatic Leader*, 21.
31. *Charismatic Leader*, 25.
32. *Jesus the Jew*, 69–82. Vermes also refers much more briefly to other Galilean holy men.
33. Vermes seems to have been, at least in part, led astray by an article by William Scott Green ('Palestinian Holy Men'), to which he refers in *Religion of Jesus*, 6. In spite of Green's title, however, he does not deal with leadership at all and presents no evidence that Ḥoni was a leader of anything. Cf. further John Meier's criticism (*Marginal Jew*, 2, 624) of using Ḥoni and Ḥanina as comparators.
34. 'Prophecy, Charisma'.
35. 'Prophecy, Charisma', 7.
36. 'Prophecy, Charisma', 11.
37. 'Prophecy, Charisma', 13.
38. *Jesus of Nazareth*.
39. *Jesus of Nazareth*, 131–51.
40. *Jesus of Nazareth*, 81.
41. *Jesus of Nazareth*, 81–94.
42. Cf. esp. *Jesus of Nazareth*, 61–4. Fuller discussion occurs throughout the book.
43. *Jesus of Nazareth*, 215.
44. *Economy and Society*, 1, 215.
45. *Economy and Society*, 1, 241.
46. *Economy and Society*, 1, 243.
47. *Economy and Society*, 1, 245.
48. *Economy and Society*, 1, 244.
49. *Economy and Society*, 2, 439–40.
50. *Economy and Society*, 2, 440.
51. *Economy and Society*, 2, 442.
52. *Economy and Society*, 2, 444.
53. *Economy and Society*, 2, 445.
54. *Economy and Society*, 2, 447.
55. *Economy and Society*, 2, 447.

56. *Economy and Society*, 2, 630.
57. *Economy and Society*, 2, 630–1.
58. *Economy and Society*, 2, 631.
59. *Economy and Society*, 2, 633.
60. *Economy and Society*, 3, 1111.
61. *Economy and Society*, 3, 1113.
62. *Economy and Society*, 3, 1114.
63. *Economy and Society*, 3, 1115. For Charles Lindholm (*Charisma*, 25) these words of Jesus 'are the core of the charismatic relation for Weber'.
64. Garrett, 'Maligned Mysticism', 218.
65. Cf. *Economy and Society*, 2, 444: 'Jesus was not at all interested in social reform as such.'
66. Especially B. R. Wilson, *Noble Savages*. Wilson refers to 'charismatic demand' (78 *et passim*); cf. further, for example, Tucker, 'Theory of Charismatic Leadership', 737–8; and Spencer, 'What Is Charisma?', 347.
67. *Economy and Society*, 2, 631.
68. Quoted in Lindholm, *Charisma*, 32. Lindholm agrees with Durkheim and emphasizes the dangerous side of the tendency, e.g., Hitler.
69. Cf. n. 66.
70. *Prophetic Charisma*, 2.
71. 'Theory of Charismatic Leadership', 738.
72. 'Social Construction', 130.
73. 'Social Construction', 150.
74. 'Charisma and Explanation', 177.
75. 'Theory of Charismatic Leadership', 737; emphasis mine.
76. *Noble Savages*, 94.
77. 'Theory of Charismatic Leadership', 742.
78. 'Theory of Charismatic Leadership', 743.
79. 'Theory of Charismatic Leadership', 749.
80. I owe the wording of the axiom to my colleague and mystagogue into the field of sociology of religion, Marion S. Goldman.
81. 'Charismatization', 183; emphasis mine.
82. In addition to his article cited above, cf. also 'Charisma and Explanation', 'Charisma, Commitment and Control', and 'Social Construction'.
83. 'Charisma, Commitment and Control', 93.
84. Routinization is, according to Weber, the normal pattern of development after the period of the prophet's leadership of an NRM. After Jesus there was the Apostolic Council.
85. 'Charisma, Commitment and Control', 121.

86. 'Charisma, Commitment and Control', 134.
87. 'Charisma, Tradition', 107.
88. 'Charisma, Tradition', 107. Peter L. Berger has also made the same point about the prophets; cf. his 'Charisma and Religious Innovation'.
89. *Theory of the Two Charismas*, 4.
90. 'Theory of Charismatic Leadership', 746.
91. Cf. also Malony, 'Psychology of Proselytism'.
92. *Prophetic Charisma*, 21–3.
93. *Prophetic Charisma*, 1–2.
94. *Charismatic Leader*, 67–71.
95. Cf. esp. E. P. Sanders, *Jesus and Judaism*, 319–20.
96. Cf. Joshi, *The Awakened One*, 112.
97. J. S. Gordon, *Golden Guru*, 24.
98. Cf. Mehta, *Modern Godmen*, 82–3.
99. Milne, *Bhagwan*, 16.
100. *Bhagwan*, 16.
101. Bultmann, *Synoptic Tradition*, 247: a legend.
102. *Marginal Jew*, 2, 101.
103. *Marginal Jew*, 2, 129.
104. *Synoptic Tradition*, 253.
105. *Marginal Jew*, 272–3.
106. *Rediscovering*, 107.
107. *Rediscovering*, 152.
108. *Rediscovering*, 205.
109. *Theology*, 67–8.
110. *Theology*, 244–5.
111. *Theology*, 247.
112. *Theology*, 248.
113. *Theology*, 275–6.
114. *Jesus the Jew*, esp. 18–82. Cf. also the previous discussion of the effectiveness of using Jewish 'charismatics' contemporary with Jesus as comparators for the purpose of understanding him.
115. *Jesus the Jew*, 83–212.
116. *Religion of Jesus*, 206–7.
117. *Jesus and Judaism*, 91.
118. *Jesus and Judaism*, 61–76.
119. *Jesus and Judaism*, 210.
120. *Jesus and Judaism*, 156.
121. *Historical Jesus*, xii.
122. *Aims of Jesus*, 122.
123. 'Jesus: Jesus Christ', 778.
124. *Aims of Jesus*, 127. Cf. also the judgment of E. P. Sanders about this

verse (*Jesus and Judaism*, 93): 'If it is true that Matt. 11.11 gives
Jesus' estimate of John, then we may conclude that he saw his own
work as being of final significance.'

125. *Jesus of Nazareth*, 50.

126. *Marginal Jew*, 122.

127. *Marginal Jew*, 144.

128. *Jesus of Nazareth*, 67.

129. Meier had earlier, in 'Jesus in Josephus', argued persuasively for the
genuineness of the bulk of this passage.

130. *Marginal Jew*, 621–2. On Jesus' uniqueness as a healer, which we
should by no means question, however we may wish to explain the
healings, cf. Kollmann, *Jesus und die Christen als Wundertäter*.

131. *Bhagwan*, 25.

132. *Bhagwan*, 71; emphasis mine.

133. *Bhagwan*, 179.

134. Barker, 'Charismatization', 194.

135. Barker, 'Charismatization', 193.

136. J. S. Gordon, *Golden Guru*, 68–70.

137. *Golden Guru*, 68.

138. *Golden Guru*, 70.

139. Wallis, 'Religion as Fun?' 191–4, gives a good summary of those
aspects of Rajneesh's teachings that appealed to the Western seekers
who responded to him in such numbers.

140. J. S. Gordon, *Golden Guru*, 59.

141. *Golden Guru*, 234–6.

142. J. S. Gordon, *Golden Guru*, 129–32.

143. J. S. Gordon, *Golden Guru*, 38.

144. Quoted in J. S. Gordon, *Golden Guru*, 38.

145. J. S. Gordon, *Golden Guru*, 163.

146. Quoted in J. S. Gordon, *Golden Guru*, 163.

147. 'Charisma and Abdication', 129.

148. 'Charisma and Abdication', 124–32.

149. See p. 26.

150. 'Charisma and Abdication', 125.

151. Palmer's point is different. She distinguishes between the performance and the responsibility of charismatic leadership ('Charisma and
Abdication', 134–5) and argues that Bhagwan was by temperament
unable to shoulder the second aspect. Thus not only did he abdicate
his position at the end, but he had abdicated responsibility all along.
In her opinion, it is not possible to make a hard distinction between
charisma and institutionalization.

152. On this point cf. J. S. Gordon, *Golden Guru*, 130–1. J. S. Gordon
judges that the fiscal motive was not a part of the decision to pro-

claim a new religion.

153. 'Jesus and Christology', 510–11.
154. Reumann, 'Jesus and Christology', 511.
155. Cf. Reumann, 'Jesus and Christology', 512.
156. *Son of Man Tradition*, 258.
157. *Theology*, 1, 26.
158. *Historical Figure*, 242.
159. *Historical Figure*, 248.
160. *Synoptic Tradition*, 262.
161. *Quest*, 387.
162. E. P. Sanders offers distinctive explanations of both. While Jesus did not claim to be Messiah, his implicit self-understanding, seen especially in his statement that the disciples would judge the twelve tribes of Israel (*Jesus and Judaism*, 98–104), is even higher: 'viceroy-to-be' (*Jesus and Judaism*, 240); and the triumphal entry into Jerusalem was triumphal only for Jesus and his followers, to whom he had explained the symbolism in advance (*Jesus and Judaism*, 306–8). Thus Sanders strikes a middle ground between authenticity and inauthenticity on the two matters that we are discussing.
163. *Jesus and Judaism*, 61–76.
164. So E. P. Sanders, *Jesus and Judaism*, 301–2.
165. J. S. Gordon, *Golden Guru*, 27.
166. J. S. Gordon, *Golden Guru*, 29.
167. J. S. Gordon, *Golden Guru*, 29.
168. *Golden Guru*, 19.
169. *Bhagwan*, 65.
170. Cf. p. 12.
171. Cf. above, p. 49.
172. *Bandits, Prophets*, 56 *et passim*.
173. *Bandits, Prophets*, 57.
174. *Bandits, Prophets*, 61.
175. *Bandits, Prophets*, 61.
176. *Spiral of Violence*, 11 (emphasis mine).
177. *Spiral of Violence*, 51.
178. *Historical Figure*, 28.
179. *Historical Figure*, 21.
180. *Historical Figure*, 26. E. P. Sanders has elsewhere argued at considerable length for the general integrity of the priesthood and the people's respect for the priests; cf. *Judaism*, 77–92.
181. *Spiral of Violence*, 44.
182. *Bandits, Prophets*, 58.
183. *Historical Figure*, 19.
184. *Historical Figure*, 21.

185. *From the Maccabees to the Mishna*, 29.
186. Cf. above, p. 28.
187. *Awakened One*, 90.
188. *Ultimate Game*, 106; emphasis mine.
189. *Bhagwan*, 65.
190. *Bhagwan*, 108.
191. J. S. Gordon, *Golden Guru*, 58; emphasis mine.
192. Paula Fredriksen, 'What You See', 96.
193. Above, p. 34.
194. *Synoptic Tradition*, 164.
195. *From Tradition to Gospel*, 244.
196. *Five Gospels*, 178.
197. *Jesus and Judaism*, 92.
198. *Theology*, 82–3.
199. *Theology*, 30.
200. *Jesus the Jew*, 32–3.
201. *Historical Jesus*, 236–8.
202. *Religion of Jesus*, 144.
203. *Synoptic Tradition*, 50.
204. *From Tradition to Gospel*, 47.
205. *Jesus the Jew*, 33–4.
206. *Historical Jesus*, 299.
207. *Synoptic Tradition*, 199.
208. *From Tradition to Gospel*, 227–8.
209. *Five Gospels*, 55.
210. *Jesus the Jew*, 27.
211. *Rediscovering*, 37.
212. These positions appear on the following pages, respectively, of *Theology*: 31, 61, 120, and 256–7.
213. *Synoptic Tradition*, 199–200.
214. *Theology*, 152; and similarly on 134–5.
215. *Rediscovering*, 115.
216. *Religion of Jesus*, 107.
217. *Five Gospels*, 358.
218. *Synoptic Tradition*, 199.
219. *Five Gospels*, 368.
220. *Religion of Jesus*, 108, 112.
221. *Rediscovering*, 129–30.
222. *Theology*, 120 (emphasis mine).
223. *Theology*, 137.
224. *Theology*, 140.
225. *Theology*, 191.
226. For evidence that the Greek verb ὑπωπιάζω carries a nuance similar

to that of this phrase, cf. Liddell-Scott-Jones, s.v.

227. *Synoptic Tradition*, 26, 48.

228. *Five Gospels*, 102.

229. *Theology*, 72.

230. *Jesus the Jew*, 36.

231. *Jesus and Judaism*, 292.

232. *Synoptic Tradition*, 278.

233. *Five Gospels*, 117.

234. *Jesus and Judaism*, 332.

235. *Religion of Jesus*, 141, 147.

236. *Theology*, 96, 100, 137.

237. *Kingdom of God*, 183; Perrin does not discuss the saying in *Rediscovering*.

238. *Historical Jesus*, 366.

239. *Historical Jesus*, xxxi–xxxiii, 427–9.

240. Anthony J. Blasi has kindly pointed out (in correspondence) that the coherence here under discussion is verbal, not social. That is of course quite correct. In spite of a lack of coherence in Jesus' teachings, in the sense of a consistent theology, there had to be a social coherence to the Jesus movement, otherwise it would have faltered and failed early on. Thus Weber referred to 'a unified attitude toward life gained by a deliberate meaningful stand taken toward it' (quoted in Parsons, *Structure*, 568). Parsons clarifies Weber's position by adding that, if the teaching of the charismatic leader is 'efficacious he gathers about him a community of disciples' (*Structure*, 569). Such efficaciousness, however, need not – and probably does not – imply logical coherence in the charismatic leader's teaching. Parsons also notes correctly (*Structure*, 669) that it is the leader's charisma that legitimates the movement – charisma, *not* an intellectually coherent theology.

241. Schweitzer, *Quest*, 396–7.

242. Above, p. 29.

243. So a number of scholars, especially Saldarini, *Matthew's Christian-Jewish Community*.

244. Cf. Bultmann, *Synoptic Tradition*, 12–27, 39–54.

245. *Jesus and Judaism*, 305.

246. *Jesus and Judaism*, 296.

247. *Jesus and Judaism*, 305.

248. *Jesus and Judaism*, 304.

249. 'Jesus: Jesus Christ', 790–2.

250. J. S. Gordon, *Golden Guru*, 171.

251. I.e., the schools supported by citizens of the town and by people in the surrounding rural areas whose children also attended the

schools.

252. J. S. Gordon, *Golden Guru*, 169.
253. J. S. Gordon, *Golden Guru*, 171.
254. J. S. Gordon, *Golden Guru*, 182–5.
255. J. S. Gordon, *Golden Guru*, 201.
256. Cf. the discussion in E. P. Sanders, *Jesus and Judaism*, 71–6.
257. Cf. Robbins, *Cults, Converts*, 82, in reliance on a number of other studies.
258. *Social Construction*, *passim*.
259. Snow, et al., 'Social Networks', 798.
260. 'The Crazies'.
261. 'The Crazies', 17.
262. 'The Crazies', 21.
263. 'The Crazies', 22.
264. 'The Crazies', 23.
265. 'The Crazies', 33.
266. 'The Crazies', 19.
267. Cf. the summary discussion by Baab, 'Marriage', 286b; furthermore, for the Talmudic period, when the situation can hardly have been appreciably different, Baron, *Social and Religious History*, 2, 219.
268. 'Theory of Revelations'.

II Why Did Gentiles Become Christians?

1. Cf. only Haenchen, *Acts*, 188–9; cf. further my review of the issue of the number of Jewish conversions in Acts in *The Jews in Luke-Acts*, 64–5, 69–71.
2. *Conversion*, 7.
3. *Conversion*, 14.
4. *Conversion*, 14–15.
5. *Conversion*, 77.
6. *Conversion*, 117–18.
7. *Conversion*, 77.
8. *Conversion*, 78.
9. *Conversion*, 80.
10. *Conversion*, 83.
11. *Conversion*, 92.
12. *Conversion*, 99.
13. *Conversion*, 116.
14. *Conversion*, 192–3.
15. *Conversion*, 194. Earlier, in 'Genius of Mithraism', Nock had argued perceptively that Mithraism had appeals that 'its natural

rivals' (113) lacked; but he concluded, nevertheless, that Mithraism could never have triumphed throughout the empire in the way that Christianity finally did, even had Christianity died out for some reason. It did not have Christianity's broad and compelling attraction.

16. *Christianizing.*
17. *Christianizing*, 5.
18. *Christianizing*, 5.
19. *Christianizing*, 26–30.
20. *Christianizing*, 34.
21. *Christianizing*, 30–1.
22. *Christianizing*, cf. esp. 37–9.
23. *Christianizing*, 41.
24. *Christianizing*, 41.
25. *Christianizing*, 36–7.
26. *Christianizing*, 41.
27. *Christianizing*, 29.
28. *Christianizing*, 23.
29. Gallagher, 'Conversion and Salvation', 28.
30. *Christianizing*, 11.
31. *Christianizing*, 16.
32. *From Darkness to Light*, 10.
33. *From Darkness to Light*, 13. The contrast between conversion and alternation was first defined by Travisano, 'Alternation and Conversion', on whose work Gaventa relied. Gaventa's introduction of transformation is an attempt to move beyond Nock's and Travisano's polarities.
34. *From Darkness to Light*, 11.
35. Cf. *From Darkness to Light*, 106, 124. On the difference between alternation/transformation, on the one hand, and conversion on the other, cf. further Greil, 'Previous Dispositions', 116.
36. *From Darkness to Light*, 124.
37. *Conversion*, 210–11.
38. *Pagans and Christians.*
39. *Religions of Rome.*
40. *Religions of Rome*, 1, 287.
41. *Religions of Rome*, 1, 288.
42. *Religions of Rome*, 1, 289.
43. *Religions of Rome*, 1, 289.
44. *Religions of Rome*, 1, 291.
45. *Religions of Rome*, 1, 293.
46. *Religions of Rome*, 1, 294.
47. *Religions of Rome*, 1, 295–6.

48. *Religions of Rome*, 1, 296.
49. *Religions of Rome*, 1, 298–9.
50. *Religions of Rome*, 1, 300–1.
51. *Religions of Rome*, 1, 303.
52. *Religions of Rome*, 1, 307.
53. *Religions of Rome*, 1, 308–9.
54. *Cults, Converts*, 64.
55. *Cults, Converts*, 66.
56. Rambo, 'Psychology of Conversion', 161.
57. *Cults, Converts*, 67–71; cf. Lofland and Skonovd, 'Conversion Motifs' and 'Patterns of Conversion'.
58. *Cults, Converts*, 68.
59. *Cults, Converts*, 69.
60. Lofland and Skonovd, 'Conversion Motifs', 375.
61. Cf. Robbins, *Cults, Converts*, 70.
62. Robbins, *Cults, Converts*, 79.
63. Quoted from Robbins, *Cults, Converts*, 79–80. In an early study (*Satan's Power*, 12) Bainbridge, who was later to become a close collaborator with Stark, chose only three necessary steps out of Lofland's and Stark's progression: 'Pre-existing, acutely felt tensions', a 'problem-solving perspective' and an 'evolving structure of personal relationships'. A highly similar analysis, although formulated differently, has been offered by Wallis in his *Elementary Forms*, under his discussion of world-rejecting religious movements; cf. esp. 41–7 and 119–22.
64. Robbins, *Cults, Converts*, 83.
65. *Cults, Converts*, 85.
66. *Cults, Converts*, 86.
67. *Cults, Converts*, 87. Wallis, 'Religion as Fun?' 195–204, has given a thorough description of people who followed Rajneesh as being structurally available.
68. 'Networks of Faith'.
69. 'Networks of Faith', 1379; on the importance of affective ties, cf. further Richardson and Stewart, 'Conversion Process Models', 832.
70. 'Networks of Faith', 1386.
71. 'Networks of Faith', 1390–1; cf. also p. 1376.
72. There are several good studies of this NRM, one of the most thorough being Snow, *Shakubuku*.
73. 'Social Networks and Social Movements', 790–1.
74. Richardson, 'Conversion Process', 79.
75. *Early Christianity*, 188.
76. 'Psychology of Proselytism', 138–41.
77. *Conversion*, 7.

78. *Conversion*, 5.
79. *Conversion*, 13–14.
80. *Conversion*, 35–6.
81. *Conversion*, 36–7.
82. *Conversion*, 37.
83. *Conversion*, 46–7.
84. *Conversion*, 53.
85. *Cults, Converts*, 60.
86. *Rise of Christianity*, 15.
87. Cf. the further discussion of relative deprivation in Hillel Schwarz, 'Millenarianism', 527–8.
88. Cf. also Dawson, *Comprehending Cults*, 76.
89. *Conversion*, 58.
90. *Conversion*, 60–2.
91. *Conversion*, 63.
92. *Conversion*, 78–9.
93. *Conversion*, 80–1.
94. *Conversion*, 81–6.
95. *Conversion*, 95.
96. *Conversion*, 97–9.
97. *Conversion*, 99–101.
98. *Conversion*, 108.
99. *Conversion*, 114–15.
100. *Conversion*, 116.
101. *Conversion*, 118–19.
102. *Conversion*, 120–3.
103. *Conversion*, 136–7.
104. *Conversion*, 169.
105. Review of Rambo, 100.
106. *Comprehending Cults*, 61.
107. *Comprehending Cults*, 69.
108. *Comprehending Cults*, 86.
109. *Comprehending Cults*, 87.
110. *Comprehending Cults*, 88.
111. *Comprehending Cults*, 88–9.
112. *Comprehending Cults*, 93.
113. A possibility that most modern students of Galatians do not entertain; cf. the following note.
114. Many moderns, e.g., Barrett, *First Corinthians*, 65–6, find it difficult to believe that Paul performed miracles and propose rather that Paul's preaching was powerful; and for Betz, *Galatians*, 99, the χάρις of Gal. 2.9 is the content of Paul's message. Robertson and Plummer (*First Corinthians*, 33) observe that 'some Greek Fathers

suppose that miracle-working power is meant, which is an idea remote from the context'. The terms 'spirit' and 'power', however, seem to point to something beyond such twentieth-century psychologizing, which is Robertson and Plummer's context. Surely the Fathers, much closer to the cultural reality, had it right. Among modern scholars one may note particularly Weder, 'Disciple, Discipleship', 209, who includes Paul, along with the Twelve, the Q tradents, the Stephen circle, and Barnabas as 'Wandercharismatikern' (wandering charismatics) who 'carried Jesus' message *and impact (Wirkung)* to people' (emphasis mine; cf. n. 2 in the previous chapter).

115. 'Conversion in the Bible', 49.
116. Cf. above, p. 82.
117. Cited in Barrett, *First Corinthians*, 57.
118. *First Urban Christians*, 51.
119. *First Urban Christians*, 51–72.
120. *First Urban Christians*, 73; emphasis mine.
121. *First Urban Christians*, 191.
122. Cf., e.g., Bainbridge, 'Sociology of Conversion', 179–81, and the discussion above, pp. 92–3.
123. I follow Schneemelcher–Wilson's *New Testament Apocrypha* in assigning only these to the second century.
124. Prieur, *Acta Andreae*; MacDonald, *Acts of Andrew*.
125. Elliott, *Apocryphal New Testament*. An abbreviated version of Prieur's discussion, including an English translation of some of the texts, appears in Schneemelcher–Wilson, 2, 101–51.
126. Schneemelcher–Wilson, 2, 122. Cf. also the discussion in Pao, 'Physical and Spiritual Restoration', 268–69.
127. Apparently baptism; cf. II Clem. 7.6; 8.6.
128. 'The Acts of John', 178–9.
129. It is perhaps these realistic aspects of the Thecla narrative that led Harnack (*Mission and Expansion*, 2, 73) to think that 'there must have really been a girl converted by a (*sic*) Paul at Iconium, whose name was Thekla, and who took an active part in the Christian mission'.
130. The pool is filled with dangerous seals! The author thus reveals his limited knowledge of the marine food chain.
131. Misset-van de Weg, 'For the Lord Always Takes Care', 99.
132. Misset-van de Weg, 'For the Lord Always Takes Care', provides in general a very good analysis of the miracles in the Apocryphal Acts of Peter.
133. This viewpoint is also supported by Prieur's analysis; cf. *Acta Andreae* 1, 382. Cf. further the observation of Hilhorst ('Apoc-

ryphal Acts', 6) that 'Andrew as well as the other characters of the story have no individuality, but are stereotypes'.

134. Cf. *Patrology*, 1, 190–253.

135. *Patrology*, 1, 251.

136. Cf. the discussion in Quasten, *Patrology*, 1, 195.

137. See Eusebius, *HE* 4, 29, 1; Quasten, *Patrology*, 1, 221.

138. Harnack, *Mission and Expansion*, 1, 490, argues that martyrdoms occurred primarily among the lower classes and that 'people belonging to the middle classes . . . were left unmolested upon the whole'; and he is followed to excess on this point by Stark, *Rise of Christianity*, 180, who asserts that 'for the rank-and-file Christians the threat of persecution was so slight as to have counted for little'. Stark, however, might have profited from reading Grant, *Augustus to Constantine*, 85–96, where the martyrdoms of the second century are summarized in some of their grisly detail.

139. Above, 103–4.

140. On this point see the excellent discussion of Cohen, 'Crossing the Boundary'.

141. Goodman, *Mission and Conversion*, 27–32, tries to show that such religious movements as those of Isis and Mithras undertook no proselytizing activity. (In the conclusion, 154, he seems to deny only *universal* proselytizing.) Their expansion came about rather, according to him, because the members moved from one place to another or because outsiders married members. Goodman even seems to endorse Livy's (39, 9, 1) explanation that the spread of such 'cults' was like the spread of a 'contagious disease' (*Mission and Conversion*, 29). This is tortured reasoning and is surely shown to be mistaken by the large number and wide geographical distribution of known shrines, temples, altars, etc. of Isis and of Mithras. When Goodman then offers the imperial cult (*Mission and Conversion*, 3–32) as a pagan religion that *was* a proselytizing movement, he has brought in a comparator that cannot accurately be labeled a new religious movement. It had no members beyond those officials appointed to administer the cult in various places.

142. Cf. our earlier discussion of this point, 79–80.

143. Cf. Edelstein and Edelstein, *Asclepius*, 2, 255–7.

144. Cf. only Burkert, *Ancient Mystery Cults*, 17: '. . . the only extant account of a mystery initiation in a first-person style'.

145. Cf. Vermaseren, *CIMRM*, 2, 498.

146. Cf. Liebeschuetz, 'Expansion of Mithraism', 212; Beck, 'Mysteries', 180–2.

147. Cf. esp. Liebeschuetz, 'Expansion of Mithraism'. Cf. also Beck, 'Mysteries', 177.

148. Liebeschuetz, 'Expansion of Mithraism', 201–2.
149. R. L. Gordon, 'Mithraism and Roman Society', 95; cf. also Beck, 'Mysteries', 178. Cf. further our earlier discussion of the importance of NRMs' creating new statuses for their converts, above, pp. 103–4.
150. Gager, *Kingdom and Community*, 116–18, gives a good summary of this traditional explanation of Christianity's early success.
151. William Babcock ('MacMullen on Conversion'), in a conference response to Ramsay MacMullen – who had again presented his theory of two modes of conversion (above), albeit from a different perspective – proposed a theory for Christianity's success that is supportive of Rambo's point about benefits. Babcock's idea was that Christianity succeeded because it successfully combined elements that appealed to MacMullen's two types of converts, the intellectuals and the underclass. Babcock's only example, however, was Augustine ('MacMullen on Conversion', 87) – a little late to be of help here; unfortunately, Babcock did not explain further.
152. Cf. the more detailed discussion of Paul's adaptive procedure here in J. T. Sanders, 'Paul between Jews and Gentiles'.
153. 'How New Religions Succeed', 13.

III *Why Did Christianity Succeed in the Roman Empire?*

1. *Early Gentile Christianity*, 32–87.
2. *Early Gentile Christianity*, 101–4.
3. Cf. the evidence presented by Wilken, *Christians as the Romans Saw Them*.
4. Cf. R. L. Gordon ('Mithraism and Roman Society', 98), who refers to 'an important quality which Mithras shares with other major gods both new and traditional – his ability to assist the believer in everyday life'.
5. Since Justin in *Dial.* 70 quotes an ethical section from Isaiah 33 in the context of a reference to Mithraism, some see here an allusion to Mithraic ethics; but Justin does not make this connection, so that the relevance of his quotation of Isaiah here for Mithraic ethics must remain uncertain. Cf. the discussion in Liebeschuetz, 'Expansion of Mithraism', 197.
6. Yet cf. Liebeschuetz, 'Expansion of Mithraism', 211: 'There surely was no Mithraic literature.'
7. Cf. the discussion in the Introduction; also Liebeschuetz, 'Expansion of Mithraism', 213–14.
8. *Rise of Christianity*.
9. *Chronicle of Higher Education* 12 July 1996, p. A10; *Newsweek* 19 August 1996, p. 62.

10. Williams, *Rethinking 'Gnosticism'*, 237.
11. *Rise of Christianity*, 3–27.
12. *Rise of Christianity*, 7.
13. *Rise of Christianity*, 11.
14. *Rise of Christianity*, 14.
15. *First Urban Christians*, 28–29.
16. Cited by Stark, *Rise of Christianity*, 21.
17. Maier, Review, 330.
18. 'Expansion of Mithraism', 203–4.
19. *Rise of Christianity*, 39.
20. Cf. the discussion of Meeks' position in the previous chapter; cf. also the excellent discussion in Countryman, *Rich Christian*, of the role that wealthy persons played in the pre-Constantinian church and of the difficulty that Christian writers had dealing with their presence.
21. See p. 119.
22. *Rise of Christianity*, 49–71.
23. *Rise of Christianity*, 54, 57–61.
24. *Rise of Christianity*, 61–71. Maier (Review, 332) observes that Stark has been led astray by the account in Acts, 'now widely argued [to be] a Lucan fiction'.
25. *Rise of Christianity*, 54.
26. Others, of course, like the parents of the US Secretary of State Albright (cf. *New York Times* and Associated Press, 4 February 1997) converted for apparently other reasons.
27. *Rise of Christianity*, 60–1.
28. Barclay, *Jews in the Mediterranean Diaspora*, 75, 105–6.
29. See the discussion below of Stark's next chapter, and also the evidence presented by Oborn below, 149.
30. *Rise of Christianity*, 60–2.
31. *Rise of Christianity*, 60.
32. *Jews in the Mediterranean Diaspora*, 161.
33. *Rise of Christianity*, 61.
34. *Rise of Christianity*, 54.
35. *Rise of Christianity*, 59.
36. *Rise of Christianity*, 52–3.
37. Cf. Barclay, *Jews in the Mediterranean Diaspora*, 55–60.
38. *Rise of Christianity*, 54–5.
39. *Rise of Christianity*, 58–9.
40. Cf. Barclay, *Jews in the Mediterranean Diaspora*.
41. Cf. J. T. Sanders, *Schismatics, Sectarians, Dissidents, Deviants*.
42. *Jews in the Mediterranean Diaspora*, 92–8.
43. *Jews in the Mediterranean Diaspora*, 181–228.
44. Cf. *Jews in the Mediterranean Diaspora*, 181–91.

45. Oppositional accommodation has also been noted by Davidman, 'Accommodation and Resistance', for an Orthodox synagogue in New York.
46. *Rise of Christianity*, 61–2.
47. 'Adolf Harnack', 119.
48. Cf. White, *Building God's House*, 104; further Maier, Review, 332.
49. *Rise of Christianity*, 68.
50. Cf. MacLennan and Kraabel, 'God-Fearers'. Stark cites the original 1986 article.
51. Cf. Stark, 'Jewish Conversion', and Kraabel, 'Disappearance'.
52. 'God-Fearers' (1992; reprint of the 1986 article), 136.
53. *Rise of Christianity*, 68–9.
54. Cf. White, *Building God's House*, 8.
55. *Building God's House*, 8, 44, 144.
56. *Rise of Christianity*, 129–45.
57. *Rise of Christianity*, 132–5.
58. Harnack, *Mission and Expansion*, Vol. 2; Meeks, *First Urban Christians*.
59. *Rise of Christianity*, 135–40.
60. *Rise of Christianity*, 139–40.
61. For a good discussion of what Romanization was, cf. White, 'Urban Development', 30–3. Romanization involved, among other things, 'Roman law and administrative organization, imperial building programs, and the use of Roman names and dress' (31), all of which, if not completely in Jerusalem, were fully present in other cities in the region like Caesarea, Tiberias, and Antioch.
62. *Jews under Roman Rule*, 120–2.
63. Ross Kraemer's recent 'prosopographic survey' of Jewish women in early Christianity also finds that, after Jesus' lifetime, 'it becomes increasingly difficult to identify Jewish women as members of early Christian churches'; cf. 'Jewish Women', 44.
64. *Rise of Christianity*, 73–94.
65. *Rise of Christianity*, 75.
66. *Rise of Christianity*, 81.
67. *World of Late Antiquity*, 60.
68. Similarly Maier, Review, 334.
69. *Rise of Christianity*, 88–91.
70. On this point, cf. further Dodds, *Pagan and Christian*, 110–16; Benko, *Pagan Rome*; Wilken, *Christians as the Romans Saw Them*.
71. 'Popular Reactions', 54.
72. Oborn, 'Economic Factors', 136–7 (emphasis mine), citing, among others, Tertullian, *Apology* 40; Cyprian, *Epistles* 74.10 (75); and Eusebius, *HE* 4, 13, 1–7.

73. 'Economic Factors', 133–6, on which see the discussion of Stark's next chapter, below.
74. 'Economic Factors', 137–8.
75. 'Economic Factors', 139; cf. Tertullian *De spec.* 15.
76. 'Economic Factors', 139–41.
77. Cf. Lampe, *Stadtrömische Christen*, 30.
78. Cf. further Harnack's discussion of pagan hatred of Christians in *Mission and Expansion*, 1.497–509.
79. Colwell, 'Popular Reactions', 53; Oborn, 'Economic Factors', 131.
80. *Rise of Christianity*, 147–62.
81. *Rise of Christianity*, 149.
82. *Rise of Christianity*, 161.
83. *Rise of Christianity*, 147–9.
84. *Rise of Christianity*, 156.
85. *Rise of Christianity*, 150.
86. *Rise of Christianity*, 151–2, quoting another writer.
87. Cf. Stambaugh, *Ancient Roman City*, 208–10, 227; 'Greco-Roman Cities', 1048.
88. *Ancient Roman City*, 240.
89. MacMullen, *Paganism*, 51.
90. Case, 'Art of Healing'; McCasland, 'Religious Healing'.
91. *Rise of Christianity*, 200.
92. *Rise of Christianity*, 97–9, 118–21, 124–5.
93. *Rise of Christianity*, 96–101.
94. *Rise of Christianity*, 122–8.
95. *Rise of Christianity*, 103–11.
96. *Rise of Christianity*, 111–15.
97. *Rise of Christianity*, 114.
98. Cf. M. MacDonald, *Early Christian Women*, 131.
99. Colwell, 'Popular Reactions', 62.
100. 'Economic Factors', 133. This point has now been underscored in great detail by M. MacDonald, *Early Christian Women*; cf. esp. pp. 122, 205.
101. *When Women Were Priests*, 155.
102. Torjesen, *When Women Were Priests*, 155–8; cf. also M. MacDonald, *Early Christian Women*, 31, 49–126, and Cardman, 'Women, Ministry'.
103. Cf. Stark, *Rise of Christianity*, 8.
104. Cf. Stark, *Rise of Christianity*, 107–10.
105. 'Attraction of Women'.
106. 'Attraction of Women', 15.
107. 'Attraction of Women', 20.
108. 'Attraction of Women', 20–1, emphasis mine.

109. 'Attraction of Women', 21. We may recall that R. L. Gordon made a similar point regarding men in Mithraism (above, p. 119).
110. *Rise of Christianity*, 163–89.
111. Quoted by Stark, *Rise of Christianity*, 181.
112. Stark, *Rise of Christianity*, 179.
113. *Rise of Christianity*, 174.
114. *Rise of Christianity*, 168. On the issue of compensators, cf. further Stark and Bainbridge, *Theory*, 36–9.
115. *Rise of Christianity*, 188–9.
116. *Rise of Christianity*, 191–208.
117. *Rise of Christianity*, 191–203.
118. *Rise of Christianity*, 203–8.
119. *Rise of Christianity*, 199.
120. *Rise of Christianity*, 139; above, p. 146.
121. Stark's final chapter presents a summary of findings and a claim for the superiority of Christian theology and practice, which call for no further discussion.
122. *Early Christianity*, 178–9.
123. Cf. J. T. Sanders, *Ethics in the New Testament*.
124. On the consistency cf. Beard, North and Price, *Religions of Rome*, 1, 303; although they stress the similarity with Christianity, not the difference.
125. We should note that Liebeschuetz ('Expansion of Mithraism', 210–11) has stressed regional differences within Mithraism, just as within Christianity.
126. *Mission and Expansion*, 2, 336.
127. *Early Christianity*, 179–80.
128. *Early Christianity*, 62.
129. *Early Christianity*, 180–2.
130. Grant, *Early Christianity and Society*, 13–43.
131. *Early Christianity and Society*, 114.
132. *Early Christianity and Society*, 116.
133. *Early Christianity and Society*, 311–12.
134. Above, p. 136.
135. Stark cites Case, 'Acceptance of Christianity'.
136. Rudolph and Piscatori, 'Preface', vii.
137. Rudolph, 'Introduction', 11.
138. Rudolph, 'Introduction', 12.
139. 'Muslim Missionaries', 47–8.
140. 'Muslim Missionaries', 51.
141. Associated Press article, 8 November 1998.
142. *World of Late Antiquity*, 67.
143. Beard, North and Price (*Religions of Rome*, 1, 303) emphasize the

degree to which all the NRMs in the Roman Empire maintained a certain level of uniformity.

144. Beard, North and Price, *Religions of Rome*, 1, 303.

145. Vermaseren and van Essen, *Excavations*, 155–8, 179. The extant part of the formula makes the emendations certain, even though the brackets in the translation do not completely reflect the broken nature of the dipinti.

146. *World of Late Antiquity*, 66.

147. Gamble, *Books and Readers*.

148. *Books and Readers*, 102–3, 108, 110.

149. It was apparently also Nock's opinion that the religion of Isis and Sarapis, not Mithraism, was Christianity's primary rival. Cf. his statement in *Early Gentile Christianity*, 11, that in the Hellenistic period 'no form of belief took the offensive with more energy *and effect* [emphasis added] than the Hellenized but Egyptian cult of Isis and Sarapis'.

150. 'Mysteries', 179.

Conclusion

1. *Mission and Expansion*, 2, 336.

Index of Subjects

Index of Modern Authors

Index of Ancient Literature and Authors

CHRISTIAN LITERATURE

JEWISH LITERATURE

GRECO-ROMAN LITERATURE